You see, I was able to fool folks because I was a really good actress. Well, I mean I *am* a good actress. I mean, I *do* have an Emmy Award, an Independent Spirit Award, a Chicago Film Critics Award, three NAACP Image Awards, and a host of award nominations that say so. And let me tell you, I had to pull out all the acting skills for this one... because for a very, very long time I made my way through life wearing this mask...but I was living with so much insecurity, so much fear, and FEAR was huge. It felt like the first emotion I was born cognizant of. It enveloped the air I breathed, it spoke for me, it ruled me and had its way with me...*IT WAS THE MONKEY ON MY BACK!*

Debbi Morgan

A MEMOIR

DEBBI MORGAN

BREAKING A GENERATIONAL CURSE

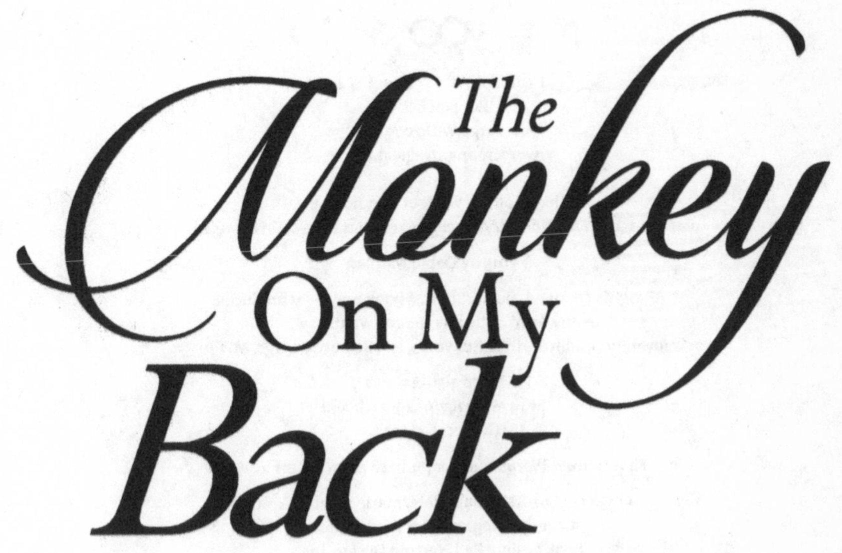

The Monkey On My Back

A MEMOIR

DEBBI MORGAN

BREAKING A GENERATIONAL CURSE

INFINITE WORDS
NEW YORK LONDON TORONTO SYDNEY

INFINITE WORDS
P.O. Box 6505
Largo, MD 20792
www.simonandschuster.com

This book is a work of non fiction.
Certain names and identifying characteristics have been changed..

For information, address Infinite Words, P.O. Box 6505, Largo, MD 20792.

ISBN 978-1-59309-642-7
ISBN 978-1-4767-9429-7 (ebook)
LCCN 2015934625

First Infinite Words trade paperback edition June 2015

Cover design: Keith Saunders/mariondesigns.com
Cover photography: © Kent Ballard
Book design: Red Herring Design, Inc.

10 9 8 7 6 5 4 3 2 1

Manufactured in the United States of America

I dedicate this book to my beautiful mother, Lora, who was still fighting the good fight after the completion of this memoir. Mom, you lost that fight, but the presence of your indomitable spirit, love, and humor will live in my heart forever. I know the trials, and the tribulations you endured both as a child and as a woman. This is because my entrance into this world, and the experiences of my life, were so akin to and intertwined with yours. It created a very strong dynamic between the two of us, which, throughout the years, often caused our relationship to be strained and contentious.

It took a long time for me to understand and accept the woman you were, only because it took me that long to understand and accept the woman I became, holding on to my fears for almost a lifetime. But it's not a cliché that it's the difficult times that make us stronger and give us a clearer perception.

My perception of you in both our lives became quite clear, Mom. You loved me every second with every morsel of your being, and never wanted me to make the same mistakes you had. I finally recognize how hard you had to work in order to persevere and maintain your sense of dignity and grace through all your adversity. I have the deepest respect, admiration, and love for you, Mother. You are and will always remain my champion.

IN MEMORY OF

LORA MORGAN

(May 22, 2014)

Preface

I can still remember that magical day sitting on the floor of director John Erman's living room. Only inches away from me was the legendary Henry Fonda, and across from him, perched daintily on the sofa, the great Olivia de Havilland. Filling out the rest of the room, draped across chairs and settled comfortably on the floor, were Georg Stanford Brown, Lynne Moody, Richard Thomas, Marc Singer, Fay Hauser, Greg Morris, Brian Stokes Mitchell, and little ole' me. I was about to embark on one of the greatest roles of my burgeoning career, and one of the most historical events in television history: *Roots: The Next Generations*.

I sat, wide-eyed, at the feet of the brilliant author, Alex Haley, as he shared with us the fascinating story of his family's history. Alex shared that, as a child, he would listen from the doorway as his elders gathered on the porch reciting tales of the old African, Kunta Kinte, being taken from his village and brought to this strange land called America, where he was stripped of his dignity, culture, security, and humanness, and forced to live as a slave.

Because we were preparing for *Roots 2*, Alex spoke mostly of Kunta's offspring, and how the African had left his mark of strength and perseverance. The later generations of family that followed would become educated, fight to vote, go off to college, build their own homes, have their own businesses, and one would even become one of the world's most prolific authors. There would be many great achievements from the Kinte lineage. The old African would have been proud to know that all his suffering had not been in vain.

Alex told us one of the most daunting, yet rewarding, journeys each of us could ever take, would be to travel back down the road our ancestors had paved for us. He implored us to question older members of our families to discover our own family histories, no matter what we unearthed.

I thought about it for a moment and wasn't too sure I'd find such an inquiry rewarding. If I started with myself and traced backward, my family history would not lend itself to a glorious re-creation.

Yet, Alex's suggestion resonated deep within, beckoning me to place a phone call that, if nothing else, would help me search for a better knowledge of the past so as to better understand my present.

I was caught up in the cinematic remaking of a family's history that had very much linked me to my own, and more significantly, to a profound conversation with my great-great-aunt and a journey through my own roots. Both the professional and personal ventures slowly drew me deeper into understanding how the repeated cycles of history can bind us all to what is familiar.

My history was Alex's history, the history of a family that continues to shape and mold its offspring with greatness, mediocrity, or far less...

Hence, I was propelled to take pen to paper and write this story of the generational cycles I'd been swept up in, particularly because of the person most near and dear... It was via her canal that I had been chosen to enter into this universe—our emotions, fates, and fears for so long knotted in destiny.

I'd often stared at my mother's still-youthful face and thought about how daunting her life had been, a common thread from one mother to the next...one daughter to the next. I knew the devastating answers. Now it was time to ask the questions.

Part I

The Apple and the Tree Before Me

Chapter 1

Wade County, North Carolina
Late 1940s

"Daddy's coming down the road and he's drunk as a skunk! Git the shotgun, Lora! Hurry up!"

Lora stood with her nine-year-old sister, Rosalie, whom everyone called Bunch, standing guard by the side of the house. They were watching their father, John Hammond Smith, staggering down the dirt path toward their four-room shack.

"Bunch, y'all go hide."

Obediently, the younger girl led the way for six-year-old Franklin and younger sisters, Virginia and Elvira. They knew the drill. They ran out to the back porch and scrunched into their familiar haven underneath the house.

Lora's two older brothers, JD and Sonny, were out at Miss Alice's juke joint. Brother Clarence, whom everyone called C, was spending the night at the home of his teacher, Miss Wallace. Baby Shirley was asleep in her makeshift crib in the front room.

Their daddy's loud drunken calls had people in neighboring shacks pulling back their tattered curtains and shaking their heads. "Here comes that crazy drunk fool, John Hammond."

Well, far be it from Hammond to disappoint any of them as he yelled loud enough to wake the dead. "Rosie! Rosie! Willie Rose Smith! Goddammit, woman, is you deaf? Hot Damn!"

When John Hammond voiced this particular profanity, everybody knew they'd better run for cover.

Darting into the kitchen, Lora found her mother seated at the table reading the Bible. "Mama! Mama! Come on outside and hide with us. Daddy's comin' down the road and he's hollerin' for you. He been drinkin' that white lightnin'; you know what's gon' happen!"

Rosie didn't even raise her eyes as she continued quoting the twenty-third Psalm. "Yea, though I walk through the valley of the shadow of death..."

Hammond was now only a few feet from the house as he threatened, "You gon'...rue the day...you didn't come runnin'...when I called you, Willie Rose!"

Rosie rocked back and forth in her chair, her petite frame hardly causing the chair to ripple. With every word, she pounded a small fist on the table. "I will fear no evil, for Thou art with me; Thy rod and Thy staff, they comfort me."

Lora didn't know what good the Bible was going to do for her mother now. "Mama, please, please git out the house 'fore Daddy come in here!"

The front porch creaked as John Hammond entered through the screen door into the front room. "Hot damn! I'm gon'...git my shotgun and...blow yo' brains out, Willie Rose, you and all the rest of these... wild-ass youngins 'round here!" he spat, filling the room with the menacing odor of alcohol from his breath.

Rosie got up from the table and gingerly crossed into the living room.

Lora stayed behind in the kitchen, out of her father's view.

"Hammond, you don't need to be comin' in here wit' all that ugliness. Why don't you go on in there and lie down?"

He laughed wickedly. "Shit! You...the one...who...gon' be lying... down... Goddamit! Six...feet...under!"

Hammond lunged to make good on his threat and fell, banging his head on the wooden floorboards. He'd slipped on Elvira's dirty, white baby doll with the hole in the center of its head.

Relief swooshed through Lora's body, freeing her to breathe normally.

"Lawd have mercy. Lora! Help me git yo' daddy up off the flo'!"

Lora felt she had no choice but to ignore her mother's command. She knew this was her last chance. She dashed through the living room, jumped over her father's head, and rushed into her parents' bedroom.

Lora hopped up on the bed and grabbed Hammond's shotgun, which hung in its usual place on the wall above their bed. She darted out the back door and scooted underneath the house with her little brother and sisters, clutching the sawed-off shotgun underneath her arm.

Too drunk to make it up from the floor on his own, Rosie struggled to help lift her five-foot-ten, 185-pound man as best she could.

"Come on now, Hammond. I need you to lift your right foot up."

Hammond complied, finally managing to get both his feet planted firmly on the floor. "Thank...you...woman," he mumbled, and then, without missing a beat, he backhanded Rosie in the eye.

Lora huddled tightly together with her four siblings. They were trying to stay warm in the cool night air when they heard their mother's scream.

Little Elvira began to cry. Lora wrapped a protective arm around her. "Shhhhh."

Lora lived in constant fear for her mama, and she swore to herself that she would never suffer like her mama, and that she would never, ever, get married.

The argument continued above them. "Why you always gots to be knockin on me, Hammond? I ain't done nothin' to you!"

Still in a drunken rage, Hammond belted, "You done knocked me... down! That's what you done! Made me...hurt my head! And where's... my...goddamn...shotgun?"

Rosie started backing away, staring fearfully through one open eye, the other now swelling into a small slit. "I ain't took that thang, Hammond. Please don't hit me no mo'!"

He put his hand up to his pounding head, stumbled and sat on the side of the bed, slightly incoherent and mumbling to himself. "I know...what, that...old...fast...ass...yaller...gal done...come...in here... and...took...took...my shotgun."

Hammond was obviously referring to his eldest daughter, Lora, whose complexion was light-skinned, like his own. When he was drunk, she was yaller gal. When he was sober, she was *pretty* gal.

It was a matter of fact that Lora Isabelle Smith was a lot more than pretty; she was stunning, with warm brown eyes set in a beautiful, oval-shaped face. Her long, soft hair fell past her shoulders when the pressing comb was used, which was only on Sundays for church. And as was a trademark of a Hammond daughter, she had gorgeous, filled-out legs. But it was fair to say that all Hammond's girls were beauties. The formidable patriarch wouldn't have had it any other way.

Lora knew things might not have gone this far if her two older brothers had been present. Hammond tended to curtail his shenanigans when one of his older sons was around. JD and Sonny feared their father as much as anyone, but when it came to their mother, whom they adored, they would attempt to protect her at all costs.

After all his fussin', cussin', and fightin', and with his head still throbbing, Hammond passed right on out.

Rosie hurried outside to rescue her babies from under the house.

They were all glad to get out of the cold and back into the warmth of their tiny dwelling. All except my mother, Lora, who took one look at her mama's battered face and wished she could get far, far away from that place. But unfortunately, she wouldn't get far enough, because her deepest, darkest fears would one day become her brightest, most stark realities...

Chapter 2

"Mama, look at your face!"

It seemed like early dawn when Lora awoke to JD shouting from the kitchen. Her brother's voice cracked with unsteadiness.

"I'm gon' kill Daddy. I swear fo' God, I'm gon' kill him!" JD fumed.

"And I'll help," Sonny seconded.

Rosie sat quietly at the table, feeding baby Shirley, but she quickly stood once Sonny added his two cents, his face filled with a silent, smoldering fury. Rosie took one look at her second eldest son and an alarm went off inside of her. She didn't underestimate the rage in either of her sons, but it was Sonny who posed the greater threat.

Hammond sat in the front room smoking his pipe, eavesdropping on his eldest son's threats. He knew they were quite serious about wanting to murder him, but Hammond also knew that neither boy was a real threat unless he was still drunk as a skunk.

Rosie's small voice bellowed through the tiny house as she took definitive authority over the Sunday morning routine. "JD, I want you to go on in there and make sho' them sleepyheads, C and Bunch, are outta that bed fo' we be late for church.

"Now, git to it; ya'll ain't about to make me miss Reverend Arnold's sermon this mornin'."

Everybody got dressed in their Sunday best, which was the exact same clothing they wore every Sunday, but they were always freshly cleaned and ironed. When they were set to depart, Rosie crossed into the front room cradling baby Shirley in her arms, leaned over, dutifully kissed her husband on the cheek, and then walked out the door.

Lora held onto little Virginia and Elvira, following behind her mother. She didn't utter one word to her father; neither did JD nor Sonny.

Her younger sister, Bunch, looked up at Hammond, and said, with a mock sweetness, "Goodbye, Daddy." Then knowing he didn't have eyes in the back of his head, she stuck out her tongue.

Franklin, with his expressive eyes and fat cheeks, smiled and said, "We gon' pray for you in church today, Daddy...all day long."

Lora was quite aware of the stares from all the churchgoers. She felt their eyes boring a hole through her and heard the whispers as her family filed down the aisle to their usual pew. Rosie's face was a shame before God, and everybody knew it.

Reverend Arnold was at the pulpit giving an untimely, and what now seemed to the children, a somewhat jarring sermon about "Christian Home Relationships."

"I'm reading from Ephesians chapter five, starting at verse twenty-two. Wives, submit yourselves unto your own husbands, as unto the Lord! For the husband is the head of the wife, even as Christ is the head of the church; and He is the savior of the body. Therefore, as the church is subject unto Christ, so let the wives be unto their own husbands in everything. Can I get an amen? I said, can I get an—"

Reverend Arnold stopped mid-sentence as the whispers caused him to look up from his place in the Bible. He must have realized why he wasn't getting the proper response from the congregation.

How could anyone believe that Willie Rose's huge, blue and purple eye was the will of the Lord?

The shame and embarrassment of her mother's battered face kept Lora's eyes glued to the floor.

The reverend was determined to grab the focus back from everyone's nosey curiosity, and seemed quite anxious to get on to the next part of his sermon.

"I said, can I get an amen? Somebody?!"

The congregation snapped to attention. "Amen! Hallelujah!"

As Reverend Arnold barreled on through his sermon, Lora grew angry. The only thing worse than everyone knowing she had a father who went on drunken binges and beat his wife was the minister somehow condoning her father's behavior.

Apparently satisfied with the crowd's response, Reverend Arnold continued with much less fervor in a directive toward the men. "So, too, husbands, love your wives, even as Christ also loved the church, and gave Himself for it. That He might sanctify and cleanse it with the washing of water by the word. That He might present a glorious church, not having a spot, or wrinkle, or any such thing, but that it should be holy and without blemish. So ought men to love their wives as their own bodies. He that loveth his wife, loveth himself!"

Reverend Arnold shouted again, "Can I get an amen?!"

Again the congregation responded. "Amen!"

The reverend wanted more fervor. "I said...can...I...get...an...amen?!"

The church appeased the reverend by roaring loud enough for their voices to reverberate through the heavens. "Yes, Jesus! Amen! Amen! Amen!"

Then Reverend Arnold uttered a quiet reprimand, "Best you pay attention and use your voices to shout the name of the Lord, and thus refrain from whispering about your neighbors' business, lest you run the risk of encouraging God to remove your vocal cords."

He moved to the side of the altar and sat in his big leather armchair. A look of serenity came over the reverend's face as the New Zion Choir began to belt out "The Old Rugged Cross."

In a moment of desperation, Lora caught Reverend Arnold's eyes. She held her breath, wishing God could let him read her thoughts, hoping he would maybe come to their house and have a word with Hammond.

But the reverend looked away. Lora realized it was just as well. Hammond wouldn't have let another man come and tell him how to run his house. Not even a preacher man.

After a small stint as a bellman in a white hotel, John Hammond had moved his family out to the country and become a sharecropper. He soon developed a Friday and Saturday night proclivity for drinking everybody else under the table, gambling, backhanding his downtrodden wife, and diligently leaving emotional scars amongst all members of his household. Enveloped by poverty during the Depression and segregation in the backwoods of a small Carolina town, and with eleven mouths to feed, this weekend recreation seemed to be his only outlet.

Bunch had a particularly rebellious and angry nature coupled with enormous feelings of insecurity that were shared by her older brother, Sonny. The two were the darkest of Hammond and Rosie's offspring and when properly intoxicated, their father would quickly spew out offensive language, referring to them as his two, ugly black tar babies.

Through the week, a decidedly sober Hammond was another sort altogether. He exuded a quiet manner, introspective and dignified. He was good to his family and provided for them as best he could, never lifting a finger to strike his precious wife. His tone was mild and respectful, though there was never a doubt who was ruler of the roost.

Hammond had a reputation outside as well as inside the home, as someone not to be tampered with. In fact, he was feared by many and had no need to demand respect. It was hard to come by a man, black or white, who was willing to stand toe-to-toe with John Hammond.

He never whipped any of his children, leaving that discipline to his wife. Sometimes, the way Rosie used a switch, Hammond's children felt she must be venting all the anger from her own multiple beatings. At times, she'd whip them across bare legs so hard, she'd draw blood. The offense could be as small as accidentally breaking a glass. Or if a child were caught looking up at guests while they conversed with Hammond and Rosie over Sunday dinner, there would be hell to pay. Before the guests could get out of the door good, Rosie would send the chosen one out into the woods to fetch a switch; if it wasn't big enough, she'd send them back for one more appropriate.

Hammond also demanded that the only whippings any of them better ever get were inside his house. If any child got beat by some bully, Hammond would have Rosie give them another beating once they got home.

One smoldering hot day, Bunch came tearing into the house, sweating and trying to catch her breath. "Daddy, Daddy! Them Wilford brothers chasing C down the road again!"

C was two steps behind Bunch, also sweating and more out of breath than his sister.

Hammond took a look through the screen and then turned to his son. "What you doin' runnin' in here like you wearin' some skirt fo', boy?"

C stared at his father incredulously.

"Don't be lookin' at me like I done lost my mind. You best git on back out there, and I mean quick and in a hurry, too."

"But, Daddy," C pleaded.

Hammond walked back to the screen door and watched four of the five Wilford boys standing down the road, daring the mama's boy to come out.

He turned to C with a quiet sternness. "Now I know ain't no mama's boy livin' in this here house, so let me tell you what you gon' do. You gon' walk out this house, and back on down the road to where them four sissies is standing. You gon' pick out the biggest and the baddest and you gon' hit him first. Now unless you gon' deaf, I spect I done made myself clear, Son."

C felt a cold chill through his body and knew he feared his father more than he'd ever fear any of the Wilford boys. Slowly, he turned, and with an iron will, marched out of the house and down the road.

"Come on, Sucker! I dare you to take a step across this line," Sam Wilford, the biggest and the baddest, threatened as he drew a line across the dirt road with a stick.

The other Wilfords chimed in. "Yeah, come on, Chicken! We dare you! Where's your mama?"

This would be the last time the brothers would ever talk about C's mother. He never broke his stride from the moment he walked out of the house. C walked down the porch steps, down the dirt road, across the line in the sand, and socked Sam with a left-handed punch that Archie Moore would have been proud of. C actually broke Sam Wilford's jaw. The Wilford brothers stood there, stunned, as their biggest and baddest brother lay on the ground screaming like a mama's boy.

Hammond, who'd been watching through the screen door, came out on the front porch with a slight grin at the corners of his mouth and hollered, "C! Time to come on in now, Son. Supper's ready."

Chapter 3

"Git on way from here now! Why can't you jus' leave me be!"

There was the piercing sound of glass breaking.

"I'm 'bout tired of yo' mess, Hammond!"

Lora, C, Bunch, Frank, Virginia, and Elvira were walking home from Friday evening Bible Study when they heard their mother's screams. Lora thought it was way too early for Hammond to be home. The night was still young and their father surely had six or seven more hours of drinking and carousing to relish.

Nonetheless, Lora took off like a colored person running from the Klan, with C and Bunch right by her side. Franklin was doing his best to keep up, as were Virginia and Elvira, that is, until the tiny tots heard their father yelling about gittin' his shotgun! Then they sat down along the side of the road and began to sob.

Franklin turned back, watching the big tears stream down his little sisters' faces. He joined them, placing an arm around their slumped shoulders. He'd probably wanted to cry, too, but held back, fearing his daddy might come and shoot him for behaving like a sissy.

Lora was the first one through the door, barely missing a glass that came flying through the kitchen. Her mother's dress was torn and yet another purple bruise had begun to blossom on her cheek.

"Now...Li'l Rosie...you best...best...stop throwin' them glasses...if... you...you...know...what's good fo' you."

Hammond ducked beneath the kitchen table as Rosie threw a cup. It crashed at Bunch's feet. Bunch was now standing in the kitchen doorway next to Lora and in front of C.

"Goodness gracious, Mama! Can't you aim better than that?! Daddy's right there underneath the table; stoop down and hit him with that empty milk jar that's behind you!"

Lora's father lifted himself up, grabbing the shotgun he'd let fall to his feet once he'd begun pounding his fists into Rosie.

Hammond raised the firearm and pointed it directly at Bunch. Everyone froze.

"Why...you li'l...smart mouth...hefa! Gon'...on...over...there and... sit...yo' yo'...li'l...li'l...skinny rump...on the flo'."

Lora stepped in front of her younger sister. "Don't you listen to Daddy. You stay right here. He can't shoot us all at the same time."

C tried his luck at manhood. "Daddy, you best leave my mama alone. You best leave my sister alone, too!"

Hammond fixed a drunken glare on the children standing before him. The room's tone was unnatural. Nobody budged.

A light-brown-skinned, weathered and scarred hand slowly raised the shotgun.

"Then...all...all...of...you...you...smart asses...go...on over there wit... yo'...mama. And I mean quick and in a hurry, Goddammit!"

They stood in solidarity, like slabs of stone.

Hammond gritted his teeth. Spat. Pointed his shotgun up toward the ceiling, pulled the trigger and blew a hole clean through the roof of the house. Everyone screamed in a panic as Bunch and C scurried over to Rosie quick and in a hurry!

C put a protective arm around Rosie as she screamed, "Hammond, please don't shoot that thang no mo'!"

But Hammond paid no attention, aiming the shotgun directly at Lora.

Rosie was beside herself. "Hammond, is you done gon' mad?!!"

"I'm talkin' to...you...too, ya...li'l yalla gal. If you don't...git on over there...wit...yo' mama you...sho...gon' wish you had!"

Lora looked into her father's face without flinching. After living with Hammond's threats for as long as she could remember, Lora knew that no matter how much liquor he'd consumed, he'd never shoot her. "You gon' be real sorry, Daddy, real sorry." And with that she tore from the house in a mad search for her two older brothers.

Meanwhile, Hammond turned back to Rosie. "If you don't... don't whip that...fast...yalla gal, I'm just...gon'...gon' have ta whip you...Li'l Rosie."

"My Lord, Hammond, these babies ain't done a thang to you! How in the world you gon' come in here and start threatenin' to shoot yo' own chilrens? Why don't you just leave 'em be?!"

This time the shotgun was aimed at Rosie.

"Now...I...I...I see where they git...git they smart...lip from. You... suppose to be a...righteous influence. I...should...shoot you and...all these...li'l hefas right...right now...you all needs to be leavin' here... tonight! Godammit!"

Rosie put her hands on her hip and courageously threatened her husband in turn.

"You can kill me, John Hammond, but you sho' can't eat me!"

The children looked up at their mother in utter bewilderment. What in the world did she mean by such foolishness? Bunch rolled her eyes and thought how much luckier their daddy was to be married to Rosie than to her. She wouldn't be wasting any time saying dumb things like their mother just had. She'd be plotting some horrific way to do away with his evil ass.

"Daddy's been beatin' on Mama!"

She'd hardly gotten the words out before JD, Otis Miller, Wesley Dobbs, and Charles Jones took off running. Lora found them at Otis Miller's having a Friday night fish fry. Sonny was the only one missing. He'd left a few minutes early to walk his girlfriend, Helen, home.

Hammond might not have been as drunk as he'd been only a short while before. He was instantly aware of the impending arrival of JD and his entourage. He rushed over to the screen door and witnessed the angry and agitated youths approaching.

"Now...where...them sons of bitches...think they goin'?!"

Bunch slithered up behind her father with an evil smile. "They comin' to kill yo' evil ass, Daddy. Look like you the one gon' be leaving here tonight."

The only reason Hammond didn't respond to Bunch's razor tongue was that he'd barely heard it. His full attention was focused on the riled-up young men.

Stepping onto the porch, Hammond raised his shotgun and aimed it directly at the foursome.

"Hot damn! Don't nobody take another step!"

Lora ignored her father, frantically slipping into the house to check on Rosie and her siblings.

Hammond looked over at Otis Miller, who was much too effeminate for his taste, then over to Wesley Dobbs, who had to be the most unattractive young man in all of Godwin County; he was lucky to even get fat, pimple-faced Arlene Hicks for a date. Then Hammond stared at Charles Jones, whose eyes were slightly crossed, and finally over at his son, JD.

The slightly drunken patriarch belched, gritted his teeth, and coughed up foul liquid that he spat out. A trace of spittle landed right between Charles's crossed eyes.

"Dammit, Daddy! Didn't I tell you 'bout beatin' on my mama?!"

"I don't give a mule's ass 'bout you tellin' nobody...nothin'! Godammit! But I'm gon'...tell...you... somethin'. If you don't git Miss Sissified... Ole Ugly...and cockeyed...Li'l Piss in the pants...away from 'round here, they mommas gon' be visitin' them over at Horton's Funeral Home tomorrow, and fo' certain, yo' mama gon' be right there wit' 'em!"

"You the only one headed over to Horton's tomorrow, Daddy! I warned you about hittin' on my mama!"

JD walked toward the steps and Hammond fired two shots to the ground, but JD kept coming.

Lora and her mother came screaming out to the porch.

Rosie shrieked, "Nooo!!! Nooo!!!"

Hammond looked over at his wife with disgust. "Shut up, woman! You disturbin' the peace!"

John Hammond pointed at JD's feet. "Boy, you take another step and you gon' be about...a crippled...dead...li'l nigga!"

Lora watched in horror as her mother threw herself in front of JD and physically blocked him from advancing any closer toward his father.

"Lawd have mercy, Hammond! Please; put that shotgun down! Please don't shoot my baby!"

"You best talk to his fool ass then, 'cause he gon' make me do somethin' I ain't 'bout to regret tomorrow."

Rosie beseeched Otis Miller. "Please take JD and ask your mama to let him and Sonny stay wit y'awl for the night."

"That's no problem, Miss Rosie. Come on, JD; let's get on back over to my place. We gotta try to head Sonny off. Can't have no family killin' each other. This ain't nothing but crazy!"

"Hell, naw! Mama, I ain't leaving you in this house wit' Daddy," JD declared, gently pushing his mother from his path.

Lora had heard stories about how the slaves were never to look a white person in the eye. Even now, there were blacks who still felt intimidated looking into the eyes of white folks. But not John Hammond. He taught his children to always look him, and everyone else in the eye when they were being spoken to. "Look me in the eye," he'd chant, "look me in the eye." At that moment, his son was doing exactly that, and with pure hatred.

Rosie shrieked, "Lawd, Jesus!!"

Lora shouted, "Daddy!" as Hammond pointed his shotgun right between JD's eyes.

Wesley Dobbs yelled out, "Jesus Christ! Mr. Hammond! What on earth are you doing?! You can't be that damn drunk!"

Hammond immediately pointed his shotgun in Wesley's face.

"Who the hell...you talkin' to?! Don't make me have to shoot yo' ole...ugly...monkey ass!"

That gave JD his opening as he knocked the gun out of his father's hand as Sonny burst through the screen door, racing to pick it up.

Sonny had caught sight of their father from the road, sneaked around and entered through the back of the house. Now with shotgun in hand, he aimed at his father with fingers ready to pull the trigger. But in the nick of time, Rosie knocked the barrel away before bullets rang out.

"Mercy! Jesus! You almost killed your daddy! Oh my Lawd! You just about killed yo' daddy!"

In a split-second, Hammond grabbed the shotgun away from Sonny and pointed it into his son's chest, backing him off the porch.

"Git the hell off of my property! Don't nobody threaten to shoot John Hammond in his own house! You li'l black nigger!!! I'm the man in this goddamn house! Always runnin' 'round here gittin' in me and Rosie's business. She might be yo' mama, goddammit! But she my goddamn wife! Now since you and yo' brother wanna be the men 'round here, you gon' git out and git yo' own damn house! Then you can be the man over there! But come sun-up tomorrow, yo' li'l narrow asses best be long gon' from here!"

Rosie clutched her chest; her eyes filled with tears. "Why would you try to shoot yo' daddy like that? What would we do wit'out yo' daddy?"

JD took Rosie firmly around the waist. "It's okay, Mama. Daddy's alive and well. Come on and let me take you back in the house."

The two went inside as the friends grabbed Sonny and pulled him away from the yard. Hammond walked off in the opposite direction. His youngest children, still sitting on the side of the road, watched their father as he drifted past, cursing obscenities and mumbling to himself.

"Next time one of you li'l niggas aim a damn shotgun at yo' daddy... you sho' best pull the trigger...'cause if you fuck up...Peter gon' be waitin' at the gate for ya."

Lora was baffled. How could her mother care one iota about what happened to their father? He was despicable. God would've been doing them all a favor to take him away.

She waited until he disappeared through the darkened fog and then went to collect her siblings. They were all clumped together sitting by the side of the road, and still scared half to death.

Lora cringed inside, tilting her throbbing head toward the sky. *God, what did any of us do to ever deserve a daddy like this?*

Harlem, New York City
Late 1950s

I skipped ahead of my mommy, who meandered behind me, speaking to a few neighbors on our block.

"Would you like a cookie, sweetie?" a man's voice called to me from his spot on the ground between two trash cans.

He waved a chocolate chip cookie at me. I remember thinking that he looked like the horses I colored in my coloring books. His giant head was mammoth, quite long and narrow. His black doe eyes would have been lovely had they not been so close together, and he was bobbing his head up and down as if he wanted to be petted.

Nonetheless, I wanted that cookie. I grabbed at the treat but missed as he quickly raised it over his head. He beckoned me forward with a grimy index finger.

"Get back, you lunatic!" Mommy intervened. She knocked the cookie to the ground and snatched me out of the man's reach.

I thought she'd done a very mean thing and *Mr. Horse* must have thought so, too. "You filthy bitch!"

A horrified look crossed Mommy's face as she stared down at the long, dirty piece of meat hanging out of *Mr. Horse*'s unzipped pants.

But it was his loud voice, and that familiar word, *bitch*, which sent the familiar jolt throughout my body. Suddenly, I felt we were in a familiar situation Mommy couldn't protect us from. *She never could.*

Mommy grabbed my hand. The chant, often played in my head, was now sung aloud, "Run, Mommy! Run!" And with that, came the ever-present twitching in the pit of my stomach.

Racing the block to our apartment, my short, chubby legs fought to keep up with Mommy's long, pretty ones, while the lecherous derelict was in hot pursuit.

At least she was smart enough to already have her key out to open the front, metal plate security door. We made it through, but Mommy closed the door with such force, she must have knocked *Mr. Horse* in the face. We certainly didn't stop to check. We just heard the scream of agony.

"You fucking whore! I'll cut your throat!"

But the two of us bolted up the three flights of stairs and into our apartment, slamming the door behind us!

Once we had safely made it into our apartment, I ran over to the sofa and tucked my knees up to my chest, trembling. I was unnerved by an ordeal I didn't quite understand, except the emotion of fear, which was all too familiar.

Mommy swooped me up in her arms, hugging me tightly.

"Debbi, you must never, ever, take anything from strangers."

I responded by obediently nodding my head.

She kissed my lips and whispered gently, "Stop shaking, sweetheart; you don't have to be afraid anymore. Everything's all right now."

But the softness in her tone did nothing to reassure me. How could I believe the declaration? I lived and breathed fear every weekday in dreadful anticipation of weekends. I recognized fear long before I learned how to spell my name. I felt like I had been born cognizant of fear. It enveloped the air I breathed; it spoke for me; it ruled me and had its way with me... it was the monkey on my back.

My mommy, Lora, my daddy, George, and little old me lived in a two-bedroom railroad flat. It was the third floor of a five-floor walk-up on 117th Street and Fifth Avenue. Technically, Harlem, and not the rich section of Fifth Avenue, but Mommy had made it as much of a showplace as she and Daddy could afford.

The entrance to the apartment was a nicely decorated living room. Its walls were painted a dusty rose with shiny white trim. In the corner of the room was a long window adorned with white embroidered curtains, which helped conceal the unattractive view of the alley. Directly across from the front door, on the largest wall in the room, sat a big, black sofa with white piping. The couch was quite unusual. It had two attached white Formica end tables. Friends commented on how impressive it was. Daddy enjoyed impressing.

To the left of the living room was my parents' bedroom. It was the only room in the apartment that faced the street. It had a beautiful mahogany dresser lined with dainty doilies and beautiful bottles topped with Mommy's perfumes.

A walk down the long, narrow hall took one past the small bathroom decorated in pink and white, through the yellow kitchen, and into my blue and white room. Blue was my favorite color and Mommy had my walls painted in all different shades of blue. In the corner, across from my bed, sat a huge, blue and white dollhouse; I was consumed by it. I didn't care much about the dolls; I loved decorating all the rooms with my pretty doll furniture.

The most prevalent marker in our home, even more than the decor, was the scent of Old Spice. My father's cologne permeated the entire place. This was somehow befitting since Daddy's presence was larger than life.

A brand-new console sat across from the couch, which housed the TV and the Hi-Fi. Its shelves held all of Daddy's hottest LPs, mostly of Ray Charles. Ray Charles was Daddy's idol, and whenever music was heard streaming from our apartment, it was a rarity not to hear Ray's melodious voice. I hated Ray's voice. B.B. King was another favorite. I hated his voice, too, but Ray Charles held the throne.

It was a Thursday night...always the calm before the storm. Mommy undressed me and began rubbing my hands and feet, which was always so soothing.

"You have to be up for nursery school at seven o'clock, so Mommy's going to give you a quick, hot bath."

"Mommy, will you read me *Goldilocks and the Three Bears?"* I stalled. Maybe, if Mommy read to me all night, Friday would not come so fast.

"Not tonight, Baby; it's late. On the weekend, Mommy will let you stay up late and tell you all the stories you want to hear."

I looked into that beatific face. The bruise underneath her eye had almost disappeared, but the memory of how she had gotten it had not. And when she smiled down at me, there was still the gaping hole where her front tooth used to be. Yet she was by far, the prettiest mommy in the whole world.

People remarked about her all the time: *"That is one gorgeous woman!"*

While he was playing cards and drinking one night, I overheard Daddy say to his friends, "Shit, Man, my woman's got an ass that would launch ships!" I didn't know what the comment meant, but from the adoring smile and gleam in Daddy's eye, he obviously adored Mommy's ass. I wished Daddy always had that adoring look in his eye.

It was highly unlikely there'd be any storytelling on the week-end. I loved Mommy so much and cried myself to sleep many nights because I was too little and too scared to protect us. Mommy was much bigger, but she couldn't protect us either.

If only I was brave and strong and could use my fists the way my father could. The only good I could do was to pray to God each night that Daddy would die.

"Dear Jesus, please take Daddy away so he can rest. He must be awfully tired of fighting and yelling all the time. If you would put your hand on his heart, so it would stop screaming, he'd be so happy, and so would Mommy and I."

As I began to drift off, I heard the front door creak as it slowly opened and realized he'd come in. The bubbles in the pit of my stomach started foaming even though it was only Thursday and Daddy hadn't stopped off at the bar before coming home...

After a half-hour or so had passed, there was an undeniable stillness in the house. It was only then was I able to fall into a deep sleep.

But tomorrow was another day.

Chapter 5

"Rise and shine, Sleepyhead."

It was 7:01 a.m. when Mommy pulled the covers away and saw my tiny form hunched into a tight, fetal position. She smothered me with kisses, but when she leaned back, she must have witnessed the brief hint of fear in my eyes. I was acutely aware that today was Friday.

"Good morning, Mommy."

I attempted a smile as she held me against her breast for the longest moment.

"Good morning, my sweet baby. You scoot on to the bathroom now while Mommy gets your breakfast ready."

I went and stood on my stool in front of the bathroom sink and squeezed a glob of peppermint toothpaste onto my toothbrush. Then I took a lick with some on my tongue. After all, why shouldn't my tongue be as clean as my teeth?

It was then that I heard her laughter. Mommy was telling Daddy about Butch, a boy in my nursery school class.

"She runs on and on about this Butch. You should hear her, George. 'He's so handsome, Mommy...and he has the prettiest hair.'"

I could not believe Mommy was telling Daddy about my dearest secret. The Friday knots in my stomach were already beginning and now I was terrified of his reaction. But surprisingly, Daddy didn't even raise his voice.

"All I know is, that little knucklehead better stay away from my baby," Daddy mumbled, with a slight chuckle.

Mommy echoed Daddy's chuckle as she bounced into the bathroom to help me finish up. Then we hurried back into my room where all my clothes were laid out.

"Mommy," I whispered, "why did you tell Daddy about Butch? You shouldn't have told him. He's gonna be really mad."

My sad dark eyes must have given away my fear of betrayal.

"Oh, Baby, Mommy's sorry. I didn't know you didn't want me to tell Daddy about Butch. But why would he be mad at you?"

Mommy must have lost all her marbles. We both knew it didn't take much to anger my father, but I couldn't form the words to tell her this.

"Don't worry, Sweetheart. I promise he won't be mad, okay? Now, your breakfast is on the table. Run in and eat it while it's nice and hot. Oh, Daddy's taking you to nursery school this morning. Mommy has to go to the dentist."

She blurted this out over her shoulder while rushing from my room.

I slowly moped my way to the kitchen and climbed up in my chair. Looking down at the plate of hot grits, eggs, and bacon, I was not very happy. I understood it was important for my mother to have her tooth put back in, but couldn't she take me to nursery school first? I didn't relish being taken by my father, not today.

These thoughts swam through my little head as I hurriedly finished my hominy grits filled with butter. I loved grits with lots of butter. They were a close third after ice cream and chocolate chip cookies, but I absolutely hated bacon and eggs.

I peeked out into the hall and saw that my parents' bedroom door was closed. I quickly grabbed my plate from the table and ran over to the broom closet where I proceeded to scrape the bacon and eggs off into a far corner. I covered the food with an old rag and shut the door.

"Scooby-Doo! Have you finished eating? Time to hit the road, Jack!" My father shouted out in the hip slang of the day. He was all of twenty-three years old, and as fine as wine, another hip slang that was used to describe a black man as beautiful and sharp as he was. At six-feet-one with a slim physique, he had a warm, toasted almond complexion, natural wavy hair that didn't need a process, a long slender nose and high cheekbones. But most apparent were the two very deep dimples in his cheek that'd been genetically passed on to me.

I'd made it back up into my chair just in time, pretending to finish my breakfast. My father walked into the kitchen with his usual swagger, dressed to kill. He had on a chocolate, double-breasted, pinstriped suit, with a white, tailor-made shirt and dark-brown alligator shoes.

I looked up at this resplendent man and saw why Mommy loved him so, even though he often made it so difficult. He was the epitome of sweetness and warmth as he helped me on with my light-blue coat with the white fake fur collar. Now as I thought about it, I realized there were many times Daddy was sweet, especially through the week when he had to work and keep a clear head.

Daddy was a butcher in one of those fancy downtown delicatessens on Park Avenue. He always changed out of his cool duds into his khaki pants and work shirt with the full apron, the one with the bib that went around the neck. If he wasn't working, he looked like a man who was too cool to have to lift a finger. Yet no matter his other faults, my father was a hard worker who supported his family and made sure we were always dressed as sharply as he.

Being a butcher didn't make us rich by any means, but it was a decent living. He also got huge tips from those wealthy, white, penthouse ladies whenever he delivered their prime sirloins. They thought he looked like a black matinee idol. So whenever Daddy, Mommy, and I walked down our Harlem street, we were always a sight to behold.

"Who's got the prettiest legs in town?" Daddy asked as we walked hand in hand toward the nursery school.

"Me, Daddy, me!"

He loved saying my fat chubby legs were the prettiest around. Every so often, Daddy tickled the inside of my palm. It made me laugh, and for a moment, I forgot there was anything to be troubled about.

"Daddy, will you come home earlier today and take Mommy and me to the Five and Dime for a banana split?"

The fantasy of the moment was over and I was back to being troubled. Maybe I could devise some plan to get my father home before he had a chance to stop off at the bar.

"I'm not sure if I'll be able to do that, Baby, but if I can't, Mommy will most definitely take you."

We reached the corner of 112th Street where the nursery school was located on the first floor of the Steven Foster housing project.

Daddy looked down at me. "So Mommy tells me you like a little boy named Butch." I was too frightened to respond, so I didn't.

"Debbi, did you hear me talking to you?"

"Uh...yes...Daddy. Please don't be mad...I only like him sometimes."

He laughed out loud, which was joy to my ears. "Baby, it's all right. Daddy's not mad at you. You're so pretty, you're going to break all the boys' hearts."

My father's reaction happily convinced me he was not upset about Butch. Then, scooping me up in his arms, he planted a kiss on my fat, dimpled cheek. "You be a good girl today, and if I don't get to go with you and Mommy to the Five and Dime, you tell her to let you have my extra scoop of ice cream, okay?"

I lovingly squeezed around his neck, wishing the moment could stand still.

As he sat me back down on my feet, I heard someone calling, "Debbi! Debbi!"

A raspy baritone was heard out of the mouth of a five-year-old boy who was running down the street with his older brother lagging behind.

"Daddy, here comes Butch!" I announced gleefully.

The handsome Butch with the pretty hair, the object of my endearment, was fast approaching. The truth of the matter was that Butch didn't have a single strand of hair on his head. He'd had a severe case of ringworm and his head had been completely shaved. I happened to find that look particularly appealing and defined it in my mind as having pretty hair.

Butch also had a few battle scars from some of his daily scuffles. All the kids in the nursery school were terrified of him, all except me. That was because Butch was in love with me and made sure no one ever bothered me. And he was always trying to come up with ways to express his love for me.

"Hey, Debbi! Wait for me!"

And as my little heart went pitter-patter at the sight of my enormous affection approaching, Bam! Butch hauled off and punched me in the stomach with his little fist. It was too bad Daddy wasn't still holding me in his arms. For a second, I felt as though the wind had been knocked out of me, but I quickly recovered.

Butch ran through the double doors with me chasing right behind. "Wait, Butch! Wait for me!"

One would think Butch presented too much of a disturbing familiarity and would therefore be incapable of kindling my heart. However, it was the brutal familiarity that oddly drew me toward him. He was also my protector, and I had such a desperate need to feel protected.

Daddy couldn't believe what had taken place, it'd happened so fast. "Come back here, you little knucklehead!"

He chased after Butch, who'd already begun rough-housing with another little boy in the hallway, and snatched him up by his pants, holding him high in the air.

"Don't you ever hit my little girl again or you'll be very sorry; you got that?!"

"Let go of me! Get offa' me!" Butch screamed defiantly.

Miss Brunson, our nursery school teacher, came running out into the hall to find the source of the commotion. All the other kids came running out behind her.

"What on earth is the matter?"

"This li'l tyrant punched my daughter in the stomach; that's what's the matter. If he ever puts his hands on her again, I'll whip his butt. Now get out of here!"

Daddy lowered Butch to the ground. The boy ran into the classroom, but I stood there frozen, not knowing what to do.

"I want everyone to go inside and wait for me, quietly, right now," Miss Brunson admonished all the children. "Debbi, Sweetheart, you go wait by the door."

Miss Brunson was so perceptive. She must have known I'd be too embarrassed to walk into the classroom alone after what'd happened. However, I wouldn't move from my spot until Daddy gave the okay.

"Debbi, did you hear what your teacher said?"

"Yes, Daddy."

I quickly ran over to the door, pretending not to pay attention, but I shuffled back close enough to hear their conversation.

I couldn't help but notice Miss Brunson's body language. Now that she was alone with my father, she seemed a bit nervous. This was only the third time Daddy had ever brought me to school. On the other two occasions, he'd simply waved to Miss Brunson who'd been standing by the door talking with another parent; then he'd whisked off to work.

As Miss Brunson spoke to my father, she had a weird, fixed smile plastered across her face, and an unusual quiver in her voice. I wondered if Daddy could see her knees knocking together. I'd never seen Miss Brunson so out of character.

"Mister...Mister... uh..."

She could hardly speak Daddy's name with any clarity, let alone look him in the eye. But finally, it seemed Miss Brunson gathered the courage to steady herself.

"You know, Butch has such a crush on Debbi, and children don't know what to do with those feelings. I'm sure he wasn't trying to hurt her. Now I do have to stay on him about fighting, but he's never hurt Debbi."

Daddy looked dumbfounded. "He's never hurt her? He rammed his fist into her stomach! You just make sure he doesn't ever do it again."

Now that Daddy had adamantly made his point, his quick fury turned amiable. He gave Miss Brunson his charming smile and said goodbye.

Miss Brunson returned it with a coy grin. "Oh, don't you worry. I'll make sure Butch doesn't lay a hand on Debbi ever again."

I watched Miss Brunson's eyes trail my daddy as he swaggered out the door. She stood there until he was long out of sight. Then my teacher shook her head and whispered under her breath, "Lord have mercy; what a beautiful man! Damn, his wife is lucky."

I could have told sweet Miss Brunson, she didn't know how unlucky my mother was.

For the rest of the day, I had a hard time interacting with the other kids, and I paid little attention to Butch. I was usually outgoing, although never loud or uncontrollable. If another child was mean or said something to hurt my feelings, I would retreat into my shell, willing myself not to cry while enduring the painful twitching in the pit of my stomach.

The only time any of the kids got away with being cruel to me was if Butch wasn't around, and there were many days the little tyrant was absent. The bullying also never happened within ear-shot of Miss Brunson. For the most part, I laughed and played quite easily with all the other children, except for Fridays, when I was probably noticeably more subdued, even without a situation like the one that morning.

"Is anyone doing anything special with their family this weekend?"

"Me! Me! Me! Miss Brunson, my mommy and daddy are taking me and my sister to the Bronx Zoo."

"Miss Brunson! Miss Brunson! I'm going to be in my aunt's wedding. I'm going to be the flower girl."

"What about you, Debbi? Are your mommy and daddy doing anything special for the weekend?"

The reference to the weekend sent a cold chill through me. I didn't look directly at Miss Brunson, but instead cast my eyes down to the floor exactly as she'd done with my father.

"Uh...I don't know. I think we're going to go to the Five and Dime for some ice cream."

"You stupid! We already had ice cream for lunch. That ain't special!" yelled out Larry, who was sitting in a corner tying his shirt around his head.

All the children broke into laughter, and Larry, who was the class clown, laughed the loudest.

I wished I could cough the lump out of my throat, but then every-one would know how humiliated I was. Instead, I dug my little fingers deep into my palms to hold back the tears.

Miss Brunson clapped her hands. "Quiet! Quiet! Larry, don't you ever call anyone stupid again, and take that shirt from around your—"

Pow! Butch knocked Larry upside the head and little Larry toppled to the floor.

Miss Brunson darted across the room before Butch could do any more damage.

"Stop it, Butch Bailey! How many times have I told you about fighting?! Go stand in the corner and don't you move until I say so. The rest of you draw in your coloring books, and I don't want to hear a sound."

Miss Brunson walked over to me and stooped down. Hugging me, she whispered, "Debbi, do you know what I do every Saturday?"

"No, Miss Brunson."

"I go to the Five and Dime and have a big bowl of chocolate ice cream, and that makes Saturday my most special day of the week."

Chapter 6

Wade County, North Carolina

"For heaven's sake, Gal! Will you hurry up! You ain't the only one gots to have they shoes shined for school."

Lora sat on a small wooden stool on the back porch with her father's shoeshine box. She shined away at the dusty, black shoes with the badly worn soles. She greatly irritated her younger brother, C, by ignoring him and purposely polishing more slowly.

"You thankin' you smart; you hear me talkin' to you gal. I ain't playin' whitcha! You better hurry up...or..."

"Or you'll what?! Git on away from here till I'm finished. Ain't nobody studyin' you!"

Suddenly, Lora plopped to the floor. C had pulled the stool right out from under her.

In a flash, she was up, and with the shoe brush still in her hand, knocked C upside the head with it. He grabbed his head and Lora began banging him across the knuckles. C collected himself and grabbed ahold of one of his sister's braids, apparently trying his best to rip it from her scalp.

She screamed in pain. "Let go of my doggone hair, C!!"

"Mama, Mama! Lora and C out here fightin' again!" Young Franklin's voice was heard in the doorway.

Lora kicked C in the leg, hard, and he let go of her hair. She tried to push him off the porch, but he grabbed her dress, causing them both to fall off. Wallowing through the dirt, they punched, kicked, bit, and scratched. No one would've believed they were any relation whatsoever.

Rosie ran up with her broom and started tanning hides.

"Stop this mess, right now, I said! Doggone, y'awl, I done told you two 'bout this cuttin' up! Now you git yo' li'l narrow behinds outta here fo' you miss that school bus!"

Because of the fight, they ended up missing the school bus, anyway. So Rosie whipped the two again and made them walk the two miles to school, torn, dirty clothes and all.

At the end of the school day, Lora rushed home to help Rosie prepare dinner. She was already on her mother's bad side and didn't waste any time giving a helping hand.

A few hours later, the entire family was gathered and seated, ready to begin the evening's meal. They waited patiently while Rosie shuffled through the cupboard looking for Hammond's coffee cup. It was the only one he'd ever drink from.

"Daddy, you won't be able to drink yo' coffee outta yo' yellow mug no more," little Virginia informed her father. "Bunch broke it. You can't glue it back together neitha' 'cuz she threw all the pieces way out in the woods."

"You a damn lie!" Bunch blurted out.

Lora was aghast as she sat staring with an open mouth at her sister. Bunch was becoming as crazy as their daddy.

With all of the fighting amongst the children, it was obvious the effect of physical violence in their home life had escaped none of them, especially Bunch. The child had a mean streak in her that was absolutely deadly. She could hold a grudge forever, and at times her vengeful tactics bordered on the criminal.

Rosie slapped Bunch hard across the mouth.

Hammond looked over to Lora. "Pretty gal, go out in dem woods and git two thick switches fo' yo' mama. Git a fat one fo' this devil here who's a liar wit' a nasty mouth, and a fatter one for this li'l tattletale sister of yorn'."

It didn't matter to Bunch that Virginia hadn't been spared; or that in bed that night she whispered how sorry she was for being a tattletale. The next evening, after preparing dinner, Lora set out to retrieve Elvira, Bunch, and Virginia from the barn where they were playing cowboys and Indians, the previous evening's events all seemingly forgotten.

Elvira and Virginia were the Indians, and Bunch was the cowboy. Bunch drew her imaginary gun and shot Elvira. Her baby sister fell to the ground with her eyes closed, pretending to be dead. When Bunch shot Virginia, she refused to die. Bunch slowly sashayed over to a corner of the barn where Hammond kept his tools and grabbed a hammer. Then she slowly walked back over to Virginia and hit her over the head. "I said die, goddammit! Die!"

Blood shot out of Virginia's head as Elvira began screaming hysterically. Lora rushed in upon hearing the cries where she found her baby sister lying on the ground and Bunch standing over her.

"Lora! Lora!" Elvira wailed. "Bunch done killed Virginia dead!"

Of course Bunch was whipped mercilessly, and thankfully Virginia did live to tell the story. But as long as she shared a bed with her sister, she would sleep with one eye open.

Summers and winters came and went and many things shifted at home, not necessarily for the best. Lora still found her daily environment disparaging, causing her and her siblings to continually lash out with their frustrations. It seemed like an eternity since that dreadful night her two older brothers had tried to shoot their father. JD was in the Navy now, and Sonny had married a lovely young girl named Hermie. But their father's behavior still very much pervaded the rest of them.

The past winter had been terrible, with most of the crops frozen. This allowed even more time for a depressed, out-of-work Hammond, to stretch his drunken binges way past Friday and Saturday nights. There were times he'd get so drunk he couldn't even hold his bowels. He'd come down the road barely able to walk, with his trousers completely soiled. The only good thing was that as he began to fall more and more into his nightly stupors, he was in less of a condition to fight with Rosie.

It was a cool and rainy evening. Lora was lying across the bed watching rain splatter against the windowpane. She'd set dinner on the table, but was waiting to call everyone to eat. Rosie had made a quick run to the outhouse. Duty called, even in the pouring rain.

Of all the animals they had on the farm, everybody's favorite was a brown and black mutt named Queenie. But Hammond didn't particularly care for the canine. She barked too much for his taste and the children were never allowed to bring her into the house.

Rosie had left the back door ajar when she'd run out, and Queenie, smelling the delicious aroma, ran in with her dripping wet hair. She jumped up on the table and happily began to feast.

Unfortunately for the innocent pup, her drunken master was walking in. Hammond stood at the kitchen doorway, staring through bloodshot eyes at the sight before him.

"Goddammit!... Fool dog! I'm gon' git...my goddamn shotgun... and shoot you...in the ass!"

These words meant absolutely nothing to Queenie, and that, too, was unfortunate. Hammond walked back into the kitchen with his shotgun and true to his word, pop...pop...pop. Three loud shots rang out as everyone came running in. They could not believe their eyes as they stared at the motionless pup. There was their beloved Queenie, dead, lying face down in a pan of chicken gravy.

Lora harbored fury for her mother as well; whose only comment had been a meek one. "Well, you know yo' daddy said he best not ever find Queenie in this house."

That following Saturday evening, Hammond was out gambling and getting drunk of course. As the hour grew late, Lora, C, and Bunch waited out on the porch and kept a close watch for their father. They needed time to run for the shotgun if necessary.

Bunch, jumping up and down the wooden steps, was in full form. "Daddy ain't nothing but a no-account, lowdown, drunk son of a bitch!"

Lora couldn't believe her ears. "Bunch, are you crazy?! You'd better not let Momma hear you talking 'bout Daddy like that. Besides, you can hardly sit down from that last whipping. You keep it up and they'll be carrying your narrow behind over to Horton's."

C fell down the steps laughing hysterically.

"Always walkin' 'round here, talkin' 'bout, I'm John Hammond; look me in the eye." Bunch strutted around the porch, imitating their father, swaying from side to side and gritting her teeth.

"My name is...John Hammond. You look me...in the eye...Goddammit!"

Bunch hacked up some spittle, and spewed, catching C on the forehead.

"Hey, watch it, Gal!"

Bunch ignored her older brother and spread her legs wide apart and placed her hands on her hips. "I want you to look me in the eye, John Hammond. I said look me in the eye, goddammit! You about... a...crazy...stinkin' can't hold shit in your pants...no-account...drunk-ass...mothafucka!!"

And at that very second, their drunk, crazy-ass father stuck his head from around the side of the house. Lora's, C's, and Bunch's eyes all grew as big as saucers.

Hammond gritted his teeth, spat, and gave his second-eldest daughter a devilish grin. "Hot damn! I...done...caught...them dice. Now...roll 'em...again. Goddammit!"

The children who stood before him knew the meaning of their father's less than poetic and derisive words. He'd heard every word out of Bunch's little foul mouth and was affording her the luxury of repeating them once again, because they'd probably be the last words she'd utter for a very long time.

Chapter 7

Harlem, New York City

"How about spaghetti and meatballs for dinner? Would you like that?"

"Oh, goody! We're gonna have SpaghettiOs and meatballs, and Daddy's going to come home earlier and take us to the Five and Dime for a banana split."

"Tell you what, why don't we get some bananas, ice cream, chocolate fudge, nuts, cherries, whipped cream, and Mommy will make you the biggest banana split ever? You can even have seconds."

On any other day, I would've pleaded, but today was scary Friday and my mother had enough to worry about, so I simply said, "Okay, Mommy."

Hours later, we'd finished our spaghetti and meatballs, and now I was standing on a chair beside my mother in the kitchen helping do the dishes. She was washing and I was drying.

"Mommy, should we wait for Daddy before we eat our banana splits?" It was about 8 p.m.

"No, Baby; he might not get home until late. Why don't you put your jammies on and you can help Mommy make our desserts."

We sat in front of the TV watching *The Three Stooges* and eating our banana splits. I saw my mother's nervous laugh as Moe poked his fingers into Curly's eyes for the hundredth time. Then she stopped mid-cackle to glance at the clock. I'd learned to tell time when I was three years old and observed that it was 8:30. That wasn't a good sign.

Sometime later, I observed Mommy checking the time again. It was now 9:05. I could see the distress in her wrinkled brow. I nodded off shortly thereafter and she must have carried me to bed.

My eyes popped open the moment I was tucked in. "Mommy, I'm not sleepy yet."

"Oh, yes, you are; now night, night."

"Mommy, will you lie down with me until I fall asleep?"

She snuggled me tightly. I could still smell the chocolate on her breath tonight, but I always loved my mother's sweet smell.

"Okay, now close your eyes."

I closed my eyes but was now far from falling asleep. So my mother began reading my favorite story: "Goldilocks and the Three Bears."

We both heard the dreaded sound of my father's key turning in the lock. He walked in, slamming the door behind him. My mother and I both jumped, and the twitching in my stomach was so painful, I thought I'd surely die.

The walk from the living room down the narrow hall was quite short, but it seemed to take my father forever. His alligator shoes sounded so slow and deliberate.

"Where the hell are you, Sweetness?"

The smell of liquor on my father's breath made it to the door of my bedroom before he did. My mother stood immediately.

"I was lying down with Debbi until she fell asleep."

I held my eyes shut, pretending to be fast asleep indeed.

"Well, she's out like a light and I'm starving. Come on in here and make me a plate."

No, Mommy, don't leave! Please stay here with me. I screamed these words in my head as my parents stepped out of my room, closing the door behind them.

I prayed that whatever happened, my mother would be smart enough not to talk back. If only she would remain quiet when he went crazy, be extra sweet; that would've made it all better. Instead, my mother screamed some of the foulest language, matching my father head to head. That is until he began trading curses with his fists.

Suddenly, I realized how badly I had to go to the bathroom, probably because I'd gotten so nervous. I put my hand between my legs, holding myself with all my might. I didn't dare leave my room.

I could hear my mother rustling a pot on the stove, obviously heating up Daddy's food.

"So...did...you get...finished gettin' your...tooth...fixed?" His speech was slurred.

I didn't hear my mother answer at first, and then...

"No. I got one more appointment before everything is complete... but I don't know why you'd care."

Holy Jesus! What was wrong with Mommy?! Had she flipped? She knew better than to talk to Daddy like that!

Daddy shouted, "If I didn't care I wouldn't...ask! See, that's what I'm talkin'...'bout. You...always gots to be...talking...some smart...ass... shit outta...yo' mouth!"

"George, please. I don't wanna go through this with you tonight."

"No, what you wanna do is shut the fuck up! That's what you wanna do!"

"Do you want me to finish making you a plate or not?"

"I bet I'll smash...this...plate...upside your fuckin'...head!"

I rocked back and forth, whispering, "Mommy, please don't say anything else. Please, please, so Daddy won't be mad anymore."

I held my hands up to my ears as I tried to shut out the frightening outburst. Then I put them back between my legs to hold myself so I wouldn't pee in the bed.

A chair dragged across the floor, screeching loudly on the linoleum. Then there was a dead silence. I crawled out of bed and peeked through the keyhole. I watched Daddy plop down and pull off his shirt, exposing his big strong arms with those bulging muscles. He tossed his shirt to the floor and sat at the table in his white tee shirt.

Mommy made an ugly scowl, probably infuriated by Daddy's bad manners.

"Do you want a soda?" she asked.

"No, I don't want no goddamn soda! Gimme a beer!"

Mommy went into the refrigerator and got out a can of beer. She opened it and handed it to Daddy. He snatched it rudely and tossed his head back. Not all the beer landed in his mouth. Some trickled down his chin and onto his white tee shirt. Mommy rolled her eyes in disgust.

Daddy burped loudly and I had a quick flash of my teacher, Miss Brunson, shooting goo-goo eyes at him. I wondered how smiley-faced she'd be if she could see Daddy now.

He shoved a forkful of spaghetti into his mouth and then grabbed the salt shaker. Unfortunately, the cap must not have been on tight because as he went to sprinkle his food, the full bottle of salt poured out all over his spaghetti.

My chest heaved up and down in terror.

"Ain't this a bitch?! Jesus fuckin' Christ! Don't you know how to screw a motha' fuckin' cap on a fuckin' bottle of salt?!"

Mommy let out a deep sigh. "There is more spaghetti on the stove, George. I can make you another plate. What is the big deal?"

And with that, my father leaped from the table, grabbed the skillet off the stove, and tossed the remainder of the spaghetti across the room, aiming the pot directly at my mother's head. She ducked just in time, and the red tomato juice with noodles slithered down the bright yellow walls. The color of the juice seemed to match Mommy's eyes, as she glared back at him.

"Now, Miss Smart-ass...clean...this mess up...and make me...some... more...damn food!"

"I'm not making you a doggone thing! And I ain't cleaning up shit!"

I whispered urgently, "Mommy, please make Daddy some more food. Please, God, tell Mommy to make some more food so he won't hurt her."

My mother attempted to walk out of the kitchen, but Daddy grabbed her by her hair. While bouncing on my tiptoes to keep myself from peeing, I watched the man who was supposed to be our protector and my hero haul Mommy across the room. She went flying through the air like a rag doll, her backside banging full force into the refrigerator.

"You bastard! Get away from me!" she managed through shallow breaths. Mommy struggled to pull herself up again by using the refrigerator door.

"You...done lost your...stark-raving...mind?! You gon'...make...me somethin'...else...to...eat before...I put my foot in yo' ass!"

He snatched my mother by the hair again and pulled her down to her knees. He dragged her across the linoleum floor like a persecuted animal.

My mother's limbs fumbled across the floor, unable to find a steady position. "Let go of me! Let me go!"

I was on the verge of throwing up my spaghetti and meatballs, and I couldn't control my bladder much longer. I ran back for safety underneath the covers and rocked back and forth, shuddering with the horror of how this night might end.

The thumping, brutal sounds, and the agony and fear in my mother's relentless cries were more than I could bear.

"Motha' fuck!" I heard my father yelp, and then came the sound of frantic footsteps.

I heard my mother's screaming voice. "Help! Help! Please! Somebody call the police!"

"Close that goddamn window before I throw yo' ass out of it!"

It was then that I realized my mother had run to her bedroom window, which faced the street.

"Please! Get the police up here! He's trying to kill me!"

A few passersby looked up at our third-floor window, shook their heads, and continued on their merry way.

As my mother would recount to me years later, my father seemed sincere about his warning as he wrestled with her, trying to throw Mommy out of the window. It was hard to tell if he was truly intent on tossing her down, or if this was his sick way of scaring her half to death.

I followed the sound of the struggle back to the kitchen and resumed my view at the keyhole. Mommy had made it out of his clutches, but she was cornered between the refrigerator and the sink.

My father wrapped his large hands around her throat, and squeezed. She scratched and clawed at his hands, but it was no use. She was no match for his strong biceps.

I ran back to my bed again, crying, hoping that somehow she would slip out of his grasp.

Lying there frightened beyond reason, I shuddered at the thought of my beautiful mother lying helpless on the other side of my bedroom door. I was too traumatized to rise from my bed to go and check. Wet, warm tears ran down my face, and wet, warm urine down my legs. Shaking uncontrollably, I tried to brace myself for what might happen next. Since my father had finished with my mother, he'd surely come for me. The thought was almost welcomed. After all, death certainly had to be better than this.

Chapter 8

"Officer, he was lying right here on the floor! I stabbed him! I thought he might be dead! And my child is in there. I have to go in and see about her."

I was floating on a cloud of joy and sweet laughter with the faces of angels surrounding me. But I was awakened from my reverie by a loud voice. Thank God it belonged to my mother. She was still alive.

A stream of light burst into the room as Mommy flung open my bedroom door. She ran to me with a tearful face as I silently stared back at her.

"Oh, my sweetheart! My baby! It's okay. Mommy's here."

I began to shiver from lying in cold urine. "Mommy, I wet the bed. Please don't tell Daddy."

She pulled me into her arms. "Don't you worry about that. Mommy will get you all cleaned up."

My mother helped me out of bed and we walked into the kitchen where two police officers were standing.

"Well, Miss, where's your husband?"

Mommy said with a confused look, "I don't know."

Then we heard the calm voice. "I'm right here."

I watched my father slither into the kitchen and felt a tiny ray of hope. He didn't look angry anymore. There was a stunned expression on everyone's face.

"Sir, your wife said she stabbed you pretty bad. She thought she might have killed you."

Daddy had on a nice white shirt buttoned up to the neck. There was no blood evident on him or anywhere else. By no means did he look like a man whose wife had sliced him up.

He smiled warmly toward my mother. "Why you wanna make up a lie like that?" He turned to the men in the room. "We just had an argument, officer. Ain't nobody stabbed nobody. She probably made up that story to get you all up here."

Mommy was speechless.

"Miss, your husband seems to be fine. So since no one's hurt, I guess we'll be leaving."

"No! What do you mean?! You can't trust him! *I'm* hurt, even if he says he isn't! He came home tonight and started beating on me! He even tried to throw me out of our bedroom window!"

I grabbed at my stomach, trying to hold in the knot piercing through, but no one seemed to notice.

Daddy shook his head. "If I was trying to throw you out of a window, you'd be lying dead on the street right now. Officer, I guess I tried to throw her out of the window like she said she stabbed me to death. Come on now, Baby Doll. I'm sorry about all the arguing tonight. It was my fault, and I apologize. Let's get Debbi back to bed so you and I can get some serious shut-eye." Daddy winked at Mommy flirtatiously.

"He's pulling a trick until you officers leave! Can't you see what a phony act he's putting on? I don't care what he says, I *did* stab him because he was trying to kill me, and he's going to jump on me as soon as you leave!"

"Baby, that is not true. I'm not going to touch you, I swear. Now let's let these officers go on about their business." Daddy's face looked like butter wouldn't melt in his mouth.

"I'm afraid to stay in this apartment with him tonight and so is my child! She wet the bed because she was so nervous and frightened!"

Oh, no! Why did Mommy have to say that? I looked down to the floor, terrified of meeting my father's eyes. My legs wobbled so badly I felt the floor moving.

"Scooby-Doo, come here. Did you have an accident?"

I stood frozen, afraid that if I moved, the whole floor might open up and I would fall in.

Daddy took two steps toward me, and then lifted me up in his arms. But I didn't cling to him. I couldn't. My arms remained limp.

"Yes, you're wet. Well, don't worry. Mommy will clean you up and put you on some dry pajamas. Daddy loves you. Now gimme some suga."

Daddy had been monster man tonight and it was difficult pressing my lips to his face. But I did as I was instructed and gave him a tentative kiss on the cheek.

"That's my girl." He lowered me back down while looking sweetly at my mother. "Why don't you get her out of those wet clothes?"

He put the finishing touches on his charade. "Officers, my wife and I can talk this all out tomorrow. It's late and we need to get our daughter back to bed."

What an amazing talent Daddy had for turning back and forth between Monster Daddy and Sweet Daddy. After going through his rages, he'd always soften with apologies and kind words. It was confusing for me because as much as I loved the Sweet Daddy, I hated and feared the Scary One. So often, I'd prayed for God to come and take away Scary Daddy, or at least take me away.

I drifted back to the moment to hear Daddy telling the policemen he was going to bed. He walked away, leaving Mommy and me standing with the two officers.

"Why do you cops keep letting him get away with this?! A few weeks ago he knocked my tooth out. When the police came, all they did was tell him to take a walk and cool off! Does he have to kill me before you people do anything?! Why can't you make him leave! I'm afraid of him!!" my mother screamed.

"Miss, I'm sorry, but we can't put the man out of his own house."

"Well, what good are you?!!"

They were staring at Mommy as if she were the crazy one.

"Look, Miss, if your husband starts up anything else tonight, give us a call, and we'll come back." With that, the men in blue promptly turned and left our apartment.

Mommy yelled after them, "Yeah, and what will you do then?!"

It wasn't difficult to figure out that when it came to my father, both God and the police were pretty powerless.

Mommy washed me up and put me in clean pajamas. My sheets were changed and I was tucked securely under the covers. My little body was so drained and exhausted from the traumatic evening that I fell into a deep slumber within moments.

Once again, I floated on a sweet cloud of bliss and once again, I was shaken from this solace, by a loud voice. It was Ray Charles moaning out the song, "Georgia." Daddy always ended one of these evenings with Ray or B.B. King crooning some woeful tune as if he were the wounded party. For a long time, hearing a Ray Charles or B. B. King song would send a frigid chill up my spine.

The music was suddenly turned down and I heard a familiar voice talking to Daddy. It was his brother, my Uncle Bill, whom I was crazy about. He and Daddy were as different as night and day. I don't think I'd ever heard my uncle so much as raise his voice before. So it was unsettling to hear him so uncharacteristically upset.

"I don't believe this shit! Let me take you to the hospital!"

"Naw, Man, I don't need to go to no hospital. I need you to stay here with Debbi so I can see where the hell this woman's run off to in the middle of the night."

"Jesus Christ! She's cut you up like this and you're worried about where the hell she is!"

I fretted all over again, wondering why Mommy had finally run away and hadn't taken me with her. Little did I know, she was fretting too, as she lay trembling on a cold cement floor in the basement of our tenement.

"On second thought, I'm going to bed. My head is killin' me. Besides, she ran outta here with no coat on, so she damn sure can't be gone that long..."

"Dammit, Man! You'd better let me carry you to the hospital!"

"It's not as bad as it looks. They're superficial cuts."

"Superficial?! Look at all this blood. Looks to me like she could've cut an artery!"

"Jesus Christ! I said I'm fine! Now I'm going in here and lying down."

I heard a door slam. I didn't know whether it was the door to my parents' room or my uncle leaving the apartment.

It was surprising how well my father had been able to hide his cuts under his white shirt from the two policemen. I hadn't seen any blood seeping through. Daddy told my uncle that Mommy had tried to cut him up real good with the butcher knife, but he conveniently left out trying to throw Mommy from our third-floor window.

Hours after midnight, Mommy, cold and shivering, crawled into my bed and rested her face next to mine. I wrapped my arms around her neck in an effort to warm her up. Realizing I was awake, she tried to form words with her lips, but none came out.

Daddy cracked his head in the door. We both froze at the faint sound of his bare feet approaching. He leaned down as the two of us clutched each other, lying still as could be.

By now, his breath really stank from the fumes of stale alcohol and vile rhetoric. "Baby, I'm sorry about all this. I really am. Things are going to be different, I promise. You know I love you. Now why don't you get up and come to bed?"

Nobody stirred, and finally, Daddy let out a deep sigh and left the room.

Slowly, our chests began to heave, in unison. Once again, I felt the warm, wet tears; only this time, they belonged to Mommy.

Chapter 9

Wade County, North Carolina

"Come on, Lora; let's ride our bikes for a while before supper." Tommy Lawrence, her favorite cousin, was already pedaling away on his. Lora, who could be a real tomboy, had no trouble catching up.

She was spending part of the summer in Dunn with her father's younger brother, Wes, and his wife, Florence. It was a real treat getting out of rural Godwin. The family had moved abruptly from Wade County after their daddy had lost the farm.

"Hey, Tommy Lawrence, let's go past my Aunt Luticia's house. Mama said she lives over on North King Avenue!"

"No kidding? My best friend, George Morgan Jr., lives on North King Avenue! Everybody calls him June on account of him having the same name as his daddy, George. Hey, come to think of it, I believe your aunt and uncle are the folks that moved in across from them. Let's head on over there. Last one's a lazy, rotten egg!"

They headed off toward Aunt Luticia's house and Tommy Lawrence pedaled as fast as he could, trying to surpass his cousin. He was way out of luck.

Lora would turn sixteen in August and enter her senior year of high school. There'd be only one more year to bear before discovering a world outside of the backwoods of Godwin. She prayed to make it out before Rosie gave Hammond yet another mouth to feed.

"Lord, Chile, you 'bout a pretty li'l thang. Ain't she as pretty as she can be, Frank? The last time I seen you, you weren't nothin' but a little ole bitty thang. You done growed all up; look like an angel!"

Tommy Lawrence and Lora were standing in Luticia's living room. Luticia was actually Rosie's much younger half-sister. The two women shared the same father but not the same mother. Her aunt lingered in a rocking chair. Lora took a seat beside her. With each compliment, Aunt Luticia would pinch Lora's cheeks, and then she'd rock back and forth, howling with laughter. She weighed more than two hundred and fifty pounds, and each belly-shaking laugh erupted with a hoarse cough.

Mr. Frank, on the other hand, didn't seem too concerned that his wife acted like she might possibly choke to death. He nodded. "Um hum, she's a real looker all right. Takes after her mama."

Lora wanted to give her aunt a chance to compose herself. So she ran over and grabbed Tommy Lawrence, still standing by the door, and led him over to her aunt.

"Aunt Luticia, this is my cousin, Tommy Lawrence."

Luticia poked the young man in the stomach and then roared again, squealing with delight. It seemed any, and everything made Aunt Luticia laugh.

"The last time yo' mama wrote me, she said some of Hammond's people lived 'round here. You a fine-lookin' young man, yes indeed!" Luticia doubled over coughing with laughter.

They drank homemade lemonade and Lora filled her aunt in on her plans to go to beauty school after graduation. She also brought her up to date on everyone else in the family; although there wasn't a whole lot to tell, except of course about their daddy losing the farm.

"Yes," Aunt Luticia growled. "Yo' momma wrote me a letter and told me all about how Carl Tucker cheated your daddy out of his land. It's a sin and a shame, after all those years of sharecropping."

Lora nodded her head. "I guess we should be getting back now. Aunt Florence told us not to be late for supper."

Aunt Luticia pulled Lora into her ample bosom, giving her a suffocating bear hug. "Chile, it's so good to see you all growed up and everythang. Now you make sho' you come back and visit. I'll make you and Tommy Lawrence some chicken and dumplings and a sweet potato pie."

Luticia struggled to rise from her rocker. "Let me walk you chilren' out to the porch."

Frank rose from his chair as well. "Here, let me help you, Motha." Mr. Frank was almost ten years older than his wife but affectionately called her Motha.

Lora gave her aunt and uncle a kiss goodbye with the promise of returning soon.

As they ran down the steps, Tommy Lawrence said, "Wait a minute. Let's go across the road and say hey to June."

Aunt Luticia quickly interjected, "Oh, the Morgans are such a nice family, and that oldest boy, George Junior, is a real dreamboat. You best run over there quick and say hello."

She gave Lora a wink and then broke into her shrill, high-pitched laughter. She began laughing and choking so hard, Mr. Frank had to take her by the arm and lead her back into the house.

Lora thought Aunt Luticia gave new meaning to the term "laughing hyena."

Lora was understandably impressed as she stepped onto the Morgans' porch. Theirs was the biggest house she'd ever seen, though she didn't have much to compare it with. It was a large, green-and-white wooden structure with the sweet scent of vibrant roses in the front yard. The enormous porch had a large, white, wooden swing topped by an inviting flowered cushion.

Tommy Lawrence yelled through the screen door. "Hey, June, you home?"

There was no answer, but Tommy barged in anyway. Lora followed close behind.

They crossed through a lovely living room with a dark-green sofa, and two large, burgundy armchairs. There was an upright piano in the corner filled with family photos, and floral curtains adorned the windows along beige walls. Lora was taken in by the warmth of the room as her nostrils filled with the aroma of fresh cornbread.

An attractive older woman stepped out of the kitchen, wiping her hands on her apron. "Why hello, Tommy Lawrence. How are you today?"

"Oh, just fine, Miss Cora."

"How's your mother?" Cora inquired.

"She's fine, too, thank you. Everybody's fine."

Cora looked at Lora. "And who is this pretty li'l girl with you?"

Tommy Lawrence put his arm around Lora, who stood back shyly. "This is my cousin, Lora. She's staying with us for part of the summer. Lora, this is Mrs. Morgan."

Cora Morgan had deep dimples in her cheeks, which were set in a soft, round face. Her warm, pleasant manner could make anyone feel comfortable immediately. "Hello, Lora, it's very nice to meet you."

"Thank you. It's nice to meet you, too, Mrs. Morgan."

"Oh, Precious, you can call me Miss Cora, the same as the rest of these children around here do."

Lora couldn't help but take an instant liking to this woman, but noticed she stared back at her as if puzzled by something.

"Wait a minute, are you John and Rosie Hammond's child?"

Lora was surprised. "Yes, ma'am."

Cora threw back her head and laughed. "Lord, have mercy. Your mama and daddy used to live down the road from here. I don't think they had anybody back then but the two boys, JD and Sonny. How are your brothers doing?"

Lora loved Cora's soft, yet commanding voice, very distinct and lyrical. She pronounced each word with clarity and without the typical Southern drawl. "JD's in the Navy. Sonny got married a while back."

"You don't say? Well, you're certainly a beautiful young lady. You make sure to tell Rosie and Hammond that Cora Morgan said hello. It's been such a long time."

Lora smiled. "Thank you, Miss Cora. I'll be sure to tell them."

They all looked toward the back porch at the sound of loud, rowdy screams.

"Tommy Lawrence, you know that's June and them out there playing baseball." She tilted her head toward the big open field in the back of the Morgans' property. "You and Lora can go on out. I need to get back in the kitchen and finish supper. George will be starving to death by the time he gets home. Hope to see you again, Lora."

With that, Miss Cora darted back into the kitchen.

Lora would've preferred staying and talking with the delightful woman of the house, but they'd been dismissed, so she followed her cousin out the back door. As soon as she did, she was ready to turn around and flee. There was a group of boys standing outside in an uproar.

"Come on, Bill! You're out!"

"No, I ain't, June!"

Lora gathered from their argument that June had been standing on third base. Bill had slid in to third, just as June caught the ball.

"Don't give me that!" June shouted.

Bill would not back down. "I made it to third base before you caught that ball, June! You know I did!" Bill's teammates shouted in agreement.

June kicked his foot in the dirt, displaying his anger. "Aw, hell! I caught the ball, took out a piece of Juicy Fruit, stuck it in my mouth, had a few good chews, and your slow butt was still running to third!"

All the boys laughed at June's audacity to make up such a blatant lie. Even his younger brother, Charles, whom Lora later learned was sometimes referred to as Bill, but was mostly called Morg, by his friends.

"June, how are you gonna stand there and tell a lie like that with a straight face?" Bill contested.

June broke out into a boyish grin, exposing beautiful white teeth and the deepest dimples in his cheeks, exactly like his mother's. It was a smile that could burn a hole through a heart. "I wanted to make sure you amateurs were paying attention, that's all."

Everyone laughed, including Bill.

Suddenly, the laughter ceased as they realized there was a girl in their midst. The young stallions, brewing with testosterone, began grinning from ear-to-ear. They whistled and shook their heads in disbelief.

Someone shouted out, "Tommy Lawrence, please tell me that's your cousin!"

Tommy Lawrence responded proudly, "Shut up, Fool! She most certainly is my cousin and I'd better not catch you breathing on her either!"

They all chuckled, except for June, who stood back. He appeared cool, calm, and collected.

"Hey, June! I brought my cousin over here to meet you."

George Junior smiled, but didn't make a move toward the porch.

Tommy Lawrence took Lora by the arm, leading her down the steps and out to the field. "Come on, Lora."

She knew that a gentleman certainly would've come over and greeted her, but Lora reluctantly allowed herself to be dragged over anyway.

Tommy Lawrence announced with excitement, "Lora, this is June, the friend I was telling you about!"

He looked down at her with eyes so mesmerizing, they seemed to dance when he spoke. "The name is George."

"Oh, listen to Mr. Big Shot!" someone yelled out. "That's yo' daddy's name! Your name is George Junior, better known as June! And you ain't never had no problem being called June any other time."

All the guys gave a hearty laugh.

Lora looked up at the six-foot-one specimen and offered nothing more than a simple, "Hello."

Feeling embarrassed and awkward, Lora hoped that George Junior couldn't hear how loudly her heart beat. Yet, strangely, her self-consciousness and shyness came across as being as calm, cool, and collected as he.

George Junior took her hand and squeezed tenderly. "Look at you. You're pretty as a peach."

No one had ever spoken to her so sweetly.

Another chuckle was heard from the peanut gallery, and with that, Lora turned on her heels, snapping her ponytail behind her. She never looked back as she made her way across the field, around the side of the house, and out to the front yard to retrieve her bike.

Lora could hear the boys cracking up, hurling friendly insults at George Junior.

"Hey, June! Oh excuse me, I mean, George. Maybe you're losing your touch!"

Another boy laughed hysterically. "June, maybe you should've said she was as pretty as a shiny red apple!"

George Junior shouted angrily, "Shut up, clown! I didn't see her looking your way!"

Tommy Lawrence joked, "Don't pay them no mind, June. Lora's just shy. I'll see you tomorrow...Mr. Peach Man!"

Everybody whooped and hollered as Tommy ran off to catch up with Lora, who'd managed to stir up quite a commotion.

Chapter 10

"I don't know why you're sitting there thinking so hard. You might as well go on and make a move."

"Aw, Girl, ain't nothing wrong with a little concentration."

Tommy Lawrence and Lora were in the middle of a game of checkers. She was about to win her third game in a row. After all, she was the *Checker Queen*.

Tommy's concentration was probably broken again by a knock at the door. "I'll get it, Mama!"

She gave her cousin a wry grin. "No use trying to get away either 'cause I'm just gonna finish whipping you when you get back."

Tommy Lawrence crossed his eyes. "Please, nobody trying to get away. I been lettin' you win, 'cause you visitin'; that's all."

Lora laughed. "Oh, don't you wish. And you keep that up, your eyes are gonna stay like that."

Tommy Lawrence crossed his eyes again and ran to the door.

George Junior stood there trying to maintain some measure of coolness. Instead, he appeared rather sheepish, looking down to the floor, trying to avoid Tommy's eyes.

"Hey, June, since when you start knocking? Why didn't you come on in?"

Pretending to meet Tommy Lawrence's gaze while peeking over his shoulder on the sly, George Junior's best friend gave a knowing grin. "So what can I do for you, June? You looking for me or somebody else?"

"I'm on my way over to Dell's grocery. I have to get Mama some cream for Daddy's coffee in the morning."

Tommy Lawrence put his hand on his friend's shoulder and stared him down. "Well, you sure as heck gone clear out of your way then. By the time you walk way over there from way over here, Dell's liable to be closed." Tommy Lawrence playfully turned George Junior around. "You'd better hop to it. Miss Cora won't be too happy if you come home without the cream for your daddy's coffee."

A seething George Junior pushed Tommy's hands away. "Cut it out, clown! I wanted to see if you'd walk to the store with me. Forget it!"

Tommy must have decided to give his best buddy a break. "Oh come on, Man; lighten up. Sure, I'll walk to the store with you, no problem. Hey, Lora, I'll finish beating you when I get back."

He rushed past George Junior down the steps. "Come on, Man. We'd better hurry!"

George Junior seemed immobile as he glanced from Tommy Lawrence to the screen door.

"What are you waiting for? Let's go!"

George Junior stood there looking dumbfounded, his lips obviously unsure of what to say next. "Uh...uh...I...ah...well, I just thought..."

Lora sat still, listening to their conversation. She'd already picked up on the game Tommy Lawrence was playing with his friend.

"Cat got your tongue or something? I've never seen you at a loss for words, June," he taunted.

George Junior turned on his heels and raced down the steps. "Oh, shut up! Just come on!"

"Tommy Lawrence! Where do you think you going right in the middle of our game?! Gosh! Talk about a sore loser." Lora came out on the porch to see her cousin standing there with George Junior. She crossed her arms and threw all her weight on one hip.

George Junior's eyes lit up like a Christmas tree. "Oh, it's all my fault; I'm sorry. I didn't realize you two were in the middle of a game. I only stopped by to see if Tommy Lawrence wanted to walk to the store with me."

Lora smiled shyly, unable to speak up again. Her heart skipped two beats. Finally, she found her voice. "That's all right. You two go on. We'll finish the game when you get back, Tommy Lawrence."

"Well, if you don't mind a long walk, why don't you come with us?" George Junior asked, his voice dripping with hope.

Tommy Lawrence began to wiggle a bit. "Hey, listen, I got to run to the bathroom. You two run on and I'll catch up with you."

Lora flashed a wide-eyed gaze at her cousin. If Uncle Wes or Aunt Florence discovered that she'd gone off with a boy all by herself, even someone they knew as well as George Morgan Junior, it wouldn't be looked at too kindly.

As though he'd read her mind, Tommy offered, "It's okay, Lora. I'll tell Mama you all walked on ahead so you could catch Dell's before closing. I'll be right behind you."

"I don't think so, Tommy Lawrence. I don't want to get into any trouble." As much as she wanted to, Lora was scared to death to walk off with George Junior. She'd never gone off alone with a boy before.

"What's the matter, Lora? I've known Mr. Wes and Miss Florence since forever. Of course they won't mind."

"June is right, Lora. Don't worry; I'm right behind you." And Tommy Lawrence ran off to relieve himself.

As they walked down the dirt road together, Lora noticed for the first time how well dressed George Junior was. He had on a crisp white shirt with perfectly creased pants, and his shoes shined as if they were brand-new. Lora looked down and her attention was grabbed by something else, George Junior's hands. She'd never seen a boy with such clean hands and nails before. Suddenly, Lora felt out of place in her drab dress and dirty shoes with the worn-out soles. She'd almost conquered her nail biting, but not quite yet, so she placed her unattractive hands behind her back.

"My mama said our folks used to live down the road from each other when I was a baby and you weren't even born yet."

"Yes, that's what she told me when I met her yesterday."

George Junior smiled. "Some coincidence, huh?"

Lora nodded her head.

"Are you going to be staying at Tommy Lawrence's with your aunt and uncle for the whole summer?"

"No, I'll be leaving at the end of June."

George Junior couldn't hide his disappointment. "So soon? How come?"

"I have to get back home to help my mama with my sisters and brothers."

"Will you be coming back to visit again?"

Was George Junior taking an interest in her? Was he really? Well, why else would he be asking all these questions? "I'm sure I will. I hope so. Everybody knows Godwin is a big hick country town. But I don't know when I'll get to visit Dunn again."

"What about next summer then?"

"No, not next summer. I won't be able to come back then," she spoke softly.

"What was that? I didn't hear you."

The thought of George Junior actually liking her summoned a sense of bashfulness. But she attempted to speak more loudly. "Next year, after graduation, I'll be going to stay with my aunt Elvira in Durham. I'm going to be working in her diner to save money for beauty school."

"Graduation?!" George Junior exclaimed. "You're going to be a senior this year?"

Lora nodded again.

"Well, I'll be doggoned! You look too young to be going into your last year. I'm going to be a senior this year, too. I figured you to be about a sophomore. How old are you?"

"I'm fifteen. I'll be sixteen at the end of August."

"Well, how is it you're going to be a senior at only sixteen?"

She didn't wish to come off like she was bragging or anything, but he was standing there waiting for her response. "Well...uh...I got skipped a grade, actually."

"Oh, you must be one of them bookworms, huh?"

Lora wasn't sure if George Junior was paying her a compliment, or being sarcastic. "I wouldn't really say I'm a bookworm, though I do like to read."

"Well, I'd have to say you were a bookworm, and a beautiful one at that."

Obviously, he'd been paying her a compliment, and now Lora was starting to feel all tingly inside.

"So you'll be living in Durham?" The words rolled off his lips like he actually liked the sound of that. Durham was only a stone's throw away from Dunn. "Come on; we'd better run the rest of the way or we'll never catch Dell's."

They ran along quickly when George Junior suddenly grabbed ahold of her small hand with the chewed fingernails. She knew if John Hammond ever got wind of her running down the road holding some boy's hand, there'd be hell to pay. But George Junior had such a take-charge attitude, she didn't have the courage to pull away. And quite frankly, she didn't want to.

Chapter 11

Harlem, New York City

"Where did you go last night? I was worried about you, Baby. I'm sorry we had to go through all that."

"You're always sorry after you've beaten the crap out of me! I don't want to hear it!"

Mommy was on her knees on the gray tile floor washing out my ears as I sat in the tub. I lowered my head and pretended to have the time of my life playing with my rubber ducky. I was really praying the situation wouldn't escalate into something bad.

Daddy squeezed into the tiny bathroom and slithered down next to Mommy. She quickly scooped me up from the tub, wrapping me in a fluffy white towel. "Excuse me," she said, and marched right past Daddy.

We hurried into my room where Mommy sat me on the side of the bed, and then began rummaging through my clothes drawers. A few moments later, we heard the front door close. Mommy whispered through clenched teeth, "Thank God," and I repeated the words silently, "Thank God."

After I was dressed, my hair was brushed and combed, and parted down the middle, with two long, thin braids, one on each side.

"Mommy, can you tie red ribbons on the ends?"

"I certainly can." She reached into a small drawer where I had all sorts of ribbons and colorful barrettes. Mommy tied one satin ribbon into a perfect bow around each braid.

"Mommy, can I tie some of my ribbons in your hair? It will look really pretty."

She tried to act as if everything was all right, but I could see how sad she was. Maybe putting some pretty ribbons in her hair would help cheer her up. Suddenly, the door opened and closed again. Mommy whispered through clenched teeth, "Shit!"

I repeated the word silently, "Shit!"

There was the familiar sound of his footsteps, and Daddy appeared at the door of my room holding a huge bouquet of flowers. He looked at Mommy with loving eyes.

"I brought you some flowers, Baby."

Mommy ignored him. "Debbi, why don't you go on into the living room and watch TV while Mommy makes your bed."

Daddy could look so sincere when he wanted to, but the worst thing was for Mommy to put him in another bad mood. I slowly left the room with Daddy staring at Mommy's back while she vigorously fluffed my pillows. My one consolation was that at least he appeared sober.

It was the wee hours of the morning when I awoke to the stream of light coming from the kitchen window into my room. Mommy hadn't shut the door tightly. I rarely woke up at night except during the fighting, but my eyes suddenly popped open.

I gasped as I saw what appeared to my fear-prone imagination as a figure in a white sheet jumping back and forth over the stream of light. There were two slits in the sheet that resembled a pair of eyes that shone with a piercing red light. Each time the sheeted figure jumped over the light, the eyes grew bigger and brighter.

I made a feeble attempt to cry out for help, but it was hard to do with my lips glued shut. No matter how hard I tried, I couldn't tear them apart. Finally, calling on every ounce of will I could muster, I slithered down the side of the bed. Crouching to the floor, I waited until the thing took another leap over the light. Then I quickly made a dash underneath it and ran down the hall to Mommy and Daddy's room.

They were sound asleep. If I woke them and told them about the hooded figure lurking in my room, they might not believe me and would send me immediately back to bed. I was not about to take that chance. There was a small space between them, big enough for me to fit in. I breathed a quiet sigh of relief the moment I was safely tucked in the middle.

A few minutes later, Daddy turned to me with his eyes still closed. I could smell his breath above my head. Then he slipped his hand underneath my nightgown and began to rub me down there.

I lay still as a dead person, bewildered as to what Daddy was doing and why. Instinctively, I realized Daddy must have thought I was Mommy because he hadn't seen or felt me sneak into their bed. What I didn't understand was why he'd be rubbing Mommy down there. You only touched down there when you made pee pee or when you took a bath. It felt odd and uneasy for Daddy to be doing it.

"Damn, Baby, what the hell did you do to yourself?" he muttered in total confusion.

Of course, I was too young to have pubic hair, and Daddy was too groggy to know he was groping his child and not his wife.

Suddenly, he jumped out of bed and I could feel him standing over me. Feigning sleep, I gently heaved with a little light breathing for good measure.

Daddy leaned down and whispered, "Debbi, is that you?" Then I heard him rush around the bed toward the door and put his pants on. It'd been ages since I'd gotten into my parents' bed in the middle of the night. Daddy must have been mad that I'd decided to do it again as he hurried from the room and whispered loudly, "Damn!"

"Debbi, you forgot your gloves. Run back and get them off your dresser."

Daddy was taking me to nursery school again because Mommy had a doctor's appointment. I rushed back to my room and grabbed my fire engine-red gloves, rushing back just as quickly.

"Bye, Sweetheart; I love you." Mommy planted a great big kiss on my lips.

"Can I get a kiss, too?" Daddy was speaking to Mommy, but she ignored him and helped me on with my gloves. We went out the door and he turned back to her sadly. "I love you, Honey."

As we walked along to school, Daddy didn't hold my hand the way he normally did, except when we had to cross the street. Upon contact, both palms appeared unsteady. Finally, he dropped me at the steps of the rust, brick building and his eyes quickly swept over me. They were awkward, cheerless, a defining moment to a cross-road of no return.

Mommy picked me up from school later that day, still looking like she wasn't feeling well. "Mommy, is your stomach hurting again?"

"No, Sweetheart, why would you ask me that?"

"I don't know. You look like it could be hurting you." She gave a faint smile, but said nothing more. However, we were barely through the front door when Mommy went racing to the bathroom. I could hear her throwing up, but this time I sat on the couch and waited for her to finish.

When she finally came out, her eyes were teary again. "Debbi, go in your room and take off your school clothes, okay? Put on your pajamas and then Mommy will make you something to eat."

What happened to the bath I always took before putting on my PJ's?

I rose from the couch to go and do as I was told and that's when I heard her crying. I'd never heard her cry like that, like a petrified, lost child. Her stomach must have been hurting a lot more than she let on, and I didn't know what to do about it. I stood there in the middle of the hallway feeling so bad for my mommy. Why couldn't our life be happier?

The next day, as my best friend, Deidre, and I played out on the stoop, I looked at her dirty white socks riding down her scraped-up little legs. "Deidre, will you pull your socks up?"

Deidre's mouth pointed down to the ground as she bent over and said, "I heard my mommy say your mommy's going to have a baby."

Chapter 12

Dunn, North Carolina

"George Junior, what do you have that's so important to be talking to Lora about all the time?"

"Oh, nothing much, Miss Florence. I was sitting here telling Lora how I'm thinking about enlisting in the service after school. And she was telling me about her brother, JD, being in the Army."

June's honest face had told an honest-faced lie. Lora had told June about JD being in the Army, but it wasn't because George Junior was interested in enlisting. In fact, he'd told her he was plain tired of school, but that he'd rather go off to college than serve in the Armed Forces. It was also a conversation that had taken place over a week earlier.

Before being interrupted by Aunt Florence, George Junior had asked Lora if she'd be his girl and he was about to make his move for their first kiss.

The summer weeks had passed much too quickly and she'd soon be returning home to Godwin. Lora was much more comfortable with George Junior now and actually cherished the time she got to spend with him. But she'd always been careful that they were never caught alone, until now.

"The service ain't too bad," Miss Florence commented.

Wes Hammond walked down the back porch, making his way over to the threesome. "What's goin' on out there? What you all doin'?"

Lora's heart beat a mile a minute. Wes Hammond was the spitting image of his older brother, John, except that he was brown-skinned. He didn't drink like his brother or beat his wife, but he instilled the same fear.

Florence said, "I was wondering where Tommy Lawrence ran off to, leaving these two out here by themselves."

"Where's Tommy Lawrence?" Lora's uncle asked.

George Junior quickly lied with yet another straight face. "At the store getting us a couple of bottles of Coca-Cola, Mr. Wes."

But who could blame him? Uncle Wes was quite intimidating lurking above the teenagers with his dark, steely eyes.

"Well, I reckon' you all tryin' to stay cool here in the shade?" Wes eyed them suspiciously.

Lying didn't come as easily for Lora. She could hardly look her uncle in the eye. "We were just talking, Uncle Wes, that's all," she uttered timidly.

"Look me in the eye when you talking to me, Gal." She could have sworn it was her father speaking.

George Junior felt the need to intervene. Lora wasn't handling this well at all. "Yes, Sir, we were talking about the Army, Mr. Wes."

Wes laughed sarcastically. "The Army, huh? When I was your age, June, if I was with a girl as pretty as my li'l niece here, I don't think we woulda' been discussing nothin' 'bout no Army."

George Junior opened his mouth to speak, but before he could get a word out, they heard Tommy Lawrence calling.

"Lora! Where you all at?" Her cousin rode up on his bike from the side of the house and was, of course, empty-handed.

"Hey there, Son, you done kept these poor, hot, thirsty souls out here waitin' for you. Ain't you got nothing for 'em?"

It didn't take a rocket scientist to size up the situation. Lora and George Junior couldn't be any tenser. Tommy Lawrence felt a trap and noticed George Junior moving his fingers stealthily in the dirt. He drew the word "cola."

"I can't believe it; I got all the way to the store and forgot I'd left my money in my other pants pocket. I'm sorry about y'all's Cokes."

George Junior wiped the sweat from his brow with one hand, and with the other, gingerly erased the word "cola" from the dirt.

Wes looked at Tommy Lawrence and then down at George Junior and Lora, still frozen on the ground. He smiled crookedly. "Um hum... Um hum. Well, ain't you three a bunch of li'l whippersnappers." Wes must have decided to let the frightened teenagers off the hook, this time. He turned around and strode back to the house, but not without offering a wink to George Junior, lest the young man forget Wes wasn't as dumb as he might think.

Chapter 13

"Girl, what you standing there like that for? Let's go inside," Tommy Lawrence commanded.

But Lora wasn't so sure. Earlier that morning, she'd seen George talking to another girl right after church service. He'd been in such close conversation with the young lady, he hadn't even been around when Miss Cora and George Sr. invited Lora and Tommy Lawrence to supper.

"Wait a minute. What if George Junior's mother didn't tell him she'd invited me for dinner? He might have invited that girl who was making goo-goo eyes at him outside the church."

"How many times do I have to tell you? If there are any goo-goo eyes going on, they're the ones June has for you. Now I can't make it no more plain and simple. So are you coming in or not?"

Lora brushed past her cousin and entered the Morgan home.

George Sr. and Cora were in the dining room, placing bowls of food on the table and engaging in a humorous conversation. The sweetness of their laughter sounded like glorious music and their love for each other couldn't be more apparent.

Cora looked up and said to her two guests standing in the doorway, "Come on in and have a seat. Food is just about ready."

Mr. George flashed a handsome smile and Lora thought Miss Cora was the luckiest wife on Earth.

"Where's my fifty cents that was up on the dresser? I know you took it, you little thief!"

"Let go of my arm! I didn't even see no fifty cents! Mama! Mama! Tell June to let go of me! He's trying to break my arm!"

"Excuse me, Lora." Cora walked through the house to a back bedroom, but her voice could still be heard.

"June! What have I told you about grabbing on your sister?! I want you two to cut this mess out right now. We have company. Wash your hands and come on in here to supper."

George Junior fumed, "Mama! You know I made that extra fifty cents yesterday. I delivered all those extra papers over to Mr. Joe's shoeshine! I came in here and put my money up on the dresser and now it's gone! Ain't nobody took it but Suge!"

The girl sobbed. "Mama, I didn't steal nothin'! Honest I didn't!"

"Mama, don't believe nothing that gal—"

"June, shush! Now I'm telling you and Suge to wash up so we can eat. We'll get to the bottom of this later; and, Suge, what did I tell you about having them skates on in this house?"

"Yes, Ma'am. I'll go outside and take them off right now."

Lora watched a big-boned, tall, pretty, young girl skate through the dining room, through the living room, and out the front door.

George Junior followed his mother back into the dining room. "Mama, why you always got to let Suge get away with every..." He stopped mid-sentence upon seeing Lora sitting at the table.

"Hi, Lora! Mama didn't tell me you were the company we were having for supper."

"You see; serves you right. Now you can be real embarrassed carrying on like that," Cora said.

George Junior didn't pay much mind to his mother. He was too choked up at this pleasant surprise. "And what are you doing sitting here at my table, Tommy Lawrence?" George Junior teased.

"This is me and your daddy's table and you'd better be glad we let you sit at it," Cora teased back.

"Well, now that we know whose table it is, I say we all sit down and eat," the senior George commanded.

"All right, you just hold your horses now, George. I told Suge to go take them skates off and I don't know where Bill disappeared to."

Lora loved the ease with which George Junior's parents talked back and forth to each other. Miss Cora was kind, but seemed not to be the subservient doormat of a woman Rosie was. And Mr. George had a commanding presence, but not the tyrannical abusiveness John Hammond possessed.

"Miss Cora, may I go into the kitchen and wash my hands for supper?" Lora asked.

"Of course, Dear. But you don't have to wash them in the kitchen; let me show you to the bathroom."

Lora had never been in any home with an indoor bathroom. She couldn't believe it! There was no outhouse at Uncle Wes's, but you did have to go out to the back porch where a small room with a toilet was enclosed.

Cora led her through a big bedroom and then through a smaller-looking boy's bedroom. "Here you go, Lora, and you'll find fresh towels hanging on the rack."

When Lora closed the door, she had to cover her mouth to keep from screaming. "Well, I'll be a monkey's uncle!" The bathroom was all pink with a clean white sink, and lo and behold, there was an actual bathtub! "My goodness," Lora whispered, "I'm gonna kill Tommy Lawrence! He didn't tell me George Junior's parents were rich! What on earth would he want with someone like me?"

Lora washed her hands and then shook them dry. She didn't wish to risk messing up the clean white towels. When she walked out of the bathroom, there again was the sound of a girl's voice.

"I'm gonna wash my hands, Mama!" The girl swung the bathroom door open, almost hitting Lora by accident. "Who are you?"

"Lora. I'm Tommy Lawrence's cousin."

For a moment, the girl was silent, staring back at Lora. "I'm Thelma, but everyone calls me Suge. You're real pretty. You sure you related to Tommy Lawrence?"

Lora giggled. "Yes, I'm sure."

"Well, I need to wash my hands before Mama has a heart attack."

"Oh, sure." As she turned to walk away, Lora happened to look back and catch Thelma pulling change out of her pants pocket. The girl, who had to be no more than twelve, quickly bent down and put the money in her shoe. It suddenly occurred to Lora that this was probably the fifty cents George Junior had accused his sister of stealing.

Thelma rose and saw Lora watching her suspiciously. Her face broke into a huge grin. "I found that money."

"Oh." Lora knew the adolescent was lying.

"You don't believe me, do you?"

Lora didn't answer, but the expression on her face must have said she clearly didn't.

Tears welled up in Thelma's eyes. She motioned for Lora to come closer. "Okay. Yeah. I stole June's money. You know why? He stole my money first. It took me a whole year to save up fifty cents to put in my piggy bank. Daddy would give me money for jawbreakers, but I would put every penny into my piggy bank instead, even though my mouth would be watering for that candy. When I'd finally saved up fifty cents, my daddy exchanged all them pennies for two shiny quarters. I was saving up to buy me a bicycle. Mama and Daddy bought me skates because they said they couldn't afford to buy me no bicycle. June came in here one day and asked if he could borrow my money, said it was for something real important and he'd pay it right back. He made me promise not to tell Mama." Thelma's pretty face slumped with sadness. "He never gave me back my fifty cents and even worse, he told Mama I ain't give him no money."

Lora was surprised June would do such a thing to his little sister.

"You girls best come on in here so we can eat dinner or we'll be starting without you!" Cora's lyrical voice was heard from the dining room.

Thelma's shaking hand reached out to Lora. "Are you gonna tell my mama and daddy I stole June's money?"

"What money...?" Lora asked, and Thelma thanked her with a beaming smile.

Wes and Florence were at a wake and Tommy Lawrence had run off somewhere. Lora was sitting out under the big oak tree after packing up her few belongings for her trip home the next morning.

Suddenly, she became aware of a dark shadow approaching from down the road. It took only a second to realize who it was. His steps turned into a rapid pace and Lora jumped up.

It was like at the picture show. The handsome lover comes tearing down the road to bid his sweetheart farewell. He reaches her, lifts her high in the air, twirling her around and around, and then, in a deep embrace, gives her a tormented, but passionate kiss.

It was their first real kiss. They'd stolen a few pecks here and there, but nothing like this.

"I'm gonna have to figure out a way to see you. You're my girl, Lora, forever and ever!"

Chapter 14

Godwin, North Carolina

"Mama said you best git your lazy bones outta that bed and come in here and make breakfast!" Virginia announced.

Lora quickly hid the letter from George underneath her pillow. She had twenty-five of the precious, handwritten notes hidden away in a shoebox underneath her bed. He always ended by saying, "Kisses, George."

Lora had mustered up the nerve to write and ask if he'd escort her to her senior prom. George had responded, "Why of course!"

"Lora! I'm in here feeding the baby and the rest of these children are starvin'! Git in this kitchen and make breakfast!"

Will you stop all that screaming, Mama! I can hear you! Maybe if you hadn't had all these damn children, you wouldn't have to worry about whether they were fed or not! Besides, they're your children, not mine. You're the one who's supposed to be taking care of them, not me! Now, for God's sake! Will...you please...just...leave me...alone!

Of course, those words were silently spoken in Lora's head. "I'll be right there, Mama," are the words that actually came out of Lora's mouth.

Lora walked into the kitchen and went over to the sink to wash her hands. Hammond was seated at the table eating a piece of fatback and some eggs.

He slid his coffee cup across the table.

"Lora, pour yo' daddy another cup of coffee." Rosie sat beside Hammond, feeding baby Shirley. Her mother had made sure their daddy and the baby of the family were fed; everyone else would have to wait on Lora.

Bunch came into the kitchen with a scowl on her face. "Lora, ain't you made breakfast yet?" Lora ignored her pain-in-the-butt sister.

"You need to git a move on now fo' Hattie and Jacob git here," Rosie said.

Hattie was Hammond's ex-sister-in-law. She'd been married to his elder brother, Moody, up until his death. Now she was married to Jacob, a man Hammond deplored, and for no other reason except the fact that Jacob was ugly. Hammond said Jacob gave the family a bad name.

"I didn't know they were coming to visit, Mama."

"They're driving us to Dunn this morning to visit yo' Aunt Luticia. Frank had to take her to the hospital. Seems like Luticia had a mild heart attack. That's why I didn't git you youngins up fo' church this mornin'."

"Excuse me, I'll be back directly." Hammond pushed himself up from the table.

"Where you goin', Hammond? It's best fo' us to git an early start so we can git back 'fo nightfall."

"I know, Rosie, I know. I'll be back in plenty of time."

Lora couldn't believe her good fortune. They were driving to Dunn and somehow, some way, she was going to get to see George. She'd count on Tommy Lawrence to help her out. It was a shame, however, about Aunt Luticia's heart attack. Lora could imagine her obese aunt laughing and coughing until she keeled over.

While everyone was waiting for Jacob and Hattie to arrive, Lora stole a few moments to finish reading George's last letter.

Dear Lora,

I cannot believe the many months that have passed without my seeing your pretty face. Tommy Lawrence may have come up with an idea. He said he could come down there for a visit and bring me along with him. Chances are that then I could find the right time to ask your daddy if I could start calling on you.

But if all else fails, I certainly plan on being at your door to escort you to your senior prom. Don't forget that I expect you to come to Dunn for mine as well. I can't wait to show you off to everybody.

Kisses, George

It was hard to know how Hammond would react to George's coming down to Godwin to call on her. Lora had recently started her period and overheard Hammond say to Rosie more than once, "Now that she done come into her time a month, you best make sho' she don't be hangin' 'round none of them li'l school fellas and that she keep them legs shut tight."

Uncle Jacob paced up and down the porch while Rosie and her sister-in-law, Aunt Mattie, rocked back and forth in rocking chairs waiting on Hammond to show up. The relatives were all supposed to be on their way to Dunn to visit Rosie's ailing sister, yet they were already running late.

Rosie had purposely scheduled the trip to Dunn on Sunday rather than Saturday because she knew Hammond never touched the bottle on the Lord's Day, which was also the only reason Jacob agreed to drive them. But Hammond had been gone a very long time and you could see the trepidation on everyone's face.

Now they saw the bobbing figure meandering down the road. As he neared, Hammond took one look at Jacob standing up on the porch and cursed aloud. "Aw, hell! What that...ugly...nigga...doin'... comin 'round here fo'?! I bet...my brotha' still turnin' over in his... his grave to see...Mattie done gon'...and married up wit...his ole ugly...donkey-lookin' ass..."

Mattie was frail and quite common-looking; her husband, on the other hand, made Mattie look like Dorothy Dandridge. The first thing you noticed about Jacob was his enormous bucked teeth, which made him unable to fully close his mouth. He'd also suffered from polio as a child and was left with a curvature in his spine that compelled him to walk slightly bent over. And Jacob's eyes were so droopy it made one wonder if he'd fallen asleep while they were speaking to him.

Jacob was far more than simply unattractive, but certainly through no fault of his own, though no one ever convinced John Hammond of this fact.

Lora knew immediately the condition her father was in. She couldn't believe he'd been drinking on the Lord's Day. She also felt real sorry for Uncle Jacob. The only reason he put up with her father had to be for the sake of Mattie's close relationship with Rosie.

Hammond approached the front steps. He stopped and stared at Mattie's unsightly husband. He shook his head real hard, and then shook it again. He stumbled with dizziness as he shook it for a third time.

"What you shakin' yo' head like that fo', Hammond?" Rosie asked. "Come on in the house so we can have supper, cuz we need to be gittin' on the road to Dunn."

Hammond took his fingers and stretched his eyelids down as far as he could as if to see more clearly. "Well, I'll...be goddamn! It gots to be that pint...of...whiskey...cuz...I...swear...if yo' old mule ass...ain't got uglier...since the last time you...showed up 'round...here! Shit! I swear fo' God...Mattie, if my brotha'...knowed you done married up and...brought somethin' this goddamn...ugly into the family...after he gon'...he might git' right on up...outta that grave...come on back here...and carry you off wit' him!"

Uncle Jacob clamped his lips tight.

Rosie pleaded, "Hammond, forget about eatin'. Can we please just git on in the car? I told you Jacob and Mattie were gon' be drivin' us up to Dunn. They done come all this way, and it's gittin' late."

"Woman, you ain't told me...no sucha' thang! Cuz you knowed...it ain't no way I'm...gon' be caught dead ridin'...in no car wit' him! If'n I was dead...I wouldn't let his funny-lookin' ass...drive me to the... funeral home! And you ain't takin' none of...my youngins neither cuz...all that...ugly liable to rub off!"

Jacob grabbed Mattie's arm. "I'm sorry, Rosie, I guess you all gon' have to find you another way to Dunn dis evenin'!"

Jacob and Mattie jumped in their car and drove away, blowing dust as they sped off.

Lora knew her father had purposely gotten drunk on a Sunday to get out of riding with Jacob, and she knew her mother was heartsick about not seeing her ailing sister. Lora was just as heartsick about missing out on her chance to see George.

Chapter 15

The night was chilly and Rosie threw extra coals into the stove. Hammond smoked his pipe, sitting in his rickety old rocker. It squeaked like a wounded bird with each movement.

Rosie had just read a letter they'd received from JD. Their long gone, but not forgotten, son would be arriving home from the Army in three short days after getting an honorable discharge due to an injury.

All the children but Lora were in bed and Rosie and Hammond seemed to be in a pleasant enough mood.

Lora seized the moment. "Daddy? May I have a date take me to my senior prom?"

"Has some boy done axed to take you to the prom?"

"Yes, Sir."

"What's his name?"

It was almost a whisper. "George Morgan."

"Who?!" Hammond was sure he hadn't heard right.

"George Morgan, Daddy. He lives over in Dunn."

"Now what in tarnation is this gal talkin' 'bout, Rosie? I only know one George Morgan in Dunn. That's George and Cora Morgan. They lived down the road from us when we wuz still livin' up there. And she fo' doggone sho' can't be talkin' 'bout him!"

"Well, Hammond," Rosie interjected, "I remember Cora had a son after they oldest girl, and I believe they named the boy after George."

"That's right, Daddy. His name is George Junior."

"Well, that's the way you shoulda' called it then. George Junior, huh? Since when you meet up wit' Cora and George's boy?"

"He's best friends with Tommy Lawrence, Daddy, and his parents go to church with Uncle Wes and Aunt Florence." Suddenly, Lora realized she might have offered too much information.

Hammond studied her for a moment. "You been talkin' to this boy when you were up there in Dunn fo' the summer?"

Lora knew better than to even attempt a lie. Besides, Hammond might decide to go back and question Uncle Wes.

"Yes, Sir." Lora figured it best to keep her honest reply succinct.

"Well, if he's Cora and George's boy, I guess he might be all right fo' you to be talkin' to. But you best not be runnin' off in 'dem bushes." Hammond rose from his chair to go to bed.

"But, Daddy, do I have permission for George Junior to take me to the prom?"

Hammond kept walking. "I'll think on it."

For once, Daddy's "thinking" produced a positive result. Hammond had agreed to let Lora go to the prom, so long as JD accompanied her. But even that wasn't totally bad news because JD was going to the prom with Lora's best friend, Claudette.

The weeks flew by quickly and the big night was finally there. Rosie had paid Sister Corrine from the church what she could to make Lora's dress, a beautiful peach organza with a soft, sweetheart neckline. The white corsage she knew George Junior was bringing would add the perfect finishing touch. Lora had expertly styled her own hair, piled high atop her head in the perfect pompadour.

George Junior was running late and Hammond took out his pocket watch. He shook his head. "If that young fella ain't here in ten mo' minutes, you and JD going to the prom wit'out him."

With one minute left, there was an anxious knock at the door. Hammond got up and answered for an out-of-breath George Junior who stood there quite flustered.

"Good evening! Sorry I'm late, but I missed my bus! It took forever for the next one to come along."

"The reason why don't much matter. The fact is, you done kept my daughter here, waitin' on you fo' almost an hour. Next time you best plan on being an hour earlier. That's if I decide it's gon' be a next time."

"Yes, Sir. It won't happen again."

"That's right, youngin', it sho' won't."

George Junior walked in and the sight simply took Lora's breath away. He was even more handsome than the last time she'd seen him. Dressed in a white suit with beige, spit-shined, wing-tip shoes, hair slicked back with pomade, and sporting a slight mustache, Lora thought he couldn't be more gorgeous if he'd tried to be. It was said that God made man in his image, and as far as Lora could see, God was standing right in front her.

George Junior raised quite an eyebrow as well. "I'd like to say how lovely you look this evening, Lora."

"Thank you, George. Well, I guess we should be going."

"You make sho' my daughter is treated proper like. Do I make myself clear, Son?"

George swallowed. "Yes, Sir, most definitely."

The threesome rushed out; they were already running late to pick up Claudette. Lora and George Junior, who smelled so good with that fine scent of manly cologne, piled in the cool, leather backseat. As soon as they were a distance from the house, George put an arm around Lora and pulled her close. They held hands and stared into each other's eyes like two lovesick puppy dogs, oblivious to the couple in the front seat.

When they arrived at the school auditorium, George Junior slipped off Lora's shawl and handed it to the coat check. JD pinned a beautiful pink flower onto Claudette's dress, and grabbed her hand. "All right, li'l sis, we'll catch you two later."

Lora faced George so he could pin on her corsage, too.

He bobbed his head up and down. "Hey, Lora, the band sounds great. Come on; let's dance!"

"George, can you pin on my corsage first?" Lora beamed with expectancy.

"Your corsage? Uh...actually, I forgot to get you one."

"You didn't get me a corsage?"

"No. I was so busy trying to catch the bus on time, and then I ended up missing it anyway. Come on, I like that song; let's dance." He didn't seem quite as disappointed as she.

Every other girl on the dance floor had a beautiful corsage pinned to her dress or tied with a bow around her arm. Lora knew she must stick out like a sore thumb. But she did her best to dismiss the slight and have a good time. After all, the most important thing was that she was with her guy.

JD was as good as his word and kept a low profile. Lora and George Junior almost forgot he was even there. They danced up a storm, thoroughly enjoying themselves. As the evening neared to a close, the band changed rhythm and began playing a slow song. Dancing cheek to cheek in each other's arms for a few seconds, they were suddenly interrupted by James Cook.

"Excuse me. May I cut in, please?"

Everyone at school knew that James harbored a secret crush on Lora. From afar, Lora had appreciated knowing that someone liked her. But James wasn't quite her type in the looks category. She opened her mouth to decline gracefully, but George interrupted, "Are you nuts? No, Chump! You most certainly may not cut in with my girl. Get outta here!"

"I'm sorry. I didn't know Lora was your girl." James seemed to back away in slow motion, quickly disappearing into the crowd.

Lora was mortified. James Cook was one of the nicest boys in school. She couldn't believe George Junior's rudeness. It was a side of him she'd never seen before.

"George, you didn't have to speak to James like that. He was asking to cut in for a dance, that's all."

The angry crease in George's brow should have been a clear warning to Lora.

The principal announced that the next song would be the last for the evening and the band began playing Nat King Cole's "Too Young."

George Junior pulled her tightly around the waist and whispered in her ear, "From now on, Lora, this is going to be our special song."

She quickly forgot his crudeness and rested her head on his chest. The sound of his heart beating was magnetic, and in that moment, all was right with the world.

Chapter 16

Dunn, North Carolina

Lora cradled the phone to her ear, listening to George's sweet nothings. "I can't wait to smother you with kisses."

"That's quite enough, Lora!" Uncle Wes startled her. She thought he'd somehow heard what George Junior was saying.

"You and June done been on that phone long enough; you got plenty of time to talk at the prom."

"Yes, Sir... I'm sorry, George, but my Uncle Wes says I have to hang up now. I'll see you when you get here. Goodbye."

George Junior had written to her after his evening in Godwin to confirm their plans for his upcoming prom.

Lora unpacked the lavender, floral satin dress with the black, velvet bow around the neck. The dress her friend Claudette had worn to their prom. Her friend had let her borrow it and Lora was thankful they were both about the same size. But she would be most thankful if George Junior didn't recognize the dress.

By seven-thirty, the young lady in waiting heard George Junior running up the steps, and right on time.

"Good evening, Miss Florence, Mr. Wes."

Florence stood, and playfully stalked around George Junior.

"Well, now, take a look at you, George Morgan, Junior. Lora, you'd better hold onto your heart."

Uncle Wes added, "That ain't all she'd better hold onto!"

Lora's fair skin flushed an embarrassing shade of rose. She swore she didn't know who was worse, her daddy or her uncle, but Lora took that thought back. No one was as bad as John Hammond.

Tommy Lawrence came out of his room decked out in a handsome navy suit.

"Well, Son, I must say you three are going to be the most outstanding-looking young folk this entire evening."

"Thanks, Mama. Well, let's get a move-on so I can pick up my date."

"You mean a real date?" George Junior joked, and everyone smiled as the two boys threw a couple of playful jabs at one another.

"Wait a sec. Lora, look what I have for you!" George Junior pinned a beautiful white corsage to her dress.

"Lora, that is lovely," Aunt Florence said admiringly.

"Thank you, George." It was indeed lovely. But Lora couldn't help but think how George Junior hadn't been as mindful when it had been *her* senior prom.

They tried to rush out, but not before Uncle Wes's farewell warnings, a 1:00 a.m. curfew and George Junior was to return his niece in exactly the same condition he'd picked her up.

The difference was immediately noticeable. The auditorium was exquisitely decorated, and there was a professional, six-piece band. All the girls were adorned in expensive evening gowns. At least George Junior hadn't noticed she was wearing Claudette's prom dress. In fact, he kept commenting about how beautiful she looked.

"You're the prettiest girl here. I can't wait to show you off."

As the evening went on, George Junior only got around to showing her off to a few people. Tommy Lawrence had been quite attentive to his date, Estelle. George Junior kept disappearing. He would dance with Lora a few times, drop her back at their table, and then vanish into the crowd.

There'd been a number of times Lora had caught Tommy Lawrence and Estelle cooing at each other. Feeling somewhat miserable and envious, she'd excused herself and gone to the ladies' room. When she returned, she found the table completely empty. Now she looked up to see George Junior running back to the table.

"Lora! Where's Tommy Lawrence?!"

"I don't know. He and Estelle were gone when I came back from the bathroom. They're probably out on the dance floor."

"Well, wait here a minute. I'm going to go look for them."

"Can I come with you?"

"I'll only be a second, Baby."

"But, George..." He'd already whipped away.

When he returned, more than twenty minutes later, Lora smelled liquor on George Junior's breath.

"Let's dance, Girl!" he said loudly. George Junior pulled her out onto the floor and began dancing a bit seductively, tilting his pelvis against hers. At first Lora was embarrassed, not to mention annoyed, by George Junior's behavior. However, she was quickly propelled into the romantic moment as she danced in his electrifying embrace.

Tommy Lawrence found them on the dance floor and tapped George Junior on the shoulder. "Listen, Estelle and I are going for a walk. We'll meet you and Lora back here by twelve-thirty, okay?" And Tommy Lawrence and Estelle scurried away.

When the music finished playing, George Junior led Lora back to the table. Lora was barely seated before he said, "There's Bill Elliott! I ain't seen him all night! I'll be right back."

She tried to offer some protest, but again, he was too quick. This was becoming infuriating, certainly not the night Lora had envisioned.

"May I have this dance?"

She looked up and saw a young man standing at the table, towering over her. He was medium height with a muscular build and an attractive face, even with the few pimples adorning his forehead.

Without thinking twice, Lora rose from her chair and allowed the young fellow to escort her to the dance floor. As he pulled her into his arms, Lora spotted George Junior through the crowd dancing with a very pretty girl. She could swear it was the one she'd seen batting her eyelashes at him in front of the church last summer!

Fuming, Lora had a good mind to walk back to Uncle Wes's and leave her arrogant boyfriend high and dry.

When the dance was over, her partner walked her back to the table. But being a gentleman, he chose not to leave Lora sitting alone. The young man told her that his date had gotten ill at the last moment, and so he'd come to the senior prom alone. After dancing with Lora, he was glad he had.

They sat down and began making polite conversation when George Junior rushed up with two friends. "Lora! You remember my friend, Bill Elliott? And this here is Delores."

George Junior suddenly became aware she was sitting with someone. Fury marred his face.

"You came to the prom with me. What are you doing sitting here, talking to someone else?!"

Lora was speechless.

George Junior abruptly turned to his schoolmate. "Why the heck are you sitting here with my girl, Jackie?!"

This was déjà vu. Lora remembered how rude and jealous George Junior had been at her prom with James Cook.

"I didn't know she was your girl, June, and if she's your girl, why'd you leave her sitting here all by herself?"

"What business is that of yours?!"

George Junior reached down and snatched Jackie by the collar, but Jackie jumped up and roughly threw him off. Bill Elliott jumped in between them. "Hey! What are you all doing?! This is prom night! Not fight night! Why you two wanna carry on like this in front of these pretty ladies?"

Lora was scared, but she was also mad as hell! How could George Junior even think of jumping on someone for talking to her? After all, he'd been running off and leaving her alone most of the night.

Jackie backed off, but the repugnance in his eyes spoke volumes. Luckily, the school photographer rushed up in the midst of the confrontation.

"You all want a group photo to show to your future kids, 'cause, June, you know how smooth you looking tonight!"

George Junior quickly pulled himself together and straightened out his clothes. He resumed his handsome posture and once again was all smiles.

"Sho nuff! Come on, Lora, Bill, Delores! Let's have our pictures taken."

Jackie had disappeared. The photographer told them to say *Cheese*, and *click*, a bright light went off as they all cheesed for the camera.

Lora forced her smile. Years later, people would look at the photo and comment on how unhappy she'd looked.

It was just after eleven-thirty and Tommy Lawrence and Estelle had not returned to the dance. But their curfew wasn't until one, so there was no immediate cause for concern. "Let's go by my house for a while."

Lora stared up at George Junior. It wasn't like she'd been having the greatest time, but she wasn't sure about going off with him anywhere right now.

"When my cousin gets back, he won't know where we are."

"We'll be back before they will. Anyway, we have until one o'clock and it's not like Tommy Lawrence is going to go home without you. Come on, Lora, please. We won't stay that long; I promise."

She was still irked by his antics, but George Junior sure knew how to beg. Against her better judgment, Lora went.

He tried to keep the front door from squeaking as he opened it. George Junior put his fingers up to his lips. "Shh...I don't want to wake Mama and Daddy."

It was too late. Miss Cora walked into the living room, wearing a warm, fuzzy nightgown.

"I thought I heard the front door. Why hello, Lora; it's nice to see you again and my, my, my, don't you look beautiful."

"Thank you, Miss Cora."

"What are you two doing back here? Is the prom over already?"

"No, Mama, we decided to stop by the house for a minute."

Cora's face filled with a dubious expression. "You all left a big dance to come back here to the house?"

"Mama, I said we just stopped by for a minute; that's all. The auditorium was jam-packed. We wanted to get away from the crowd for a while. But we have to go back and meet Tommy Lawrence and Estelle. You can go on to bed. I'll be in after I take Lora home to her uncle's house."

"All right, but don't you kids stay in here too long. Goodnight, Lora."

"Goodnight, Miss Cora."

As soon as George Junior's mother left the room, he went around closing all the doors—the door in the living room that led to the dining room and the kitchen, and the door that led to his older sister, Margaret's room.

Lora hoped closing all the doors was truly meant to keep from disturbing George Junior's parents and not for some ulterior motive.

As if reading her mind, George Junior tried to reassure her. "Lora, I don't want to bother my folks while we're in here talking, and I sure as heck don't want that nosey Suge popping in. Are you okay?"

There was a draft in the room and Lora was feeling a bit chilly. She'd unconsciously wrapped her arms around herself.

"Yeah, I'm fine."

"Aw, you look like you're cold, Baby. Here, let me put the heater on."

They sat on the couch across from the big electric heater, which got nice and toasty pretty quickly.

"I wish you didn't have to go back home tomorrow. I wish I could spend every minute with you."

Lora found this statement rather absurd. She rolled her eyes and remained stiff. George Junior certainly hadn't acted like he wanted to spend every minute with her back at the prom. But he always knew the right words to say.

He wrapped his arm around her and she tentatively laid her head on his chest. The small amber lamp cast a soft glow in the room, and the mood was beginning to pump adrenaline through both their young bodies.

"You're the prettiest girl in the world, and definitely the sweetest. You know that?"

It was a wonderful compliment, but Lora was starting to feel a little uneasy. George Junior gently squeezed both his arms around her, nuzzling the side of her face. "I love you, and I mean that from the bottom of my heart."

He began to kiss her softly, gently parting her lips with his tongue.

The tender words made her feel special as their kisses became more heated. George Junior slipped his tongue in her mouth. Lora wasn't sure what to do, so she waited for his lead. He began exploring the inside of her mouth. She enjoyed it immensely, but a part of her wished they'd get back to the hugging and the sweet words of affection.

His movement was so smooth as he gently pushed her back on the couch and whispered, "You are so precious to me." Now his kisses ran down the soft bone of her neck, and then he cupped his hand and began to fondle her breasts.

She wanted him to stop. Right now. But the feeling was so intense, Lora could only manage a feeble attempt. "I think we'd better stop."

He was slowly moving on top of her now and she could feel the growth between his thighs. "Baby, I love you. Do you love me?"

"Yes," she mumbled. But Lora lay very still. It seemed that at the tiniest movement, the more excited George Junior became. Now his hand was attempting to lift her dress.

Lora tried to push it away. "George, no. Don't do that; I'm scared."

He pressed down on her even harder, and the electricity that went through her seemed to take away any power she had to put an end to this.

"I don't want you to be scared...I would never do anything to hurt you. I want to show you how much I love you."

It was disorienting; her mind was completely out of touch with her body.

The temperature in the room had gotten hotter and the massive body writhing on top of her was most definitely in heat. Lora knew that what she was allowing George Junior to do was terribly wrong. But crazy as it seemed, she was as fearful to stop, as she was to go on. If only he'd stop whispering sweet nothings in her ear. It was clouding her good sense.

George Junior continued to smother her with kisses and words of his undying love. Then he pulled something out of his pocket that he began to struggle with. Lora wasn't quite sure what it was, and for the life of her, couldn't remember when he'd pulled down her panties. In the blink of an eye, she felt him thrust himself inside of her and the excruciating pain that accompanied it.

She panted, "George!"

Apparently, this only excited him more. He quickly covered her mouth with his and began swiftly moving in and out of her, for every bit of ten seconds. Then a contorted look came over his face as his body jerked for another ten seconds. He froze, and then collapsed.

The inside of her thighs felt wet and sticky. Lora turned away, and buried her face into the deep hollow of the green sofa.

"Shit! The damn thing broke!"

Slowly twisting around, Lora saw George Junior holding a torn Trojan in his hand.

"Wait here. I'll be right back."

Lora was so scared of being discovered there in her condition, she stood to follow George as he ran from the room. But the fact that she was sore and scared shitless with blood and semen running down her thighs stopped her from going anywhere.

In a total panic, Lora raised her dress and tried wiping herself and Miss Cora's couch with her slip. She tripped in the rush to put her panties back on. So much for her father's warning of keeping her dress down and her legs shut tight, or Uncle Wes's admonition of returning in the same condition as she'd left.

George Junior ran back into the room. "Lora, it's a quarter to one! We'd better head on over to the school!"

To say she was shamed and confused would've been a gross understatement, and right here in his parents' home while they lay asleep. Lora prayed they were asleep. Had it even been worth it? The actual act had not been enjoyable in the least, and Lora had no intention of ever repeating it again.

As they hurried back to campus, George Junior stopped and took hold of her hand. "Look at me." Lora felt terribly awkward, but obeyed. "I want you to know that you have my heart, forever and ever."

She guessed that was some consolation, but all she could offer in return was a sorrowful, half-hearted smile.

Chapter 17

Durham, North Carolina

Lora had come back home from Dunn and exhausted herself with details of preparing for graduation. There'd been measurements for cap and gown, her responsibilities on the yearbook committee, and last-minute packing and preparation for her move to Durham. Yet none of those duties could block out the evening she'd spent with George Junior on his prom night.

She'd sat in the back of the Greyhound bus oblivious to all the bumps in the road, lost in deep thought. Rosie had filled her brown paper bag with more than enough food for the trip to Aunt Elvira's, but she hadn't been hungry. Lora had tried focusing on the beauty of the trees and pastures whisking by her window, trying to feel exhilarated about her move to the big city. She'd graduated at the top of her class, but unfortunately, would have no mementoes to look back on. Their principal, Mr. Anderson, had stolen all the money that'd been set aside for their yearbook.

"You go on up there and make me and your mama proud now," her father had said. "You a Hammond and don't ever forget it. Anybody don't treat my baby right, you tell 'em they gone have to look John Hammond in the eye."

Neither parent gave too much display of affection. Rosie hugged her lightly and gave her a pat on the back. "You be good now and don't forget to write."

Her brothers and sisters begged her to send them something from the big city. Bunch said, "Lora, when I finish school, can I come to Durham and live with you?"

Hammond hushed her. "If you don't be keepin' yo' mind in dem school books 'stead of always nosey'en in grown folks bizness, you ain't gon' make it to tomorrow, never mind makin' it to Durham."

Still staring back at the continuous stretch of greenery, Lora took only two bites of her bologna sandwich laced with sandwich spread and wrapped between two pieces of Wonder Bread. She read another one of George's love letters for the hundredth time.

She rested her head against the window and fantasized about the long walks they'd take together, holding hands and all the things romantic to a young teenaged girl blooming into womanhood.

Then Lora closed her eyes and took in three deep breaths, determined to erase from her memory what had taken place in the Morgan home. At least she'd give it her best shot.

Lora couldn't worry about that now. She had made it to Durham and started her first job, working in Aunt Elvira's diner. Spending time with the free-spirited woman had done Lora much good, and she wanted to thank her aunt by making herself an asset to the restaurant.

Johnny B, the cook, was well into his sixties and often took his sweet time preparing the food. Good thing the food wasn't the only reason people came to the diner. Many of them came for Aunt Elvira's bright smile and free laughter—or one of the flirty, bosom-laced hugs she often gave male customers who might have had a mind to complain about the slow cook.

"Child, what is that drab thing you puttin' on? Your beau is coming to see you and you looking like some poor stepchild."

Lora stared at her aunt in the doorway and then at her reflection in the mirror.

"I know, Aunt Elvira, but it's about the nicest thing I have, being that it's such a warm evening and all."

Today had been a real busy Saturday in the diner and Lora had thirty minutes to get herself ready. It was the first evening she'd be seeing George Junior since arriving in Durham.

"Well, we've got ourselves a few extra dollars. We're gonna have to do something about that. I can't have no niece of mine walking around like she's from the backwoods or something, though that would be about the truth." Elvira teasingly laughed at her remark. "That's all right, Darlin', Aunt Elvira's gonna take you downtown to a real nice department store tomorrow. We'll get you some pretty things for school, all kinds of weather, and for dates with your beau."

It'd been a whole week since a bunch of boys had come in and stolen dozens of boxes of supplies from Aunt Elvira's store on Lora's watch, but it seemed like the incident had never taken place. Elvira had the affection of many suitors who all chipped in to restock her diner, above and beyond what she even needed. Her aunt's kindness should have been a comfort, but it only made Lora feel guiltier.

At Elvira's, she had her own room in the back of the restaurant, right across the hall from her aunt. She even had a full-length mirror on the door of the armoire. What a luxury to be able to see herself while she dressed.

Her aunt seemed happy to have her living at the diner. Elvira, who had never been married and had no children of her own, would take joy in showering Lora with whatever material things Elvira could afford. She must have seen that the teenager could use a little sophistication as well. Elvira could take pride in the fact that Lora's mama and daddy had sent her to the right place.

By the same token, Lora was just as happy to be there for Elvira. For all of her aunt's flamboyant energy and colorfulness, Lora sensed a bit of loneliness. She was glad to fill whatever void she could.

Elvira left Lora to finish primping and then returned, holding a pretty bottle with a red tassel on it.

"Li'l Darlin', let me dab a touch of this Midnight Rose behind each of those little ears and Mr. George Junior won't know what hit him. My love juice is liable to put him under some kind of spell. Make sure he don't be puttin' his hands in the cookie jar, if you know what I mean."

Lora knew exactly what her aunt meant. Unfortunately, George Junior had already been in the cookie jar, deep into the cookie jar.

There was a loud knock. Elvira bounced out of the room and rushed to answer it.

"Dab a little Midnight Rose on the inside of your arms, too, Lora!" she yelled over her shoulder.

After taking the suggestion, Lora sniffed the inside of her arm. Her aunt was right; the scent was divine.

Was that George's voice she heard? She wasn't sure. There were a couple of voices. After a few seconds, she was certain one definitely belonged to George Junior.

Elvira hurried back to Lora's room, exuding a grand smile.

"Chile, you got company out there, and I must say that beau of yours is one handsome fella! Them other two ain't too bad neither. You and George Junior can go off on your date and leave them friends of his here with me."

The friends were Bill Elliott and Andrew Gilmore. Lora went out to greet them, disappointed that George Junior would come to pick her up for a date with his two friends in tow.

"Hey, Lora! How you doing? You remember Bill Elliott and Andrew Gilmore?"

Yes, she remembered. But she couldn't say she was happy to see them. "Hi, Bill. Hi, Andrew."

Elvira probably couldn't help but notice the displeasure in her niece's eyes, and struck a sassy pose with her hands on curvaceous hips. "Well, they say three's a crowd, so what exactly are you two planning to do?" Elvira was staring at Bill and Andrew.

George Junior didn't get the hint. "Miss Elvira, they have a dance at the park on Saturday nights. I decided we'd go out there."

Elvira wasn't letting him off the hook that easy. "Then you and Lora should run along and let me and these two sweet young thangs get acquainted. They can meet up with you all a little later. You boys know your way out to the park?"

Andrew was glued to his stool at the counter, staring at Elvira like a hungry young pup. "Oh yes, Miss Elvira, we come to Durham quite a bit to go to the dances they have out at the park."

Bill Elliott, who was on the shy and quiet side, said softly, "Sho nuff."

Then Andrew blurted out, "June, why don't you and Lora go on ahead. Bill and me will meet you two up there."

George Junior snatched the door open, obviously irritated. "Yeah, fine. Let's go, Lora."

Once outside, they had walked a few paces when George Junior stopped. "You still feel like going to the park?" He seemed to bark the question at her.

It was the first time she'd seen him since that night at his parents' house. The moment suddenly felt tense and awkward, and now she wished Andrew and Bill had tagged along.

"Say something. Do you want to go or not?"

Why was he so exasperated? He'd already decided they were going to the park. Why was it all up to her now?

George Junior had written how much he'd missed her and how he couldn't wait for them to be together again, and now here he was behaving so horribly.

"I don't mind going to the park, George. It'll be fun to dance."

"Fine, then."

George Junior turned on his heels and she had to walk double time to keep up.

Once they got to the park and began to get into the groove of things, George Junior became the usual life of the party—that was, until it hit him that Andrew and Bill hadn't shown up.

Now they made their way back to the diner, and again at breakneck speed.

"If those jokers went back to Dunn without me, they can forget about ever having another meal at my house!"

They'd actually had a fun evening at the dance, and now here he was switching gears again. George Junior was boiling mad that the guys had ditched meeting them, and had apparently headed back to Dunn without him.

"Why are you so upset? At least we got to be alone and have a good time."

George Junior cut her off. "That's not the point! They said they were gonna meet us at the park. Then they turn around and head back to Dunn without me!"

Lora had had about enough. Maybe she'd look for another boyfriend, right here in Durham, one who didn't display a six-year-old childishness when things didn't go his way.

As they rounded the corner, loud laughter could be heard coming through the windows of the diner. They walked in and saw Bill and Andrew sitting at a table with Elvira eating plates of fried cabbage and oxtails, having a merry old time.

"Thank the Lord you two decided to come on back here," Elvira said. "Andrew and Bill just about talked my head off!" Well, at least Andrew had. Bill had simply smiled shyly. "Now it's time for me to go and get my beauty rest."

Bill and Andrew were practically foaming at the mouth as they watched Elvira's hourglass figure depart to her room.

"Gee whiz, Lora!" Andrew gushed. "Your aunt is something else! She gave us all kinds of advice on women—how to tell a lady from a tramp. It's like she's showin' us the playbook. Bill and I can't wait to come back and visit!"

"Yeah, Aunt Elvira's a real nice lady. I'm looking forward to seeing her again," Bill gleefully chimed in.

"What are you clowns talking about? We waited up at the park for you half the night. That's the last time I'm ever bringing you up here with me!"

But George Junior was only pretending to still be annoyed.

Andrew came right back. "Oh shut up, Man! Like we don't know how to get on the bus without you! You heard Aunt Elvira; she told Bill and me to come on back and see her sometime. We certainly wouldn't want to disappoint her."

Bill said, "That's right." And the young men cracked up laughing.

They kidded each other back and forth for a little bit and then the boys said goodnight to Lora, and stepped outside to wait for George Junior.

"I had a great time with you tonight, Baby."

Now it was Baby again, now that Bill and Andrew hadn't gone back to Dunn without him. Lora was displeased with George's attitude tonight and was about to tell him so. But when he kissed her with those soft lips, all displeasure flew out the window.

And true to Aunt Elvira's words, at that moment, George Junior was only thinking with one thang.

"Let's go back to your room for a minute."

"No, George! Are you crazy?! If my aunt catches the two of us in my bedroom, she'll have me on the next bus home."

"I want to spend a little time alone with you before I go. Besides, your aunt is already sound asleep."

This was true. Elvira's loud snoring could already be heard all the way out in the diner.

"Please, Lora. I'll only stay a second. I don't want to keep Bill and Andrew waiting that long, though they both deserve it."

She didn't believe him for one minute. Lora knew George Junior didn't care how long he kept his friends waiting. Besides that, the two of them had already been alone, all evening. No, she knew how persuasive George Junior could be, and she was not ever going down that road again.

Oh, God! Why was he looking at her like that? Those piercing dark eyes staring straight through her; they were enough to drive a girl crazy! She couldn't believe it. Here she was again, not using the common sense the good Lord had given her.

They tiptoed back to Lora's room.

"This room sure is small," he observed rudely.

"At least I don't have to share it with six other people."

"Six! You had to sleep in a room with six other people?" George Junior smiled. "Then it'd be nice to only have to sleep with *one*."

And there were those gorgeous dimples, exposing those pearly whites.

George Junior pulled her down on the bed next to him, planting the sweetest kisses on her mouth.

God, pleeese pleeese pleeese, hellllllp! she screamed in her head. Then Lora made a secret deal with herself. She'd allow the kissing, but that was absolutely all she'd allow. It didn't matter how crazy George Junior was driving her.

But unfortunately, Lora found she was rendered powerless yet again.

George Junior smoothly pushed her back on the bed, gently spreading her legs ever so slightly. He raised his hand high underneath her dress and stroked the place, filling her with an urgent wetness. A loose cannon went off inside of him and he was not alone. But Lora couldn't understand what was making her go forward, because as good as the moment felt, she remembered how humiliating and painful the actual act had been the first time.

Aunt Elvira rolled over and ejected a loud cough, and that was all it took to spring Lora off the bed and out of George's hungry trap.

"Stop it, George!" she whispered loudly. "You have to go right now before my aunt finds you in here!"

George Junior tried to pull her back down, but this time she stood her ground.

"Come on, George; you have to leave! I mean it!"

"Okay, okay. But I don't know what you're getting all scared about; your aunt is still snoring."

Lora listened for a moment and heard Elvira's snore. But there was no way she was getting back on that bed with George Junior, no way!

"Come on, George. I'm walking you to the door."

He was not pleased, not to mention hard as a rock, which had to be absolutely painful. But George Junior had no choice except to follow Lora out to the front door.

Clearly, he was disappointed, but right now Lora couldn't care less. What they were doing could get them into a mess of trouble, and once was definitely enough.

"Bye, George. Will you call me?"

"Yeah, sure I will. See you later."

He didn't even kiss her goodbye. Maybe it was for the best, because George Junior's kisses were too damn dangerous!

Chapter 18

"Come on, Child. Come on in here, to the back." Lora felt Aunt Elvira's soft hand touch the back of her neck as she lifted her head up from the counter.

"But, Aunt Elvira, I've got all these folks waiting for their orders. I felt a little dizzy for a moment, but I'm all right now."

"That's fine; they'll have to wait a little longer; and trust me, they'll wait."

Time was whipping by and life had been going great. George Morgan Junior came up almost every other weekend, and Lora had gotten into a real groove at the diner. Johnnie B came to adore her. For the first time, Lora had her own money. She sent a few dollars home and was still able to put away some for beauty school, which would be starting in a few short weeks. She couldn't have been more excited.

On this beautiful sunny morning, business was jumping with the usual breakfast rush. Lora had grabbed a plate of ham and eggs from Johnnie B in the kitchen and was delivering it to a customer sitting at the counter. Suddenly, she felt queasy and had to hold onto the counter until both she and the room stopped spinning. Taking a moment to try and pull herself together, she'd placed her head down on the counter feeling terribly hot, like she might pass out or something.

Aunt Elvira held onto her arm and led her back to the bedroom where she all but collapsed onto the bed. Elvira went out to the bathroom and returned with a cold, wet towel, which she placed on Lora's forehead.

"You know I'm gonna have to get in touch with your daddy and mama, don't you?"

Lora had no idea what her aunt was talking about. Surely, she wasn't dying.

"I felt dizzy for a minute, Aunt Elvira, but it's passed now. There's no reason to get in touch with Mama and Daddy."

Lora looked at the serious expression on her aunt's face. It made her nervous.

"Chile, you're pregnant."

She couldn't have heard Elvira right. Feeling like the breath had been knocked out of her, she struggled to speak. Her words were barely a whisper. "I'm not pregnant, Aunt Elvira. Why would you think something like that?"

"Now, Lora, you know what you and George Junior have obviously been up to. Your Mama told me you'd already started your time of month before you left home, and you haven't had no monthly since you been up here."

From the depths of her soul, Lora knew her aunt was right, and the reality was that she had missed her period. She'd explained it away by the fact that since she'd only started it a few months ago, maybe missed periods in the first year were a usual occurrence. Yet she knew there was no explaining this away. She'd done something sinful and now she'd be bringing nothing but shame and embarrassment to her family.

But how could this have happened? It'd only been one time. The second time, she'd gotten George Junior out of the diner before they ever went that far. After that, Lora made sure she was never alone with George Junior in any compromising position.

"But, Aunt Elvira, it only happened once, I swear! I've never done anything like that again."

"Oh, Sugar Plum, it's unfortunate, but it only takes one time, just one time to change all your hopes and dreams." And then Lora had a sudden flashback of George Junior holding the torn Trojan in his hand.

As soon as the rooster crowed that next morning, her eyes popped open. She'd hardly slept the entire night. And a few short hours later, Lora was back on a bus headed for Godwin, away from what had been a world full of promise.

Aunt Elvira had kissed her forehead and held her tight as the tears flowed inconsolably. "Now, Li'l Darlin', it's way past crying time. You're going to have to pick yourself up because you're about to become a woman now. Just know how much your Aunt Elvira loves you and I'll be praying to the Good Lord to see you through this."

As the bus pulled away from the depot, her aunt waved. It would be the last time Lora would ever see her. Aunt Elvira would pass away in her sleep a few short months later.

It was early afternoon when Lora tentatively walked up the porch steps. Entering the front room, she saw Hammond sitting in his rickety old rocker. It squeaked back and forth as he stared up at her. Lora shamefully lowered her eyes to the floor.

The house was conspicuously silent. Then she heard the toot of a car horn. She looked out the front screen and saw Uncle Jacob. Rosie was in the front seat beside him. Lora had no idea where everyone else was.

Hammond rose from his chair and walked out to the car. Without any instruction, Lora instinctively knew to follow. She climbed into the backseat next to her father. Jacob took off. No words were spoken.

It didn't dawn on her where they were headed until she saw the sign: *Dunn, City Limit.* It must have been pushing about sixty-five degrees this winter morning, but Lora felt the coldest chill in the air.

When they pulled up to the front of the Morgan house, Rosie got out, and then Lora and her father climbed out of the back. Uncle Jacob respectfully stayed in the car.

Bill and Thelma were sitting out on the porch, sucking on Tootsie Roll pops. They didn't speak to these strangers entering their home. The only one they recognized was Lora, but she avoided eye contact as she followed into the house behind her parents.

Hammond didn't even bother to knock; he barged right through the front door like he owned the place.

Thelma got up to follow, but Bill gave a strong reprimand. "If you don't sit your nosey behind down! Didn't Mama say to stay outside until she said different?!"

"Oh shut up! How come Lora didn't even speak? Why was she acting like she didn't know nobody?" And with that, Thelma skipped off down the road.

There was no friendly smell of corn bread baking or jovial laughter filtering through the house, only the somber face of George Junior standing next to his father, George Senior, who sat in his big, overstuffed chair. There was no sign of Miss Cora either.

Mr. George stood as they entered into his living room.

"Been a long time, Hammond; good to see you. It's good to see you, too, Rosie."

Lora's mother smiled graciously. "Thank you, George. It has been a mighty long time."

Hammond grunted. "I'd say it ain't been long enough."

Mr. George ignored Hammond's sarcasm and said, "Well, looks like we've got ourselves a little problem here."

Hammond looked around the room. "I don't wanna talk to you. I wanna talk to the Boss Lady."

Lora couldn't believe her father's audacity, and he wasn't even drunk.

"Is that Rosie and Hammond?"

Thank God! There was the sound of that sweet, lyrical voice, breaking the tension between the two men as Cora ran in. "Oh, my Lord! It's mighty good to see you, Rosie. You too, Hammond."

George Senior probably knew the situation was too delicate to allow Hammond to draw him into a confrontation. Perhaps it would be best to let Cora handle things diplomatically.

The two teenagers kept their eyes plastered to the wall while Hammond waved his hand in frustration. "Well, now that we done got all the niceties outta the way, I wanna know what yo' boy here is gon' do 'bout my daughter. He done gon' and got her pregnant, and I wanna know what he plannin' on doin' 'bout it?"

Miss Cora looked Hammond squarely in the eye. "George Junior knows he's going to have to take responsibility for this, Hammond. There is no question about that. I can assure you, he's going to do the right thing."

"He should've been doing the right thing long before now," Hammond quipped. "And I'll tell you what, he don't have to marry my girl if he don't want to. I sure ain't gon' force him. She gon' always have a home wit' her daddy, that's fo' sho'. But he best be gittin' some kinda work 'cause this here baby sho' as hell gon' have to eat."

George Junior cleared his throat. "I *want* to marry Lora, Mr. Hammond. I plan on marrying her and getting a good job so I can take care of her and the baby."

Hammond's eyes narrowed. "Then you best make sho' you come through wit' that promise, too...plain and simple. All right then; good day to you folks."

Her father had come to say what he had to say and that was all there was. Everyone had remained silent while the two bosses decided what would be. Now Lora and Rosie obediently followed Hammond back out to the car without another word being spoken.

Lora was frightened and still in a state of shock. Things seemed to be going from bad to worse. No one had given any thought or care as to how Lora felt; no one even bothered to ask. It didn't seem pertinent whether or not she wanted to marry George Junior, and the fact was, she didn't.

Lora cared for George Junior, and up until now, even thought she might be in love with him. But now that reality had set in, it was a different story. Lora was insecure about the kind of husband George Junior would be. He drank alcohol on occasion and had somewhat of a controlling streak. If only she could turn back the clock and once again be in Durham with Aunt Elvira at the diner. Lora would be preparing to attend beauty school instead of preparing for the birth of a child when she was only a child herself. But she couldn't turn back the clock, no matter how much she wished to. The die was already cast.

The following morning, George Junior showed up at her front door. He informed Lora that he'd been given money from his father for them to get married. He told her to pack a suitcase because she'd be coming to live with him at his parents' home.

"Under different circumstances, I wouldn't be giving you no kinda permission to be marryin' up wit' my daughter. But seeing how you done made a mess of her life, the best way fo' you to clean that all up is doin' the respectable thing."

George Junior nodded his head in response to Hammond's words and then sat quietly on the sofa waiting for her to go and pack.

Lora had never seen that kind of sadness in her father's eyes. At that moment, she realized how much he truly loved her, and how truly disappointed she'd made him.

Her sisters and brothers were all at school and Lora was sorry she wouldn't get to say goodbye. She hugged Willie Rose, and when she saw the tears well up in her mother's eyes, Lora ran quickly out the door before she fell apart.

The soon-to-be newlyweds sat in abject silence riding the bus to Dillon, S.C. to be married by a justice of the peace. In Dillon, they were able to wed without having to show proof of age. There were no compassionate words, or reassuring caresses. In truth, the reality had hit them both hard. Neither knew what to say to the other, nor how to comfort the other.

The ceremony, if one could call it that, void of pomp and ceremony, was over in less than five minutes. The two quickly repeated their vows. It was done. Then the naive young girl and the immature young boy were pronounced man and wife. When George Junior was told he could kiss the bride, he gave Lora a swift, perfunctory kiss on the lips and they fled from the chapel.

Bride and groom sat again in silence riding the bus to Dunn. They were bound for Lora's temporary new home, and the beginning of a new life, one she was ill prepared for, to say the least.

Then and there, Lora realized that a line had been drawn in her life's sand. She recognized the crushing death of her dreams and aspirations; and sadly, she received the weight of the monkey that would pounce on her back for decades to come.

Chapter 19

Dunn, North Carolina

"Ummmm... Uggghhhh... Oohhhh..." He was making all sorts of grunting noises moving up and down inside her, causing the bed to squeak. Lora was mortified and couldn't wait for it to be over. She imagined everyone in the house to be awake and listening at the door.

Finally, it was over. George Junior stopped and rolled over, immediately falling asleep.

The Morgans had gone out of their way to make things pleasant for her, and Lora had to admit she enjoyed living in their comfortable home. If anything was difficult, it was the sleeping arrangements. She and George Junior had been given his older sister, Margaret's room, which was right next to George Junior's parents' room. Margaret was away at college.

Although they were now married, Lora was still uptight and uncomfortable about having sex with George Junior, especially in such close proximity to his parents. She did enjoy, however, the occasional foreplay, and wished it went on a lot longer. The actual act was less than thrilling. She was relieved this would be the last night, for a while, anyway. George Junior was leaving for the Big Apple, New York City, to find work.

The months passed by quickly and Lora enjoyed the daily pampering of her new family. They couldn't have been kinder, including Thelma, who'd developed a real liking for her new sister-in-law. Since they were much closer in age than Thelma and her older sister, Margaret, Thelma now felt she had a sister she could confide in.

Thelma constantly questioned Lora about growing up on a farm, and what it was like having a houseful of brothers and sisters. Lora found herself developing a fondness for the wayward teenager, but her biggest soft spot was held for Mr. George. It was quite apparent how different George Junior was from his father. In fact, it was the younger son, Bill, who was more like the patriarch. Both were soft-spoken, happy-go- lucky and playful, and unlike George Junior, they never displayed temper-tantrums.

George Senior would pop in from work, plant a kiss on Miss Cora's cheek, and then go to calling, "Where's Lora?!"

"Here I am, Mr. George," would be the usual reply, unless she was visiting over at her Uncle Wes's, with Tommy Lawrence, or across the street at Aunt Luticia's.

"How was your day today?"

"Oh, just fine, Mr. George."

Sometimes, Mr. George would question if she'd been bored sitting around all day. He was always genuinely concerned about her feelings as well as her welfare.

As it turned out, Miss Cora worked part of the day, doing house cleaning for some prominent white family in town. Lora came to realize that she'd had a false perception about George Junior's parents being rich—far from it. Mr. George worked as a railroad conductor and did carpentry on the side. Both husband and wife worked hard to make ends meet, and to keep their oldest child, Margaret, in college.

Bill had met a girl named Beatrice, over in Benson, whom he visited on the weekends. Eventually, Beatrice would become his wife. During the week, Bill would come in from school and he and Lora would sit and laugh, and often play checkers. Bill was the only person who'd ever been able to beat her. However, Lora could tell when he was purposely letting her win, which was most of the time. When she would call him on it, her brother-in-law would only laugh and deny it. He had such a pure, sweet nature, and after receiving a scathing letter from George Junior one day, Lora couldn't help but wish her love were with the other brother.

George Junior had included some money in his last letter for her to buy some things for the baby. He'd found a job as superintendent of a Harlem apartment building, and one of the perks of the job was free rental of the basement apartment.

Lora had written back, congratulating him on finding work so quickly. She also explained everything she'd bought with the money.

George, I spent three bucks on baby clothes, two bucks on a pretty yellow blanket and a baby rattle, and I still had a buck left over.

He'd written back, skipping any pleasantries.

Lora,

You're not in the country anymore. Stop acting like you're still living on a farm! The word is dollar, not buck! I hope you're not using that kind of country talk around my mama and daddy!

Anyway, I won't be able to send you any more money until my next paycheck. I get paid every two weeks.

I'm lovin' it here in New York! It's a swingin' place! Tell Mama and Daddy I'll write soon.

George

Lora had torn the letter into tiny pieces. It hurt her feelings deeply to be referred to as country.

The next afternoon, when she came in from visiting over at Aunt Luticia's, she passed by the living room and caught a glimpse of an older girl standing with Miss Cora. The girl looked a lot like Miss Cora and she looked up as Lora passed, their eyes locking for only a moment.

"Lora, hold on a minute. I'd like you to meet someone," Cora shouted out before Lora could get too far.

"This is my oldest daughter, Margaret, and, Margaret, this is your brother's wife, Lora."

"Hi, Margaret."

"Hi, Lora. It's nice to finally meet you."

Margaret was nice enough, but she seemed reserved. Lora guessed she had a right to be standoffish. It's not every day that one meets her teenage brother's pregnant wife.

Lora felt shy and intimidated in George's older sister's presence, so she would pretty much keep her distance. Margaret was usually out with friends, anyway, so Lora saw very little of her during the short times her new sister-in-law was home visiting.

Lora wanted to be happy for Margaret. The young woman was smart. She was making her way through college, making something out of her life, and making her parents proud. But it was sad and difficult to see Margaret's good fortune as anything but a cruel reminder of what had been lost to Lora forever.

Chapter 20

"How's my little lady?" Doctor Melbourne had come rushing in.

A tight grimace crossed Lora's face as she mumbled, "It's starting to really hurt, Doctor Melbourne."

"Well, don't you worry. I'll give you something to take care of that right now."

That was the last she remembered. A short while later, my mother awoke to a nurse bringing me in to her for the first time since my delivery, and I was delicately placed in her arms. Mom said it was a momentous day looking into the precious face staring up at her. All the dreaded feelings of motherhood quickly disappeared. She held my little round body and placed a kiss on my tiny lips. Granddaddy Hammond had requested I be named Deborah, and so I was, but I would grow up with the nickname Debbi.

There were the same deep dimples in my cheeks as my father and grandmother, and I wasn't all wrinkled like most babies. Everyone said I'd capitalized on both parents' best attributes, and for the first time, Mom was madly in love.

The relatives came piling in: Granddaddy George, Grandma Cora, Tommy Lawrence, Uncle Wes and Aunt Florence, Aunt Luticia and her husband, Mr. Frank, Bill Elliott, and Andrew Gilmore. And as soon as school let out, Aunt Thelma and Uncle Bill were on their bikes racing to the hospital to join the others.

"Lora! She's got big ole dimples in her cheeks exactly like Mama and June," voiced the exuberant Suge.

"She's definitely a Morgan, laying back, cool as a cucumber, and smiling. The rest of them babies in there are screaming at the top of their lungs. They probably mad 'cause they came out so doggone ugly!"

Granddaddy George said, "Now, Son, bite your tongue. Just because the rest of them tots look like wrinkled prunes, that's no reason to call them ugly."

Everyone laughed and Grandma Cora swatted Granddaddy on the arm. "George, you and Bill cut that out now."

Daddy called from New York and they each got on the phone giving their opinions about his new daughter. When he finally spoke to Mom, it was brief because Daddy was worried about the long distance telephone bill. He promised to phone later, when he could call the house collect.

After that, everything was a whirlwind. My mother brought me back to my grandparents' home only briefly because with them both working, and Uncle Bill and Aunt Thelma in school, there'd be no one at the house to look after mother and child. So Mom packed us up and moved us on to Goldston, North Carolina, where her parents were now living, until Daddy sent for us to come to New York.

My mother was actually sad to leave the Morgan home. Her stay there had been the best, warm, tension-free, and loving home environment she'd ever had. She'd cherished the kind and gentle spirit of George Morgan Senior, and often thought of how lucky his children had been to have such a wonderful father.

Once Mommy was back with her own parents, everyone doted on me. Granddaddy Hammond couldn't have been more enamored with his new grandbaby, holding me constantly. My mother was able to get some much-needed rest. Because her birth canal was so small, I'd ripped her apart as I came tearing into the world. Mom had to have numerous stitches and was in tremendous pain. But Grandma Rosie came to the rescue giving her child daily sitz baths in a huge basin filled with Epsom salts to get her healed up quickly.

Nothing much had changed, except that the family was cramped in a new, small dwelling. There was still a houseful of kids and everything inside the house was still old and stale. But life would move on...

Chapter 21

Bronx, New York
Mid-1960s

"Leave my mommy alone! You leave my mommy alone!!" My five-year-old sister, Terry, ran into the kitchen where our father had our mother pinned up against the wall with a crowbar under her neck.

We were now living in the South Bronx, in the McKinley Housing Projects on 161st Street and Tinton Avenue. Our apartment didn't come with a dead bolt, but my mother had called in a locksmith earlier that afternoon and installed one for extra security. Daddy had been making threats and was becoming much more violent. More frightening was the fact that the violence was now erupting even when he was stone-cold sober. His mood swings intensified and could ignite at any given moment. Mommy, Terry, and I walked around in constant dreadful anticipation.

I'd been staring in the dark at the big red letters on our Popeye clock, listening to the tick, tick, anticipating the moment that was here. Daddy turned his key in the lock but found that the door wouldn't open. Either it failed to do the job or the idiot locksmith hadn't installed it properly. Whatever the reason, the dead bolt, along with the skimpy door chain, came flying off when my father kicked the front door in at 11:22 p.m.

When I'd first heard the familiar screams I'd heard all my life, I jumped out of my twin bed to awaken my younger sister. "Terry! Terry!" I whispered frantically, "Daddy's hurting Mommy!"

I didn't know whom my baby sister had taken after, but she certainly wasn't the scaredy-cat I was. That's why I'd chosen to arouse her to confront the situation at hand. In one quick movement, Terry leapt up from her bed. It was as if I'd charged a battery remote in her brain and channeled her to the kitchen.

At only five years of age, Terry Janelle Morgan seemed to fear nothing, least of all our father. Perhaps a bit of that had to do with the fact that our father seemed to favor her. Ever since the episode years ago when I sneaked into my parents' bedroom in the middle of the night, things between my father and me were never quite the same, and the distance I felt from him only heightened my fear of him.

Seeming to operate on impulse, instead of running to the kitchen, my sister stopped in the hallway and grabbed the princess phone.

"Call the police! Please send police to our house! My daddy is—"

"Give me that damn phone!"

I hadn't even seen him run up. My father snatched the phone from my little sister and shoved her away, ripping the phone from the wall. That's when Mommy made a run for the window. She opened the window and tried screaming for help. But Daddy yanked her away, shoving her hard into the wall.

Terry had run behind my father to the kitchen and now she kicked at his legs with her tiny, bare feet. I stood in the doorway, my mother and me gasping for the same air while our father brutally shoved the crowbar against her delicate skin.

Then he stopped as his crazed eyes glared down at his baby daughter.

"Go back to bed! You get back to bed right now!"

Daddy dropped the pole and chased Terry from the kitchen. I

immediately fled back to my room for fear I'd be caught standing there as well.

"If you get out of that bed again, I'll whip your butt! Do you hear me!?"

I'd mastered feigned sleep ages ago. It was as if the blast of fire engines, bull horns, or the blood-curdling screams from a mother in peril could not stir me from deep slumber.

The cover was pulled high up on my face, but I pulled it down ever so slightly, peeking through the tiny slit of a moist eye.

Terry stared my father down without so much as a tremble, as if daring him to raise his hand, but knowing all along he'd never strike her. He never had. To be honest, I couldn't remember my father ever spanking either one of us. It seemed that parental discipline was relegated to our mother alone.

Mommy took advantage of the suspended seconds when Daddy chased Terry back to bed and took flight, once again searching for protection that the authorities never seemed to offer.

My ears wide-awake, I heard the door open minutes later and the distinct voices of two officers. They continued to quiet my father's interjections as they tried to listen to my mother's story. Daddy kept trying to offer up one lie or another. But the cops took one look around the battlefield apartment and surmised there'd been more than, in Daddy's words, a *verbal disagreement*.

Footsteps approached our room and it felt safe to open my eyes. Terry had already fallen back to sleep, snoring ever so slightly.

"Debbi, get up and get dressed. We're going to Aunt Sport's house."

"She's not going any goddamn place!" my father snapped back.

As always, I avoided his eyes, and trembled, looking toward the two officers.

"Would you like to go with your mother, or do you want to stay here with your father?"

I said ever so softly, "I want to go with my mother." I could feel Daddy's eyes boring a hole through me.

"Then you get up and go on with your mother!" He'd never spoken to me in that tone and I shuddered, unable to move. "But Terry's staying right here."

My sister's eyes fluttered open as she squinted at the faces above her.

Mommy pulled back the covers and lifted her up. "Come on, Baby; let's get you dressed."

"Where are we going, Mommy?"

"To your Aunt Sport and Uncle Bill's house."

"I told you she's not going anywhere! Go back to sleep, Terry!"

Terry looked at my father for a moment, and then seemed to recall what had transpired. "No! I'm going with my mommy!"

"Listen, Mister. That's enough. It's obvious your children want to go with their mother. We suggest you come on back into the living room with us until your wife can get herself and the kids out of here. Make it quick, Miss."

Daddy started to argue again, but then shrugged and stomped away. The two officers followed and Mommy hurriedly began throwing some things into a small suitcase. Maybe things were changing. I could remember a time when the cops would've done nothing except tell Daddy to take a walk and cool off.

"Mommy, don't forget Barbie," Terry whined.

"You can take Barbie in your arms, Sweetheart."

I wished my sister would shut up about her Barbie doll, and let our mother concentrate on getting us out of there before Daddy somehow managed to stop us.

A few minutes later, we were heading out the door and racing to the elevator.

"Don't you bring your ass back here either!"

"Listen, we don't want to have to arrest you for disturbing the peace. We suggest you get back inside and close the door." The police looked like they meant it, so Daddy slammed the door.

Oh, my goodness, I'd forgotten! The next day was Easter Sunday and my mother had bought me a beautiful dress to wear. I'd anxiously watched her pack and knew we'd both forgotten it.

"Mommy, what about my new Easter dress? It's in the closet." I looked at the police, hoping they'd offer to go back and get it.

Instead, they simply stared over at my mother. "You can run back and get your child's dress. We'll wait." Were they crazy?! They couldn't possibly think of sending my mother back into that apartment alone.

Our door suddenly swung open. Daddy wanted to see if we'd gotten on the elevator yet. His cold stare was ominous and Mommy seemed terrified of walking anywhere near him.

"That's okay, Mommy. You don't have to get it."

The tall, Italian-looking cop looked down at me sweetly. "I tell you what, you run back in and get your Easter dress, okay?" Then he looked down the hall to my father. "Your daughter forgot one of her dresses."

I looked at the cop with pleading eyes. Why couldn't he simply go to my closet and get my Easter dress? Why were cops so stupid? Did neither of them realize how frightened both my mother and I were to go anywhere near Daddy? It was obvious they did not.

"Go ahead, little girl, run and get your dress. Your mommy will wait right here for you."

If I thought about it too long, I'd never do it. I ran as quickly as I could past my father into my bedroom and snatched the yellow dress unceremoniously from its hanger. When I ran back toward the door, I skidded to a stop. This time, my father stood wide-legged in front of the door, making it impossible for me to skirt by him again.

I approached slowly as tears began to well up and I stuttered. "Ex...excuse...me, Daddy."

He was obviously angered by my betrayal. "I paid for that dress, and I shouldn't let you take it out of this house." He sighed heavily, but then stepped back to let me pass. My legs almost gave way as I bolted toward the elevator to safety.

My mother's younger sister, Rosalie, was called Bunch as a child. But then she'd changed her name to Rosalind, and after that was nicknamed Sport. Go figure. Anyway, Aunt Sport lived about fifteen minutes away with her husband, Bill Elliott. Uncle Bill had served in the Army, and was a quiet, distinguished man who seemed to worship Aunt Sport. So it was understandably shocking to discover some thirty years later that Uncle Bill was gay. He and my father had been high school buddies for years. Dad had introduced the pair after they'd all moved to New York City.

Uncle Bill Elliott didn't have much respect for his friend knocking his sister-in-law around. What on earth had gotten into George Junior?

"I don't know why June carries on like that," I heard my uncle mumble.

Aunt Sport was more vocal. "Because he's a jackass! I told my sister she shoulda' left that nigga a long time ago! I wish I were married to his stupid ass. I'd have somethin' for him, all right!"

Easter Sunday was pretty sad. Mommy stayed up most of the night discussing her plans with Aunt Sport to finally get my father put out once and for all. My mother didn't even get up to attend Easter Sunday Mass. Aunt Sport forbade us to disturb her. So I got myself dressed while Aunt Sport got Terry ready in the one plain jumper my mother had packed for her. Then Aunt Sport took us to

Mass. When we returned home, Mommy was still in bed, and that's where she stayed until the following morning.

While Mommy waited for the court to determine which of them would get to stay in the apartment, she did get a restraining order. Daddy was not to come within so many feet of her. In the interim, we went back to the projects to collect more of our belongings until a decision was made.

Two police officers escorted us to the front door and I waited with bated breath as Mommy stepped in. After a few seconds, it seemed apparent that Daddy wasn't home.

"Debbi, get as much as you can fit into your suitcase, and make sure you get all your underwear."

"Okay, Mommy."

The officers waited out in the hall, which I thought was a good thing. That way they could head my father off at the pass in case he suddenly appeared. My mother darted off toward her room and I was about to follow when something in the living room caught my eye. I froze.

Across the room on top of the TV console was a newspaper. Cutting through the newspaper and right into our console was a seven-inch butcher knife. I slowly crossed the room and stared down at the gory headline: *Husband Slashes Wife To Death.* Underneath the headline was a picture of a woman laid in a spiral twist soaked in her own blood. I couldn't tell if she was black or white, not that it mattered. But the whites of her eyes looked up in shock as if she couldn't believe someone had actually done this to her.

My mouth agape, I squeaked out, "Mommy," while clamping down on my jaw.

I heard my mother scream from her bedroom. *Oh, my God!* My immediate thought was that my father must have been hiding in the closet, waiting to jump out and slash my mother to shreds.

The officers bolted into the apartment and ran down the hallway.

I could not bear to follow them, absolutely horrified of seeing my mother lying on the floor, soaked in her own blood. It wasn't until I heard my mother's second outburst that I had the courage to run to her room.

"I cannot believe that lunatic did this!"

Thank Jesus, my mother wasn't lying on the floor, slashed to pieces, but all of her clothes were. Every single stitch of clothing she owned, including her slips, bras, panties, and stockings, had been sliced to smithereens!

"He's crazy! He's absolutely crazy!"

There was a dead silence as everyone looked down at Mommy's pretty things, all of which had been destroyed. Suddenly, I rushed from my mother's room into my own and threw open my closet, half expecting to see my entire wardrobe shredded as well. But not one of my darling dresses had been harmed. I smiled to myself, and then immediately felt guilty. How could I possibly take joy in being spared after my mother's awful misfortune?

"Miss, if it's any consolation, you're lucky your clothes are all that got cut up. Believe me, we've come upon these kinds of situations before and seen a whole lot worse. Now I'm sure the judge will put your husband out of the apartment, but until then, you and your child need to leave. We'll escort you out."

My mother realized how right the cop was, and quickly dried her eyes.

Exactly one week later, the court granted Mommy a legal separation and ordered my father to vacate the premises. My only hope was that this time it'd be for good.

There had been another time a few years before when she'd gotten Daddy put out. We'd been living on the top floor of a five-floor walk-up. The judge had ordered him to stay away until after he and Mommy had gone to court. In the meantime, Daddy was only allowed Sunday visits with my little sister and me.

It was a Friday night when my mother's younger sister, Virginia, showed up at our house with a huge black eye. She and her husband had moved to New York where my aunt had given birth to a baby boy named Robbie. Robbie was born with an Rh-negative blood type, and was extremely fair-skinned, although both his parents were dark-skinned. The child was the spitting image of his father. Anybody with eyeballs could see the resemblance. But because of his light complexion, my uncle had been making accusations to my Aunt Virginia that the child couldn't be his. They'd gotten into another huge fight about it, and he'd given my aunt a black eye and thrown her out in the snow. It was admirable that he'd allowed his son to remain home in his warm crib.

My mother burst into tears when she opened the door to her baby sister, bruised and practically frozen to death. They clung to each other and cried. It was a sorrowful truth that except for one, Aunt Sport, all four of John Hammond's girls had married violent and abusive men.

Saturday morning, Mommy got up and made us all a big breakfast. Then she decided we were going to go see a movie, something that would hopefully take Aunt Virginia's mind off of the predicament she was in. Then Daddy called to say he wanted to take Terry and me somewhere with him that day. Mommy told him "no." She told him it was not his visitation day and that we had other plans. I could hear Daddy screaming through the phone as Mommy hung up.

We were all on our way out the door when Aunt Virginia looked out the kitchen window and let out a blood-curdling scream. There was Daddy on the fire escape gaping through the window. In the next second, he assumed the position of Superman as he jumped through the window.

"Run! Run!! Run!!!" We were all screaming, "Run!" And we were running as fast as we could down the five flights of stairs. Before we could reach the bottom, there was a wrenching scream. Aunt

Virginia had slipped and fallen down the last set of stairs, lacerating her leg.

My poor aunt had come to us with a big black eye from her no-account husband, and now my father had caused her to split her leg, which would leave a permanent scar.

This time, Daddy had to move out all of his belongings, begrudgingly I'm sure. We weren't present. He moved in with his brother, Bill, and Bill's wife, Bea.

That first night, I still listened for his footsteps, still listened for his key turning in the lock. It was a while before I was truly convinced Daddy wasn't coming home again. Finally, I drifted off to sleep. I slept more soundly than I ever had before that night.

Chapter 22

"Daddy, come on! Why do you keep stopping?"

"I'm coming, Baby. You run on. Daddy will catch up with you."

As Terry ran ahead, I looked back and saw my father leaning up against a building. For a moment, I thought he was going to slide down the wall, but then he seemed to get his bearings.

Daddy had been out of the apartment for almost nine months and we were having one of our court-ordered visitations. He'd taken us to see a Disney movie: *Snow White and the Seven Dwarfs*. At first, the visitations had been difficult. I was fearful and unsure of my father and what his attitude would be toward me. In fact, there seemed to be apprehension that hung in the air for both of us. But Daddy seemed to go out of his way to make sure Terry and I always had a good time.

Thankfully, he never spoke badly about our mother either. In time, I began to feel less uptight and more able to enjoy our outings. But always in the back of my mind was the hurt, the insecurity, and the fear. I'd never let go of the fear.

I noticed the dark circles under his eyes, and how weak Daddy appeared to be. In fact, he'd seemed to be a bit ill on each of the last three visits we'd had. And looking at him now, I was struck by how vulnerable he seemed.

"Daddy, are you okay?" I walked back and tentatively touched his hand.

He smiled and placed a shaky arm around my shoulder. "Yes, Sweetheart, Daddy's a little tired."

I didn't believe him. I looked up and saw the fear in his eyes. I could smell it. It was so recognizable to me. It was strange to feel scared for him, instead of scared *of* him.

Terry was laughing and sliding in the snow. I walked slowly along with my father as he held on to my small shoulder for support. When we finally reached our building, he sadly looked up at our window.

"I see your mom put new curtains up. They look nice."

He looked so pitiful, like he wished he could somehow take back all the mean things he'd done to his wife and family.

"Daddy, will you come back home today? We miss you!" Terry wrapped herself around our father's leg, her innocence and youth quickly forgetting the reason he was no longer living with us. All she knew now was that she wanted her daddy back home.

"I'm sorry, Sweet Pea, but Daddy can't do that." He picked Terry up to hug her and wobbled a bit. So he gently put her back down and stroked the back of her head, trying to stop her from shedding the tears that were now forming.

"But why, Daddy?" she sniveled. "You're supposed to live in the house with the mommy and the children."

"I know; I know. Don't you worry, one day soon you're going to wake up and Daddy's going to be right there."

That proclamation sent a nervous jolt through my body.

"Now give me a big kiss so you can get upstairs; it's cold out here."

Daddy leaned down to plant a kiss on Terry's cheek and I watched a tear fall down his. "Okay, now scoot."

My little sister ran off toward the building howling in despair.

"Debbi, give your daddy a kiss." I couldn't remember the last time he'd hugged me so tenderly, or maybe I'd missed it because I was always full of so many disturbing and fearful emotions.

He peered deep into my eyes. "Debbi... You know Daddy loves you very, very much. I'm really sorry you had to see me and your mother fight sometimes. I...I...just wish I could take it all back and things could be different. I wish that so much, because I'd really like to be home with my girls again. I'd like to be back home with your mommy, too. I really miss her. Well...I wanted you to know that. You'd better run on upstairs now."

His words had honesty, even if only in that moment, for I had no doubt that if my father were ever allowed to come back, it'd be the same thing all over again. I suppose there were times that hadn't been so bad, laughter here and there. Somehow I recalled my parents in a warm caress, a softly spoken word; two hips gyrating in a seductive slow dance. It would probably be an inaccuracy to say that my father was completely evil, that he abused my mother on a daily basis, or caused nothing but heartache for every moment of our lives. Yet the good times were fleeting; they held no weight. They were always overshadowed by the loud thumps, the crashing glass, the piercing screams, or the bottomless pit of vomit that rested in my belly. It's not merely a cliché. We do remember more of the bad than we do the good.

I looked at his still strikingly handsome face with the circles beneath his eyes; the huge dimples that attempted a lasting smile. The young man standing before me was my father, the only one I'd ever have. He wanted to make amends and perhaps start anew, but it was too late. He'd robbed me of a role model, robbed me of the sense of security, confidence, and courage that I'd need to make it in the big, bad world. And my relationship with him would forever set up the relationships I would have with other men.

On February 15, 1965, while radio announcers relayed news of the death of Nat King Cole, my mother called me into her bedroom and told me my father had died of leukemia. He was twenty-seven years old.

For a long time, I pondered over my father's death at such an early age. Could it truly be because of all the prayers I'd put in to the Man upstairs to deliver us from evil? I was sure I'd be greatly punished for causing such an act. In time, I would understand that it had simply been Daddy's time to go.

But the time it would take to stop suffering the fear woven into me as a child would not come so soon. In fact, freedom from fear would continue to elude me for decades to come.

Part II

Pass the Monkey

Chapter 23

Bronx, New York
Late 1960s

It would be a lie to say that I was saddened by the loss of my father. That sadness wouldn't come until decades later. But at the time, a part of me could breathe easier because I thought my fears, the monkey on my back, had gone with him.

Unfortunately, that feeling of calm and tranquility was short-lived. Within a few years, my life was impacted by yet *more* fear, as I became a victim of teenage bullying.

I was being chased through my neighborhood by a couple of hoodlum girls who got a real kick out of teasing me about my plaid uniform, and going to parochial school. I swear, bullies are a real pain in the ass. And I was quite an easy target, standing at a little over five feet and not quite a hundred pounds.

Evelyn towered over me at about five feet, seven inches, easily packing about 175 pounds. Everyone called her "Big Ev." She probably could've run Joe Frazier around the ring. I swear I must've had nightmares that Big Ev was still coming for me until I was pushing twenty-five. Now that we were living in the projects, I was constantly exhausted, running up fourteen flights of stairs trying to get away from Big Ev, and her evil sidekick Yvette, who'd be ranting at the top of her lungs that she was going to drag my flat behind up to the roof, and kick my ass off the ledge.

But the worst and very last bullying experience had taken place the day after my sixteenth birthday. I'd become quite enamored with an incredibly handsome boy from Puerto Rico, named Robert Santiago, who spoke very little English. But he'd clearly made me understand he really liked me. He started walking me home from school almost every day, but seemed a bit confused as to why I always wanted to go through the back entrance.

However, my innocent fling quickly came to an end when my girl, Rhonda Mitchell, whom I played jack rocks with from time to time, informed me that Big Ev had a real thing for Robert.

"Holy Shit!" Well, forget about her evil sidekick Yvette dragging my flat behind up to the roof and kicking my ass off, I was 'bout ready to jump!! So the very next day, I tried to explain to Robert as slowly as I could that Big Ev really liked him, and I couldn't see him anymore.

Robert tried desperately to persuade me in his broken English. "Me no like Big E; me like ju'..."

I was just as desperate. "Me no care if ju' lik' me; me can't see ju' no more, ever..." And sadly, that was that...or so I thought.

A few weeks later, the day after my sixteenth birthday, I was sitting around, bored, when Rhonda gave me a call. "Hi, Debbi. This is Rhonda."

"Hey, Rhonda!"

"Listen, you wanna come over to my house to play some jacks?"

Rhonda lived over on Union Avenue, which was only a couple of blocks away. I rushed right over, delighted she was saving me from a lonely Sunday afternoon.

When I arrived at Rhonda's door, I knocked several times, but she didn't open it. I was about to turn and leave when the door slowly opened. Rhonda's eyes looked as big as saucers and she acted as if she didn't want to open the door all the way to let me in.

"Rhonda, if you want to play jacks another time, that's fine."

"No, that's okay. Come on in." But I could swear Rhonda was shaking her head "no."

I stood there looking at the nervous Nelly look on her face. She'd seemed so excited about my coming over ten minutes earlier. I wasn't quite sure what to make of her strange demeanor.

Finally, she stood back, allowing me to enter. "Come in," she said timidly.

Then the door slammed shut, causing me to jump.

"What the fuck you doing talking to my boyfriend?" It was Big Ev. She'd been standing behind the door the whole time.

Petrified, I backed away from Big Ev. There was a bedroom doorway off to the side, and I slowly backed through it.

"Big Ev, whatcha gonna do? Debbi ain't even seein' Robert no more." Rhonda looked as scared as I was as we saw her explanation didn't mean shit to Big Ev!

"Shut up, Rhonda. Shut up! She think she cute wit them ugly-ass holes in her face!"

Maybe now Rhonda regretted getting me here under false pretenses. But it was more likely that Big Ev had threatened Rhonda to help carry out her devious plan.

Big Ev now turned her venom toward me. "You must've told Robert some lyin' shit about me, cúz now he won't even speak to me!"

I was thinking to myself...*no, it's probably 'cause your crazy ass is psychotic!*

The next thing I knew, Big Ev lifted me high up in the air, with her two bare hands, as if she was some sumo wrestler; and then...

Swoosh! Big Ev threw me clear across the room like a doggone Raggedy Ann doll! I hit the wood floor with a thud!

"Big Ev! Big Ev!" Rhonda screamed hysterically. "Oh, my God! I'ma call the police if you don't get outta here. I'm callin' the police on you! Oh, my God! You mighta kilt her! You mighta kilt her!"

Truthfully, I could understand why Rhonda would think this because I lay on that floor as still as could be, pretending I was dead for sure! Dead, very dead, real dead!

Then I heard Big Ev's big clubfeet race out of the apartment. When I was sure she was gone, I slowly began to try and lift myself from the floor. I was still shaking and terrified, as Rhonda grabbed me by the back of my arms.

"Oh, my God, are you all right, Debbi?! I thought that fat bitch done kilt you!"

I tried to hold back the tears that were stinging at my eyes, and I could see that Rhonda was trying to do the same.

I made my way to the door and Rhonda whispered, "I'm sorry. I'm so sorry, Debbi. She tricked me." But I barely heard her as I ran like the dickens!

Daddy was dead and yet I'd been given only a short reprieve. Was it really my destiny to go through life in constant fear of someone... some*thing?* I didn't know what it was to stand up for myself, to fight back. All I knew was what I'd always known...trying to fight back would get you really hurt, unless, of course there was someone, someone there to protect you...

I was coming out of the Safeway supermarket with my arms full of groceries. I dropped one of the bags when I saw Big Ev and her cronies standing there. A jar of mayonnaise lay splattered across the ground.

"Look at Miss Scaredy Cat. You better run home quick before we decide we feel like kicking yo' ass again today."

It was Big Ev's friend, Yvette, who'd made the threat. But Big Ev nodded her head toward me, letting me know Yvette spoke the truth.

"Hey, what you gangsta girls up to now?"

They all began to blush and uncharacteristically dropped their menacing tone.

"What are you talking about, Dizzy? We're no gangstas," said Yvette.

Then Big Ev, strange as it was, actually smiled, demurely. "Yeah, Dizzy, why you wanna say that? It's just this girl always trying to act like she's *Miss It*. You know, all cute and shit."

Dizzy looked at me, and then back at the girls. He laughed. "Now you know you all are jealous. That's all that is."

Oh, my God! Why on earth did he have to go and say that?

"Here, Sweetie, let me help you with your bags, okay?"

Dizzy picked up the bag from the ground. It was too late for the jar of mayo. He grabbed the rest of the bags from my arms.

"What are you all standing there staring at? Get outta here. And don't let me catch any of you li'l monsters messin' with her again, you understand? Especially you, Big Ev, wit' yo' big ole ass. You know you need to pick on somebody your own size."

Big Ev rolled her eyes and walked away in a huff. Her gangsta girls trailed behind. Thank the Lord! No longer would I have to worry about being chased through the projects, or running up fourteen flights of stairs trying to get away from Big Ev, and the evil-ass Yvette!

Everyone around knew of Dizzy. He was fine; he was popular; and most importantly, he was feared. Nobody ever messed with Dizzy and lived to tell about it.

"Come on; let me walk you to your building." Dizzy winked at me. "I was always wondering who that cute, little Catholic schoolgirl was."

I looked up at him with surprise.

"Yeah, I be seein' you walk home in your little uniform."

"My name is Debbi," I said shyly. "Thank you for helping me out with Big Ev and them."

"You don't have to thank me. But I'll tell you what. You don't ever have to be afraid of those girls or anyone else around here ever trying to hurt you. Not unless they want to answer to me. You got that?"

Oh, yes! I got it. Dizzy had said the magic words. *You don't ever have to be afraid...*

Chapter 24

"Hey, ain't that Diz and them over there?"

"Yeah, sure is. I swear, that Dizzy be cleaner than the board of health!"

The two girls were giggling, and admiring Dizzy's good looks. He always looked good. I'd sneaked over to the park by Woodstock Terrace to meet Dizzy. In fact I'd been sneaking around to see Dizzy for the past six months. When I'd told him that I was sixteen, and my mother had forbidden me to go out with anybody older than me, Dizzy shrugged. "It's no biggie. In the meantime, we'll have to be careful."

I walked past the two girls.

"Hi, Debbi!"

"Hi," I said. I had no idea who the girls were, and no idea how they knew my name.

Then I overheard one of the girls say to the other, "That's Dizzy's people," which meant I was Dizzy's girlfriend.

So that was it. Now I had this important rep and respect because I was Dizzy's girl. No one made fun of me anymore as I walked home in my Catholic school uniform. And no longer did I fear walking through the neighborhood and running into the wrong person. I felt such a sense of freedom. I felt wonderful!

Dizzy was standing next to the monkey bars talking with a group of guys. He was smoking a cigarette, looking ultra-cool. Dizzy had on a pair of black silk pants; a lime-green, alpaca knit sweater; and black alligator shoes. He wore horn-rimmed, wire-framed glasses that made him look like a sexy student. When he looked over and saw me, he started strutting toward me with that sensual gait.

"Hey, Sweetness," he called out.

Ooh, I felt all gooey inside.

"Hi, Diz."

He lifted my chin and gave me a light kiss on the lips.

Dizzy left all the other guys behind, except one.

"Charlie, this is my girl, Debbi. Debbi, this is my li'l man, Charlie. But everybody calls him Fast Charlie, 'cause he's always gettin' into some shit. I be trying to give the young brotha some education. But this big head he got is rock hard."

I smiled. "Hi, Charlie."

Charlie smiled back. "Hi."

He was very soft-spoken, and Charlie had some of the brightest, whitest teeth I'd ever seen. They probably looked even whiter because Charlie's complexion was so black, black and beautiful. Charlie was sixteen, too, but if not for his large, muscular physique, Charlie's baby face could've passed for ten. His ebony skin was like silk, and his dark, curly hair, was an adorable, uncontrolled mess. Charlie had deep dimples in his cheeks, just like me, and was as cute as a button.

"All right, Li'l Man, I'ma catch you later. And don't go stickin' nobody up today either. Yo' ass just got home."

"Naw, Diz. I'm gonna listen up. I swear, Man." Charlie burst out with a devilish grin, and walked away.

I called out to him. "Bye, Charlie. It was nice to meet you."

Charlie looked back, seemingly touched by my politeness. "Oh, yeah...yeah...thanks...yeah, you too."

I turned back to Dizzy. "Diz, what did you mean when you said Charlie better not stick up anybody?"

Dizzy put an arm around me. "Come on; let's go get something to drink. I'm thirsty."

We walked over to Union Avenue, hand-in-hand. Everyone on the street corners acknowledged Dizzy, and me, the prince and his princess, saying hello and nodding their heads.

"Fast Charlie just got out of juvie, upstate. He stuck up a liquor store."

"What?! He doesn't look like he'd hurt a fly."

"Yeah, don't let that li'l nigga fool ya'. You see how he be giving that li'l smile and shit. But you let somebody mess with Fast Charlie, he'll put a cap in they ass so fast."

I was aghast. "You mean he'd shoot somebody?!"

Dizzy laughed. "You damn right! I be trying to talk to the li'l nigga, 'cause I got a soft spot for him. But listen, you don't need to know about all that. Come on; let's go downtown to my house for a while before my moms gets home."

We went to Dizzy's and got comfortable, playing music and dancing. We were slow-grinding when things began to heat up, especially when Dizzy started tongue-kissing me. But I didn't have to worry. Dizzy never tried to push me into anything. As soon as things got a little carried away, he'd always say, "Okay, let's blow this place."

What made that day different? I don't know, except just that it was a different day. Before Billy Stewart finished singing "Sitting in the Park," Dizzy sat me down on the couch, still kissing me as he eased me back and rolled over on top of me. Now he was moving up and down, hard and slow. I could feel his maleness growing. I would be lying if I said I wasn't enjoying it, but we were on dangerous ground. Then Dizzy reached under my dress.

"Diz, please. Don't do that."

"It's okay," he whispered in my ear. "I'll take care of it. I'm not going to let anything happen to you."

Now he was tugging at my panties.

"Dizzy! No! I don't want to!"

"Okay, already!"

He jumped up off the couch in a huff.

"Come on. Let's blow this place."

Dizzy dropped me off a few blocks from my building, and gave me a quick peck.

"Okay, Sweetness. I'll check you tomorrow."

"Diz, you're not mad at me, are you?"

"No, I'm not mad at you. When the time is right, it'll be right. Go ahead now, I gotta meet Memphis and take care of some business."

Dizzy was always saying he had to take care of some business. He didn't have a job, so I often wondered what kind of business he was taking care of. But since he never offered any explanation, I didn't ask.

I hoped Dizzy didn't think I was too much of a baby for him. Dizzy was eighteen, and holding hands and tongue-kissing would probably only satisfy him but for so long.

"Debbi, what are you going to do if your mother finds out you're seeing Dizzy?"

Carol and I were stretched out across her bed. Carol Brunson was one of my three best friends. We lived in the same building, but Carol was down on the ninth floor. She was a little ahead of me in high school and attended Evander High.

"Hopefully, she won't. You know she'll kill me!"

I was head over heels in love with Dizzy. So now I'd gone a step further, playing hooky, and sneaking Dizzy into my house while my mother was at work, and my sister at school. Dizzy and I were into some serious petting now, but I'd still been able to stave him off before any actual penetration.

"You know he hangs out with those hoodlums, Bobo, Popeye, and Memphis. They say Memphis is the one who shot that boy last month on Evander's High School boat ride."

I took a big gulp at the mention of something so violent having anything to do with Dizzy. "Carol, if Memphis had shot someone, wouldn't he be in jail? Besides, Dizzy's nothing like that. You should see how he talks to his friend, Charlie. Dizzy stays on him about cleaning up his act and keeping out of trouble."

"Fast Charlie?"

"Yeah! Do you know him?'

"Everybody knows Fast Charlie. He hangs outside Evander all the time. He's an eighth-grade dropout and always has his behind in trouble. Girl, he be ripping people off for their watches, jewelry and stuff, all the time. He's crazy as they come."

"I know. That's what Dizzy said. But I've run into Charlie a couple of times, and he's always so sweet."

"Girl, please. He's crazier than some of those fools Dizzy be runnin' with. And I'm telling you, I don't care what Dizzy be saying about what Charlie's into. From what I hear, Dizzy is in to all kinds of stuff himself. I heard they all got caught outside of Evander High smoking reefer, too."

Carol was scaring me. I'd never seen Dizzy do drugs, and I refused to believe anything negative about him. Dizzy most definitely had a reputation for being a tough guy. I didn't have a problem with that. It's what made me feel safe. And Dizzy was never tough with me. He treated me like an angel, his angel. But other than having a tough-guy image, I'd not heard anything that might taint Dizzy's image, until now.

I was at the lunch table in school the next day, sitting with my other two best friends, Denise Roman and Vanessa Townsend. I wanted to tell them about Carol's accusations.

"Carol said she's been hearing a lot of bad stuff about Dizzy. She said she heard he smokes reefer, too. I've never seen him do drugs." My heart was racing. "I love Dizzy so much. I don't believe he's into anything like that."

Denise said, "You know Carol thinks she's a walking encyclopedia. You're the one going out with Dizzy. So Carol can't know him better than you. But I'll see if I can get anything out of my boyfriend, Pecky. He might tell me if Dizzy's smoking reefer or not. He'll certainly know more than Carol." Then she asked, "Debbi, has Dizzy tried to get you to do the deed yet?"

Vanessa took another bite of her doughnut and quickly put it down, looking at me for an answer to Denise's question.

"Yeah, and we've gotten pretty close. But I'm scared. Once, I almost let him put it in, and it hurt so badly, I begged him to stop. Plus, the last thing I'd want to do is get pregnant. Dizzy said he'd use protection, but I don't even want to think about feeling that kind of pain again. Also, I wonder if he wouldn't have as much respect for me if I gave in. I'm not sure. I know I'm still not ready. But Dizzy has been getting a little upset about it lately."

I looked over at Vanessa, wondering if Dizzy might start cheating on me the way Vanessa's boyfriend, Brother, was doing with her, simply because she wouldn't go all the way either.

Vanessa said, "What about you, Denise? Have you and Pecky done it?'

"No, not yet." Denise wasn't telling Vanessa the truth. She'd already told Carol and me she'd had sex with Pecky, but Denise wasn't as close to Vanessa as I was.

There was an announcement over the PA system about auditions being held in the auditorium for the year-end school musical. On a whim, I'd decided to try out. I gathered up my belongings, cutting short our girls' pow-wow, and headed to the auditorium.

That one choice would become a turning point in my life.

Chapter 25

"Debbi Morgan, you're next. Will you come up on stage, please?"

Our Monsignor put on a huge musical production at the end of every school year. I'd never auditioned for any of the school musicals because I couldn't sing. Our school was about ninety percent white. The only black students that'd ever been in the musicals had been in the chorus, never in a lead speaking role.

I was terribly freaked when I heard my name called to read for the role of "Puck." But it was weird; something overtook me. I started reciting the dialogue, and it was no longer me up there. Miraculously, all my inhibitions seemed to vanish. Even more miraculous was that I won the part!

Monsignor O'Malley, who always put on our school plays, had come down with a severe bout with his asthma, but didn't want to disappoint the girls. So he'd convinced his brother, a man by the name of Jim Mendenhall, who happened to be an off-Broadway producer, to take over the reins. Mr. Mendenhall decided to mount his own version of Shakespeare's *A Midsummer's Night Dream*.

Jim worked really hard with me, and became so impressed with my potential, that he began putting me in more and more scenes. He even wrote two songs for me to open and close the play. At first, I thought the man had lost it because I was no singer! However, after a number of music rehearsals, I discovered I was far from tone deaf. Some of the other actors got a little jealous and began referring to the production as "Puck" instead of *A Midsummer's Night Dream.*

Dizzy was walking me home from rehearsal one evening when we ran straight into my mother. She was coming out of the candy store after buying a pack of cigarettes.

"Oh! Ah... Hi, Mom."

"Well...who is your friend, Debbi?"

I couldn't really read her face. "Mom, this is...uh...Dizzy...I mean that's his nickname. His real name is James Noble. James, this is my mom."

"Hi, Mrs. Morgan. It's a pleasure to meet you."

I could see Mom studying Dizzy with probably a million thoughts racing through her mind. Gosh, for a while it really looked like we'd make it through another six months before we were ever discovered.

"Do you mind if I ask how old you are, James?"

"Not at all. I'm eighteen."

"Eighteen, huh? So that means you're legal. Debbi is only sixteen."

"I'll be seventeen in September, Mom," which was a whole six-and-a-half months away.

"I'm not speaking to you. Debbi is only sixteen, and she doesn't have permission to date anyone eighteen. But it was a pleasure meeting you, Dizzy. Debbi, I want you upstairs in two minutes."

"Yes, Mom."

My mother walked off and I didn't know what I'd do. "Diz, I think I'm dead. Maybe I should run away."

Dizzy laughed. "Get outta here. She didn't even seem that upset to me. I can't believe that's your moms, though. She looks so young. She's fine, too."

"Yeah, well, you don't want to be around her when she's pissed."

"But she didn't look pissed."

"That's what scares me. I think she's setting me up, making me think she's not too angry. And then when I get home, she's going to kill me."

"The best thing for you to do is go upstairs, and confront the situation. It certainly ain't gonna help you trying to imagine what your moms is, or isn't, going to do. But if she does kill you, at least I can tell the police I know who the murderer is." Dizzy burst out laughing, and I swatted him.

"Diz, it's not funny. I'm scared."

"Okay, I'm sorry. I know it's not. But I think you'd better hurry on home. Try to call me tonight... if you're still alive."

Dizzy ran off giggling.

When I walked into the apartment, Mom was sitting on the sofa smoking a cigarette. "Come sit down over here, Debbi."

I went and sat at the far end of the couch.

"So, how long have you been seeing this boy, Dizzy? Well, actually, he's not a boy; he's a young man."

"Mom, I only started talking to him a few months ago, but only talking. I'm not dating him or anything like that."

I hated lying, but telling the truth was not an option.

"I want one thing absolutely clear. You are not to spend any time alone with him, none, but you can talk to him on the phone. However, that's it, until you...and I'm giving you a reprieve, until you turn seventeen."

Well, that was at least something. I wouldn't have to wait all the way to eighteen like she'd always preached before.

But things didn't exactly turn out that way. Dizzy could be so charming, and he charmed my mother, at least to a point. He knew how to make her laugh, and always showed the utmost respect. So my mother started letting Dizzy come up to the apartment to see me, only when she was at home, and no more than an hour or so.

After weeks and weeks of rehearsal, we were finally at opening night. I'd not sweated a bit during the rehearsal period. I couldn't wait to get up on that stage and perform. But now, knowing that Dizzy would be sitting out front, my nerves were completely rattled.

The chorus began with a big opening number. And then it would be my turn to come out and sing a song to start the play. Alexis, who was in my homeroom, was in the chorus and was one of the fairies. Alexis was really pretty, and a real busybody. She was always talking about somebody else's business, as well as her own. Alexis loved talking about all the guys who were dying to get into her pants. When we left the school grounds at the end of the day, Alexis would hike her uniform skirt up so far, you could almost see where the sun didn't shine.

She came running backstage after the chorus's number. "Debbi, your mother is sitting right out front in the first row. Who's that light-skinned boy with the wavy hair sitting next to her?'

I was so proud. "That's my boyfriend, Dizzy."

"Well, he must be tired."

"What do you mean?'

"He's asleep."

"Asleep?" What on earth was Alexis talking about? There was no way Dizzy could be asleep.

"That's right, he's asleep, right on the front row. You can't miss him. We were all on stage, trying not to laugh."

I took a quick peep from behind the curtain before the stage manager gave me my cue to go on. Dizzy was definitely asleep, and nodding off, right onto Mom's shoulder! But why would Dizzy be so sleepy at eight o'clock in the evening?! Mom gave him a quick bop upside the head, and he jerked up, looking completely displaced.

When I made my entrance, there was huge applause. Besides my mom and grandmother, my aunts and some of their friends were in the audience. Jim had written a song for my opening number, "A

Beauty Lies Asleep in the Forest." I began softly singing the lyrics as I'd been coached, and then really began to belt the song out. It was a surprise for all in the audience who knew me, especially Mom. She'd never heard me sing a lick, and from the audience's reaction, I obviously wasn't doing too badly.

Halfway through my number, I stole a glance at Dizzy. I was relieved to see that he was now wide-awake. In fact, he let out a big whistle.

Opening night turned out to be a huge success, and I became an instant celebrity at the school. Later, when I questioned Dizzy about his behavior, he was extremely apologetic, saying he'd been up for almost twenty-four hours the night before playing cards, and hadn't slept.

My mother, on the other hand, was not so forgiving. She was furious about the way Dizzy kept nodding off. She said, if he hadn't had any sleep, he should've stayed home and come to the play another night.

But in the back of my mind, I wondered if there was any truth to what Carol had said about Dizzy smoking reefer. Little did I know, his problem was way beyond marijuana.

On the last day of school before summer, a bunch of us were gathered in the bathroom after the last bell rang. I was washing my hands, waiting for Vanessa. We always walked to the train station together.

When Vanessa exited the stall, I looked at her and giggled. "Vanessa, I think you'd better lay off those jelly doughnuts." She laughed, too, but of course on the way to the train station, Vanessa stopped off and bought three jelly doughnuts.

About three weeks later, Vanessa called and said she had something important to tell me, and that I had to swear not to tell a soul. I immediately assumed I knew exactly what Vanessa was going to say.

"I already know."

"You do?"

"Yeah, Alexis is pregnant."

Vanessa was quiet.

"Vanessa, isn't that what you were going to tell me?"

"Uh...no." I heard the tremble in Vanessa's voice. "Debbi...*I'm* pregnant."

I held the phone. I just held the phone and didn't say a word. The tears ran down my face and I couldn't speak.

All the time I thought Vanessa was too afraid of her mother to sneak around and see Brother; she was more afraid of forever losing Brother to Brenda, the girl with whom he was cheating on Vanessa. But unbeknownst to me, my close friend had been sneaking Brother into her house, and having sex with him for the past year. When I went to see her a few weeks later at New York's Foundling Hospital, my barely sixteen-year-old best friend was already six months along. Vanessa met me on the corner outside the hospital in a blue-and-white polka dot maternity dress. I looked at her, standing there with that huge belly, and wept.

Chapter 26

My mother had let me throw a Halloween party, but she was furious when Dizzy hadn't shown up until the very end. When he finally did show up, Mom almost didn't let him in. But when Dizzy pulled me into his arms and whispered in my ear that he loved me, all was forgotten.

As we danced cheek-to-cheek, Dizzy whispered something else in my ear. "You're not getting any younger, you know. It's about time for me to make you a woman now."

But as much as I wanted to be *that* intimate with Dizzy, I still found it difficult to cross the line.

It was a Friday morning, and I'd pretended to leave for school. But I'd waited in the stairwell, until I saw my mother leave for work.

Five minutes later, Dizzy showed up. In no time at all, we were in my bed, under the covers, kissing, and dry-humping. Dizzy quickly informed me there would be no more pretenses. He slowly began to thrust himself inside me, but the pain was too intense. I began to stiffen up, trying to close my legs.

"Come on, Debbi! Will you relax and open your legs?!"

Dizzy had been quite sweet and patient with me, but after almost eight months, his patience had run out.

I began to cry, and Dizzy began making threats. "If you start with all that cryin' again, I'm outta here. Now, either you're ready to grow up, or we're gonna have to call it quits!"

It was frightening to think of Dizzy leaving me. I told him I was scared, but that I loved him, and couldn't live without him.

"Please, don't leave me, Dizzy. I want to do it, I do. It's just that it hurts so bad. I can't help it. Will you give me a little more time, please? I love you. I love you so much!"

"If you loved me all that much, you'd show me. All right, all right, stop crying."

Then Dizzy placed my hand on his penis, and I began to arouse him to a point where he was fulfilled, at least for now. Afterward, we cradled each other in a spoon position, and dozed off.

Eventually my sweet slumber was interrupted by a strange dream. I was lost in a sea of red. Was it a bed of roses? Was it a red room? Was it blood?! No, it was much worse! It was the red skirt my mother was wearing!

She loomed over us like a red inferno, breathing out a fiery rage. Without raising my head, I ever so gently poked Dizzy in the back. He stirred, and then looked up.

"Oh, shit!" he exclaimed, jumping out of bed and grabbing at his pants on the floor.

"You get outta here!" My mother was beating Dizzy over the head with her belt buckle. "Are you crazy?! I'll kill you! Get ouut! Get ouuut!"

Dizzy tried to protect his head and face by crouching down and covering them with his hands. But Mom was unrelenting. Then she started in with me. I was still lying on the bed, trying to protect myself with the covers. But she snatched them away, and started wailing on me across my back and arms. Suddenly, she stopped and ran from the room.

Dizzy was tripping over himself trying to get his clothes on.

"I need the police at 731 East 161st Street, apartment 14G! There's a man in here molesting my daughter! Please hurry!"

"Your moms is crazy!" I could see a trickle of blood dripping from the top of Dizzy's head as he ran out with just his pants, tee shirt, and one shoe.

Mom came back into my room, and began searching in my closet through my box of sanitary napkins. She wanted to see if they'd been used, and if they hadn't, she'd know that maybe I was already pregnant. And she hadn't really called the police. My mother had just wanted to scare Dizzy and me even more out of our wits.

I got off easy, compared to Dizzy. He'd had to go to Harlem Hospital and get five stitches in his head, thanks to the beating Mom gave him.

My mother promptly instructed me to get my clothes on because we were going to the doctor. After an embarrassing examination by Dr. Lachine, he politely informed my mother that I was still a virgin. However, my mom wasn't taking any chances that history might repeat itself.

When we returned home, she lit into me. "Listen, Young Lady, just because I allowed Dr. Lachine to put you on birth control pills, doesn't mean I'm giving you the license to start having sex. And furthermore, I don't want you seeing Dizzy anymore until I say so, *if* I say so. I'm not very happy with the way he's been treating you lately. Showing up at the very end of your party, and now this!"

Then my mother got quiet, really quiet. She said, "I really don't believe he's the right boy for you, Debbi."

We were looking at each other and I could see the sadness in her eyes. My mother looked like she felt trapped. Maybe she knew where I was headed, and maybe she knew there was nothing she could do to stop it.

I told Charlie about Mom catching Dizzy and me together. I told him how my mother had beaten Dizzy and how he had to get five stitches in his head. I hadn't talked to Dizzy since that night.

"He's never home when I call, Charlie. I always get his mother. And he can't call me because of my mom."

"Don't worry. I'll catch up with him for you. I promise."

"Thanks, Charlie."

"Come on. I'll walk you home."

The McKinley Projects were directly across from the Forest Housing Projects. But Charlie and I took the long route around the park by Woodstock Terrace. Simultaneously, we both saw Dizzy getting out of a blue Lincoln.

"Charlie, there's Dizzy!" I ran on ahead, and thought I heard Charlie say, "I'll catch you later."

When I approached the car, Dizzy had a strange look on his face.

"Debbi, what are you doing over here?'

"What do you mean?" Yeah, what did he mean? I lived over here, at least very near to here. Or had Dizzy forgotten that?

"Dizzy, why haven't I been able to get you on the phone? I know you're still mad about what happened with my mother. I'm so sorry, but—"

"Dizzy, who is this?"

An attractive Hispanic girl exited the car. She was tall, almost Dizzy's height, with golden-blonde, curly hair pulled high atop her head.

I felt my knees get a bit wobbly as I heard her proprietary attitude. Obviously, the girl felt she had the right to demand who Dizzy was speaking with.

"Carmen, will you get back in the car and let me handle this."

Let him handle this?! What on earth was Dizzy talking about?! And what was he doing with this girl, Carmen?! As if I didn't know.

"No! I'm not getting back in the car! Who is this?!"

Carmen was feisty, and she didn't mind that she was making a scene. People were starting to gather around, and I overheard someone say, "Oh, shit, Dizzy done got busted."

Meanwhile, I was so overcome with shock and humiliation, that all I could do was walk away.

"Debbi! Wait!" Dizzy had shoved Carmen back into the car, and was running after me. I was a dribbling basket case.

"Debbi, listen, meet me up by the train station in an hour so I can talk to you. It's not what you think. I'll explain it all to you later. Come on, Sweetness; don't be lettin' these fools out here see you crying like this, and over nothing. I swear."

"But, Diz, who is that girl? What are you doing riding around in a car with her?"

"I told you I'd explain all of that. Now meet me in an hour."

I ran to my building and sat in the stairwell, sobbing. All sorts of thoughts and would-be explanations filled my head. There was no denying my mother had been part of the cause for chasing Dizzy away. She'd almost given him a concussion. And the fact that I still hadn't gone all the way with Dizzy. That had most likely been the final straw that drove him elsewhere.

But I was hell-bent on remedying all of that. I couldn't live without Dizzy. And it was unthinkable to go back to the way my daily life had been, existing in constant anxiety and fear.

Chapter 27

Dizzy gave me a lame excuse for the incident with Carmen. He said he'd been introduced to her at a party and that he was working for her uncle. I wasn't that naïve, yet I agreed to take our relationship to the next level because I simply could not lose him. Dizzy was the only thing standing between the fear and me.

Our special occasion was to take place at a hotel, if you could call it that. The room was more dingy and bleak than the lobby. It stank of stale liquor and cigarettes. The crumpled-up bed looked like it hadn't been changed since the last occupant. I stood at the foot of the bed, which was only a few feet from the door, and swore I saw something crawling across the floor in the moonlight.

"Ahhh! What was that?"

"What was what? Debbi, will you get a grip. I don't see nothin'. Here, let me help you with your coat."

I didn't want to take off my coat, or anything else, not in this filthy room. I didn't even want to sit on the bed, never mind get into it.

"Dizzy, this room is so nasty. Do we have to stay here?"

"I already paid for the room! Come on, now. It's not that bad."

Then Dizzy put his arms around me and started kissing me. I always enjoyed his kisses a lot. I could feel myself loosening up as we stood in the middle of the floor, passionately tongue-kissing. Dizzy pulled off my coat, but once he started sliding me down to the soiled bed, I tensed up all over again.

"Come, on, Baby. Will you stop trippin'? I'm here with you. Everything's gonna be fine. I promise. You're safe with me."

You could smell someone else's odor in the sheets. I wanted to puke. But Dizzy continued to work his magic, getting me hot and ready. Like a seasoned expert, he slipped me out of my clothes, and slipped out of his. Finally, the desire was so powerful, we both knew it was time.

Whether I was built too small, or Dizzy was too big, or too much in a hurry to finally get in there, the whole thing turned into a fiasco. Dizzy tried to insert his penis inside me, and the pain was intolerable. I was risking our relationship, but I begged for him to stop.

"Listen, we're not going through this bullshit again! Now lay back and relax. This time I'll take it real slow, okay?"

I nodded my head, and bit down on my lip.

Dizzy suddenly stopped. "Wait a minute; I almost forgot." He reached over to the nightstand and grabbed the brown paper bag he'd brought with him. Dizzy pulled out a jar of Vaseline.

We must have used the entire jar, but it still hurt like hell. I tried with all my might not to squirm. I scrunched up my face, and took in a deep breath. But I was still rigid and not relaxed. It was like Dizzy was trying to break through a brick wall.

"Get up. Let's blow this place."

Dizzy got up out of bed and was getting dressed. And I had no doubt he was headed back to the welcoming arms of Carmen. I caught my breath and I pleaded with Dizzy for the umpteenth time to try again. However, Dizzy implied he was exhausted with all the work.

"But, Dizzy, I love you!"

As crazy as it sounds, I honestly believed myself.

"Yeah, sure you do."

"I do. I swear! I'd do anything for you!"

But Dizzy waved me away, saying he had to meet with Carmen's uncle to take care of some business for him.

When I got back home that night, I made up in my mind that I would prove to Dizzy once and for all how much love I truly had for him.

"Debbi, a lot of girls go to this doctor so that it won't be so painful the first time. Let him know why you're there. He'll give you an exam and take care of it."

I'd had that conversation with Denise a while back. She knew I was having a real problem having intercourse with Dizzy. Denise had made the suggestion before. But now, with the threat of another girl in the picture, I was finally going through with it.

Now here I was, sitting alone in Dr. Habry's office on 116th Street in Harlem. The nurse called my name, and I entered the sterile, white room.

"You can undress and put on this gown. The doctor will be right in to see you."

A few moments later, a large, black man with very broad features entered. He spoke with an accent, like he might be from Africa. "So what can I do for you?"

I sat on the metal table with my dressing gown on and a sheet across my lap. Then I looked at the nurse standing there, feeling too embarrassed to speak.

The doctor nodded his head, and the nurse politely left the room.

"Now what are you here to see me for...," he said, looking in his folder. "Debbi?"

"Well...uh...I have a...friend who said...who said you could help me with...with my boyfriend."

He looked at me kindly, like a father, knowing how difficult this was for me to get through.

"Okay, I think I understand. How old are you, Debbi?"

"Eighteen," I lied.

"Really? You don't look eighteen." The doctor was staring at me. Then he smiled. "Are you trying to have sex with your boyfriend?"

"Well...sort of. But every time we try, it hurts so bad, I can't take it."

"I understand. It's very uncomfortable and painful for a lot of young girls when their hymen is broken. Does your boyfriend have a large penis?"

My God! The whole thing was so embarrassing. "Uh...yes. He does," I guessed.

The doctor smiled again. "Well, just look at you. You're a tiny little thing. Your boyfriend has to be extra gentle with you. But most of them don't know how to do that."

I was thankful Denise had sent me to the right place. Dr. Habry truly understood the dilemma I was in.

"Okay, Debbi. Just lie back for me."

I looked over at the cold, metal instruments sitting on the side table. The doctor was staring at me again. I guess waiting for me to lie back, or perhaps waiting for the nurse to come back in before he started with whatever procedure he was planning to do.

"Go ahead; you can lie back."

I did as I was instructed, looking up at the doctor nervously.

"This must be a little embarrassing for you. Tell you what, I'm going to cover your face with this sheet, and then you won't have to feel so awkward."

So Dr. Habry covered my face, and gently lifted my legs into stirrups. I heard him walk away, and then heard the clinking sound of metal. Hopefully, whatever instrument he was going to use would not be too painful.

Then it was quiet. There wasn't a sound. I wondered if the doctor was standing there waiting for the nurse to come in. But I heard no one enter.

There was an eerie silence. I braced myself for some sharp instrument about to cut me open. Finally, what I felt, were warm, gloved fingers applying something jelly-like to my vagina. It took me by surprise, and I flinched a bit. But the doctor's hands lightly held my thighs, as if to let me know everything was all right. I guess he wanted his instrument to be as painless as possible.

Dr. Habry was ever so slowly sliding something inside me. He'd get to a certain point and when it wouldn't go any further, he'd stop. Then he would start from that same point, slowly, extremely slowly, sliding in a bit farther.

Actually, this wasn't as bad as I'd thought it'd be. Truth be told, it actually felt good, really good. And it was odd, but the doctor's instrument didn't feel like metal at all. In fact, it felt an awful lot like a...like a... *Oh, My God! Oh, My God! It couldn't be! It couldn't be!* That's when I became aware of the doctor's lab coat brushing back and forth along my thighs.

The realization hit me hard in the chest. I had to struggle for a moment. I had to struggle to let go of how good the feeling was. Now I was panicked! And I was terribly afraid of pulling the sheet from my face. How could I look at the doctor and confront him for what he was doing to me. What would I say? So I lay there, unable to move.

There was a sudden, but painless thrust. And then his movements stopped. Now I could hear him crossing the room. It seemed like an eternity before he spoke.

"Just wait for a moment. The nurse will be right in."

I heard the sound of the door open and close. But I just lay there, covered by this sheet, like a mummy. Slowly, I pulled the sheet away and sat up. I looked straight ahead at the big, white, blank wall. And that's precisely how I felt...*blank*.

My virginity had finally been taken, in a way I would've never expected.

The nurse entered the room, but I kept staring at the wall.

"Okay, young lady. You can get dressed now."

When I rushed from Dr. Habry's office, there was only one way to look at what'd happened. It was something that never happened. Yes, I'd probably imagined the whole thing.

I never spoke about the incident that never happened, to anyone, not even Denise. I would never have any idea what her experience had been.

It would be over fifteen years later before I ever repeated to a soul that something did indeed happen in Dr. Habry's office. And that soul would be my mother, who would immediately tear through a phone book trying to find this good ol' *helpful* Dr. Habry. Fortunately for him, she could never find him.

Chapter 28

"Ummm. That was good." Dizzy gave me a quick peck on the lips and then rolled over. "Listen, I gotta make some runs for Hector. Get up and get your clothes on."

Dizzy and I had been sneaking off and having sex for months now. The hotels had gotten better than the first one, but not much else had. Dizzy was still working for Carmen's uncle, and he was also still seeing Carmen. I'd caught him in so many lies, had my heart broken so many times, and still feared letting him go. I was too young and dumb to realize my fear should have been in *keeping* him.

"Aren't you really going to see Carmen?"

Dizzy didn't answer. I looked over at him. Dizzy had nodded off to sleep, or maybe, just nodded off. But a few minutes later, his eyes fluttered open.

Dizzy dropped me off near my building with a quick kiss, and then hurried off.

The rumors were rampant now. Carol had been putting her two cents in for a while. But when Denise told me she'd heard the same things from her boyfriend, Pecky, the stories seemed to have more validity.

Word was that Dizzy was indeed working for Carmen's uncle, Hector Sanchez. But he wasn't driving moving trucks for Hector. Supposedly, Dizzy was selling drugs for Hector. I'd also heard Dizzy was using drugs, and so was Carmen. Whenever I approached Dizzy about these stories, there was always a huge denial. Dizzy said people were becoming jealous of him because he was making so much money. However, he did admit that Carmen was *tooting*, sniffing drugs, from time to time. Dizzy said he was hanging around her trying to get her to stop. Dizzy always had some phony reason about why he was with Carmen.

And although I'd seen him nod off on occasion, I never saw Dizzy doing drugs. He certainly never tried to get me to do any. That's why I found it hard to believe Dizzy was doing drugs with Carmen. Whenever I asked about his nodding off, Dizzy would explain that he was working almost around the clock for Hector, and that he was exhausted. Well, in retrospect, I assume he was working almost around the clock.

The fact of the matter was, practically our entire neighborhood had been swept up in the drug epidemic. Heroin was taking its toll on so many young lives.

Even Fast Charlie had become a victim. Poor Mrs. Carter was going through hell. Charlie was injecting heroin into his veins, sticking up folks and robbing them blind. Yet, whenever I was with him, he was like this angelic spirit.

Mrs. Carter said to me one day, "Debbi, Charlie's such a different person when he's around you. I wish you could talk to him about these bad things he's doing."

I did talk to Charlie the very next time I saw him. He was coming out of the candy store, eating a fat chocolate chip cookie. Charlie ran up and scooped me up in his arms, but he seemed a bit shaky.

"Charlie, put me down." Charlie lowered me back to the ground. "Your mother is so upset about the things you're doing. And she's so afraid for you."

"Nothing gonna happen to Fast Charlie, Debbi. Will you go for a walk with me?"

We walked down by Third Avenue, near the El station. Charlie admitted to me that he was using, but said it wasn't all the time. Then he put his arms around me and looked into my eyes.

"If you tell me to stop shooting dope, Debbi, I will. I'll do anything for you."

And I was stupid enough to believe him. That's because Charlie believed it. At least he wanted to. But I could never hold the kind of power over Charlie that his new love could...never.

I was officially sleeping with Dizzy now. I thought I'd become the woman he wanted, the only woman. It was odd how Dizzy never mentioned how much easier it was when we'd finally had sex. Maybe he thought we'd been trying for so long, the twentieth time was the charm.

But that still hadn't been enough. Dizzy continued to cheat on me, and continued to lie about it. Dizzy was tired of my accusing him of being with Carmen. He rarely saw the woman anymore, according to him.

For the next week, I feigned having the worst menstrual cramps, because I literally couldn't get out of bed. But when my mother saw my eyes swollen and red, she knew my sickness had nothing whatsoever to do with cramps, not cramps from having my period. So she kicked me out of bed and sent me to school.

My mother sent me with a warning. "Debbi, you need to stop crying over Dizzy. He's no good for you, Baby. Any man who makes you cry like this can never bring you anything but pain."

I'd soon learn Mom didn't exactly practice what she preached.

I didn't go to school; I went to Charlie's house. Mrs. Carter would be at work. Charlie was asleep when I knocked on the door. I was about to leave when he finally heard me.

"Debbi! Hi. I'm sorry. I didn't hear you knocking."

"That's okay; may I come in?"

"Are you kidding?" Charlie put a gentle arm around me and I lost it. I boohooed like a six-year-old, and Charlie held me close and rocked me. After I'd cried my eyes out and there were no more tears left, Charlie made me look at him.

"It's Dizzy, huh?"

"Charlie, it's all because of Carmen. Everything was fine until she came into the picture. I think I might have lost him to her, and I don't know what I'm going to do. How can I live without Dizzy? I love him so much, Charlie!"

"Come on. We're gonna take a ride."

Charlie had a car parked downstairs he said he'd borrowed from a friend, but I wasn't sure Charlie hadn't stolen it.

"Where are we going in this car, Charlie?"

"We gonna take a drive somewhere. Don't worry, it ain't stolen. I wouldn't have you in no stolen car and risk the cops pulling us over. Honest, Baby, I borrowed it from a friend."

Charlie drove downtown to Spanish Harlem. Carmen lived in Spanish Harlem. When he pulled up in front of a five-story apartment building, I asked, "Charlie, whose building is this?"

"I had to meet Dizzy over here one night. This is where Carmen lives. But I'm gonna have to come back without you so I can case the place. I need to check out Carmen's comings and goings. Plus, when I decide it's the right time to smoke her, I don't want you anywhere around."

Smoke her?! "Charlie, what are you talking about? Smoke her!"

"I'm gonna take her out for you, Baby."

"Take her out! Oh, my God, Charlie. You mean kill her?"

"Well...uh...yeah. You said you wanted Carmen out of Dizzy's life. And I hate seeing you crying and so upset all the time."

"But, Charlie, I didn't mean that I wanted you to kill her!"

"Look, I want you to forget about all this, okay? You don't need to know anything else. I have to keep you protected, first and foremost. I gave you my promise it will be handled, and it will. That's all you need to know."

"No, Charlie! Noooo!!! What I need to know is that you're not going to go through with anything like this! I never meant for you to kill anybody, never!"

"Debbi, it's okay. Calm down."

"It's not okay! Promise me, Charlie! Promise me you're not going to do anything so horrible and stupid! I'll never speak to you again! And I'll never forgive you either! Please, Charlie! Promise me!"

When we got back uptown, I sat in the car with Charlie until I could be certain he wasn't going to carry out his unspeakable plan. "I swear to you, Debbi. You have my word. I won't do anything to Carmen. I'd never do anything that would make you not speak to me again."

But knowing what Charlie was capable of, I made a vow to myself. Never again...never...would I discuss with Charlie my feelings toward Carmen and Dizzy!

Fortunately, I would have no more worries about Charlie taking Carmen out because he was arrested on another drug possession charge, and was sent straight to prison.

Chapter 29

Charlie had been doing time on Rikers Island, but it wasn't as long a stay as it could've been. Something to do with the way the evidence was presented got Charlie a lot less jail time. At least it'd been enough time to get him away from shooting heroin. I prayed he'd be cured because I adored Charlie and his mother more than anything.

"What about you, Dizzy? Are you done messing around, too?"

"Come on, Sweetness. I told you that's all in the past. Besides, you can't compare me to Fast Charlie. I was never shootin' no dope in my arms. Look, I'm starting my job as a tech with the phone company next week, and I can't be gettin' high starting no new gig; enough said."

Dizzy decided he needed a change in his life. He stopped selling drugs after Hector found out that Carmen was stealing from him. Diz also stopped seeing Carmen. He concentrated on giving our relationship a fresh start.

My mom was still none too thrilled about my relationship with Dizzy; that is, until *she* fell in love.

My mother was working two part-time, bar maid jobs when she met Sam Allen. Sam was a pharmacist who apparently made plenty of money. He lavished Mom with all kinds of expensive gifts. In fact, Sam insisted my mother stop working her second job a short while after the two seriously began dating. It was the first time in her life my mother had been so pampered. I was happy for her. I was also happy that Mom's new love life was occupying a lot of her time, time taken away from her issues about Dizzy and me. The sound of her laughter was often heard throughout the apartment, and she became like a free spirit.

Mom was thirty-four years old, and still looked every bit of eighteen. People often mistook us for sisters. I wasn't sure how old Sam was, but I could tell he was older than Mom. Sam was tall, very fair, and very round. He had a thick, dark brown Afro, and large, dark brown eyes. One might say he was attractive...I guess.

But to my mom, I'm sure Sam was her knight-in-shining-armor, riding in on his chariot to take all her woes away.

It was a Friday night, and Dizzy and I had just gotten out of the car in front of my building when suddenly Carmen was right in front of us, screaming and crying! "I'm tired of your lies, Dizzy! You're so full of shit!!"

Dizzy tried to take her by the arm and lead her away while telling me to go on upstairs. "Debbi, go on up. I'll talk to you later. I don't know why this girl keeps acting crazy."

"Oh, you know damn well why! Did you tell her why I can't fasten my skirt, why the shit is so damn tight?! I'm pregnant! Did you tell her that?!"

Now I noticed Carmen's pop belly for the first time, and I thought I might throw up. I stood there staring at her protruding tummy like a baby might pop out at any moment.

I turned and ran into the building as fast as my legs would carry me. Thank God Mom and Sam were not around when I rushed into our apartment, and luckily Terry wasn't either. They must have all gone out somewhere. I never heard when any of them came in either because I'd cried myself into a coma-like sleep. The next day, I refused to answer any of Dizzy's phone calls and played like I was real sick with my period again so Mom wouldn't ask me a lot of questions about staying in bed.

A few days later, I was met with yet another surprising turn of events. My connection with Jim Mendenhall, who had directed me in my high school production of *A Midsummer Night's Dream*, had proved to be a very good thing. Jim had become a mentor, and would be the key to finally help me turn away from the cesspool I'd been wading in being with Dizzy.

After several meetings with talent agencies, and a few advertising agencies that Jim had set up for me, I got my first commercial agent and booked a national commercial spot for AT&T as a cheerleader at a football game. I even signed with the Black Beauty Talent Agency! I was thrilled!

Jim also helped me get into a good acting workshop. He suggested auditioning for the Negro Ensemble Company (NEC), which had produced so many great black talents like Esther Rolle, Robert Hooks, Denise Nicholas, Diana Sands, Roxie Roker, Charles Weldon (more about Charles later), Adolph Caesar, and Hattie Winston, to name just a few.

Auditions for the company required doing a monologue and a scene from a play. Mom had done some acting in high school. She had a natural innate talent, not to mention a wonderful resonance to her voice. In contrast, I had a very high, pitchy voice that would take years to train and deepen.

The afternoon I had my audition with the resident director, Chris Kaiser, I was a nervous wreck. My mother was reading lines with me as I performed a scene from *A Raisin in the Sun*. Mom was cool as a cucumber. The next day, we received a call saying I was still a bit young and not quite ready at this point to join the company. However, an invitation was extended to my mother; she declined. I don't think she felt right joining, not after I'd been turned down. But I'm sure it'll always be one of the big regrets of her life.

It took a week or so to get over my disappointment about not getting into NEC, but then I got back up on my horse, especially after my commercial agents were sending me out for a Secret deodorant commercial. That would be another national spot.

On the morning of my audition, I'd gotten myself primped up, and was on my way out the door when the telephone rang.

"Hi, Debbi, do you know who this is?"

"Of course, I know who this is! Dizzy told me a few weeks ago that you were back home, Charlie."

"Well, listen, I want to see you!"

"I want to see you, too."

"Can you come over?"

"Look, I'm on my way out to a very important appointment. But as soon as I get back, I'll be right over."

I knew how I'd felt the last time I was around Charlie, with the whole attempt to kill Carmen craziness! But that was all over, and I really needed someone to confide in.

I made good on my promise to meet with him after the audition. Charlie had gained some more weight, but he was still as adorable as ever. We hugged each other like one of us might die tomorrow.

"You look so good. But what have you been eating in there, cake every day?"

Charlie laughed, and gave me a big kiss on the lips.

Mrs. Carter walked into the living room all smiles. "Hi, Debbi! I'm so glad to see you! You know you didn't have to be a stranger just because Charlie wasn't around."

"I'm sorry, Mrs. Carter. I'm going to make it up to you."

"Oh, Honey, that's okay. I'm glad to see you whenever I see you. Charlie looks real good, doesn't he?"

"He looks great!"

"Uh, uh, Mama. Debbi said I looked like I been eatin' too many cakes!"

We all laughed. "No, I didn't say that!"

"My baby did put on some weight, but he looks good and healthy. And he's gonna stay that way. Right, Baby?"

"That's a promise, Mama. I'm not puttin' you through no more worry."

Mrs. Carter gave Charlie a kiss on the cheek, and then wrapped her arms around him in a big bear hug. I saw the tears in Mrs. Carter's eyes from the joy of having her son back home, and back from the living dead.

The phone rang. Mrs. Carter answered it and told Charlie it was for him—his parole officer. Charlie jumped up to go to the phone.

Charlie's mother and I continued talking. "You know you're all Charlie's talked about since he got back home. I'm sure you know how he feels about you."

I nodded my head.

"I think he's felt that way about you from the day he met you. It's selfish of me to say, but I wish you and Charlie had met first. You would've been such a good influence on him."

Mrs. Carter gave me way too much credit. I knew how much Charlie cared for me. However, I don't know if our being together would've necessarily been a deterrent from all the negative things in his life.

"Charlie said he's been home for a little while now. How's it been going for him?"

"Debbi, actually he's been staying inside the house, which is what I asked him to do."

"Really? Why is that?"

"Because it's too much going on out there in them streets, Debbi. Charlie is trying so hard not to go back to any of his old ways. And I think he's been a little afraid; probably wants to give himself some more time until he's sure he's ready."

"I understand that, Mrs. Carter."

Charlie came back and sat down, right in between his mom and me.

"Well, Debbi, I guess this boy is trying to tell me something." Mrs. Carter gave Charlie a playful swat on the head and left the room.

"Your mother is so happy to have you home, Charlie."

"Yeah, I know. That's my ladylove. So, what's going on with you and Diz?"

That was it...the floodgates opened right up. Charlie cradled me in his arms.

"What's the matter, Baby? Did he do something to you? Did he hurt you?"

"He... He got Carmen pregnant, Charlie. Carmen's pregnant."

He lifted my head and peered into my eyes. "What are you going to do? Are you going to stay with him?"

"You must think I'm crazy. I still love him. I can't help it. But I really don't know how much more I can take; I deserve so much better."

Charlie pulled me close and kissed me tenderly; I allowed him that.

"For what I wish coulda' been. Dizzy has no idea what a good woman he's got. And if he keeps on hurtin' you like this, he's gonna have to answer to me, and that's on the real tip. Hey, try to take your mind off Dizzy's bullshit right now, okay? Would you like to go get some ice cream?"

"I'd love some ice cream. But your mom said you weren't ready to start hanging out."

"Who's hanging out? I'm just taking you to get some ice cream."

"Okay, yeah. I'd like that."

"Hey, Mom, I'm gonna run out for a minute."

Mrs. Carter walked into the living room. "Where are you going, Charlie?'

"Out to get some ice cream."

"Debbi, are you going with him?"

"Yes, Mrs. Carter. Would you like us to bring you some?"

Mrs. Carter smiled. "No thanks. I'm already too pudgy around the middle. I'll see you two when you get back."

Charlie and I decided to walk down toward the El and up Third Avenue to the shopping district. Along the way, we chitchatted about our plans for the future. He said he was going to work on getting back in school. I shared my good luck with acting. Charlie was so happy for me.

"And I'll tell you something else," he added. "Your plans don't seem to fit too good with being involved with Dizzy either." Charlie's words had definitely struck a chord.

We were passing a building, and Charlie stopped, looking up at one of the windows. Then he grabbed my hand and we continued walking. But we only took a few steps when Charlie stopped again, looking up at the same window.

"Charlie, what are you doing?"

"My friend José called me this morning. He heard I was home. He lives right here. I was thinking I might stop up real quick to say hello. But that's okay. I can do it another time."

We got about half a block, and Charlie stopped for a third time. He stood there, staring up at the same window again.

"Charlie, what is it?"

"Aw, what the hell? Let me run up there for two minutes and surprise him."

"Okay, I'll go with you."

"No, that's okay, Baby. I'm gonna say hello real quick and that's it."

Charlie ran into the building and I leaned up against a car and waited. Charlie was back downstairs within a few minutes, carrying an attaché case.

"Charlie, what's that?"

"Uh... José took his GED a couple of weeks ago. He let me have some of his books to look at so I can have sort of a jump start on this learnin' thing."

"Oh, that was nice of him. You know, Charlie, I don't mind helping you, too."

I started to continue our walk down the hill toward Third Avenue, but Charlie had turned back in the opposite direction.

"Charlie, where are you going? I thought we were getting ice cream."

"We are. But I don't want to carry these books with me. Let's walk back to my house so I can drop them off. It won't take that long."

It seemed a little odd to me, and Charlie was walking so fast.

"Hey, where's the fire?"

Charlie laughed. "I wanna hurry and drop off these books so we can get some butter pecan." Charlie knew butter pecan ice cream was my favorite.

When we got back to Charlie's apartment, I stood by the door to wait for him.

"Give me one more sec, Baby. I gotta run to the bathroom."

So I went and sat on the sofa. But Charlie was taking an awful long time. Mrs. Carter came out of her bedroom.

"I thought I heard you two. Back so soon? Did you get your ice cream?"

"Not yet. Charlie wanted to drop off some books he picked up from a friend of his, Mrs. Carter. As soon as he comes out of the bathroom, we're going."

The expression on Mrs. Carter's face was like she'd seen Lucifer. She ran down the hall to the bathroom.

"Charlie! Charlie! Charlieeeee! What are you doing in there?! Open this door! Open this door right now!"

I rose from the sofa and crept down the hall. I couldn't understand why Mrs. Carter was screaming such a primal pain from her gut. Her screams brought up old familiar feelings in the pit of my belly. I began to feel lightheaded.

"Mrs. Carter, what is it? What's the matter?" But my whispers couldn't be heard over Mrs. Carter's tormented yells.

"Nooooo, Charlie! NOOOOOOO!"

Charlie obviously heard his mother breaking down outside the bathroom door. Why on earth wasn't he coming out?

Mrs. Carter started clawing at the bathroom door like a caged animal until her fingernails broke off, leaving long streaks of blood. And then she collapsed on the floor. It was an image I'd never forget for the rest of my life.

The gravity of realizing what Charlie was doing in the bathroom set in, beggaring description. And I couldn't help but feel blame. Why had I agreed to go out with Charlie for ice cream? His mother had just warned me that Charlie felt he wasn't ready to be out. Why hadn't I listened? And why did I let Charlie go into that building? Why didn't I demand to see the "books" in the attaché case? Why had I been so damn trusting? Why? Why? Why?

It was a moot point now. And it certainly wouldn't fix the nightmarish hell Mrs. Carter was suffering.

When Charlie opened the door, his mother sprang up from the floor like a bat. She was all over Charlie, hitting, slapping, and punching. But Charlie didn't look as if he felt a thing in his dream-like state.

Then Mrs. Carter stopped her battery, walked to her room, and quietly shut the door.

Charlie walked into his room, and I followed him. "Why, Charlie?" I cried. "Why did you have to go and do this?"

Charlie slumped across his bed and said softly, "Tell my mama I'm sorry. I am. This is the last time. I'm gonna get straight, you'll see. I swear."

Charlie nodded off after that, his face so serene, so guiltless, and so pure. And then I stared down at the tiny bloodstain seeping through his shirt from the middle of his arm. I leaned over, kissed Charlie's forehead, and left his apartment for the last time. Charlie ended up strung out again, went back to prison, and would be killed two short years later in a knife fight, over a pack of cigarettes.

Chapter 30

"Oh, my gosh! Oooo, my gosh!!!!"

Terry and I ran into the living room to see what all the commotion was. We found Sam twirling Mom around in a huge embrace.

"Look, girls!" My mother stuck out her hand and showed my sister and me the large diamond engagement ring on her finger. Sam had poured her a glass of wine, and somehow managed to sneak the ring into her drink.

It was a pear-shaped diamond, and it was beautiful. "Oh, Mom, I love it! Congratulations, you guys!"

Then my mother gave my sister a closer look. "What do you think, Terry?"

"Wow! Is it real?"

Mom laughed. "It better be, Honey."

Sam put his arms around my sister. "Don't worry, Terry, nothing but the best for your mother; nothing but the best for all of you."

My mother was finally getting the happiness she deserved. Finally, it seemed like God was paying attention.

"Give me a hug, you." Sam and I squeezed each other tightly.

One day, not long after Mom and Sam had gotten engaged, my mother accompanied him to his baseball game. He'd sent her back to his car to retrieve something from his wallet, obviously, forgetting what she'd find in there. Mom had recently turned thirty-five, still looking so many years younger. Sam, maybe because of his heavy poundage, looked to be at least five years older than my mother. According to what Sam had told Mom when they met, he was heading toward forty.

My mother grabbed Sam's jacket from the car and pulled out his wallet. She had to grab the car door for support when she glanced at Sam's driver's license. Sam was twenty-four years old—only eight years older than me! Mom could not believe it. No wonder he'd been such an ally, convincing my Mom to ease up on Dizzy. Sam thought like a kid because he wasn't far from being one himself.

Mom had decided not to say anything until they returned home. But when they got home, there was a young woman waiting outside the door.

"Veronica, what are you doing here?" Sam demanded.

It was obvious Veronica had been crying, and when she saw my mother, she became hysterical. Just as Dizzy had done with Carmen, Sam grabbed Veronica by the arm, and dragged her away, telling my mother he'd be right back. Mom stood in the hallway speechless and quivering, looking after them.

When Sam had first met Mom, he said he'd been divorced for five years, and that he had a twelve-year-old daughter who lived with her mother in Martinique. Sam was not only big and fat. As it turned out, he was also a big, fat liar! He was still very much married to Veronica, and had deserted both her and his ten-month-old infant daughter soon after he'd begun seeing my mother.

Not long after, my mother hurtled head-first into a deep, dark place. Terry was the one who found her passed out after she had taken an overdose of pills. The utter sadness and depression took its toll on my dear mother, who had already suffered so much in life. She was admitted to the psychiatric ward at Mount Sinai and put on suicide watch.

Initially, Mom refused to see Sam when he tried to visit her. But Mom could play a good game, even with herself. At some point, she accepted the yellow roses from Sam. In the end, she accepted Sam, too.

Sam finally did divorce his poor wife, lucky her, and married my mother, who was all too glad to have him.

Looking back, I realize that the phrase "like mother like daughter" is more than just something people say. When we girls look in the mirror, we see the faces of our mothers. I'd been handicapped all the way around, having neither father nor mother to set good examples. I thought my father had been one of my mother's childhood mistakes. But in many ways, the mistake had nothing to do with Daddy, and everything to do with Mommy.

And one day, I'd have to face the fact that the problematic men I allowed in my life only had to do with me.

Chapter 31

Dizzy claimed he'd tried to talk Carmen into getting an abortion, but she'd refused just to get back at him for leaving her. As devastating as that was, worse was Carmen delivering a child addicted to heroin. That innocent child would have many hurdles to get through in life, but in the end, he'd far surpass mother *and* father in becoming a healthy, functioning, and worthwhile human being.

Carmen's life had taken a tailspin with her involvement with Dizzy, and if I didn't manage to get my head screwed on right, mine was about to do the same.

It was a Saturday night, and we were driving through Harlem in Dizzy's new Mercury Montego, when he stopped off at a bar to pick up his friend, Bobo. I sat in the car waiting for them to come back, watching all the dope fiends and unsavory characters standing on the street corner, praying Dizzy would hurry up so we could get the heck outta there.

Finally, he and Bobo came rushing out of the bar. Thank God! The two of them hopped in and off we went.

Damn! We hadn't driven more than a block or two, when we all heard the police siren.

"Aw, Man! What we gone do wit this shit?! What we gon' do wit all the dope?!"

Oh, God! Oh, my God! Dope?! For the most part, he'd been keeping his hustling and drugs away from me...well, at least up until that point.

I could feel the knots forming in my stomach, as I heard Bobo in the back seat on the verge of hysteria about what they were going to do with all the dope they obviously had on them.

Then Dizzy glared over at me, looking like a wild outlaw. He pulled out a big plastic bag of white powder from the inside of his jacket.

What is he doing?!

"Shove this down the back of your pants!" he ordered.

"No, no, I don't want—"

That was the last word I got out before he knocked me upside the head.

"You do what the fuck I tell you to do! Now take it and stuff it down the back of your pants!"

Reeling from the pain of his fist, I grabbed the bag of white powder, but I had to unbutton the front of my pants before I could squeeze all that dope into the back of my jeans.

"Pull over and step out of the car," blared from the car behind us.

Dizzy pulled over to the curb. "Don't get outta the fuckin' car!"

There were two male officers. One searched Dizzy while the other searched Bobo. The one who looked like Hercules walked up to the passenger window. I sat trembling and scared out of my dumb-ass mind!

"Do you want to step out of the car, Miss?"

I looked up at that officer and squeaked with the utmost sincerity, "No, Officer, I don't; thank you."

"Step out of the car, Miss, with your pocketbook."

I put one foot in front of the other as I slowly got out of the car with that same, old, familiar fear...Daddy's footsteps walking down the hall...his key turning in the lock...Evil Yvette chasing me up fourteen flights of stairs...Big Ev looming over me in a darkened foyer...and now this police officer asking me if I was carrying any drugs on me.

I shook my head no when he asked the question because when I tried to say the word, nothing came out. Then I looked over at Dizzy, who shot me with a look so menacing, I realized I'd probably be safer having that cop cart me off to jail.

The officer searched through my purse. When he didn't find any drugs, he looked over at his partner. "I bet she got it on her."

That's when the words finally came tumbling out. "I don't do drugs! I've never done drugs! And I'm not carrying any drugs on me!! I'm not...honest...I swear!"

Tears were streaming down my face, and out of the sides of my eyes. I could see Dizzy mouthing the words, "Shut the fuck up!"

But then the officer looked from me to my boyfriend, and then back to me with a rather sad expression in his eyes. He shook his head, after which he issued a serious warning to Dizzy. "We got our eyes on you, Youngblood. Better not catch you hangin' 'round that bar again."

After the men in blue had driven off, Dizzy grabbed me by the back of the neck and shoved me into the car. "Get yo' stupid ass in the mutha fuckin' car; you almost got us busted!"

Okay, if we'd been Bonnie and Clyde...I surely wouldn't have made a good Bonnie.

For years I wondered why the cops hadn't searched me that night, or at least radioed in for a female cop to come to the scene to frisk me; I had no doubt they knew I was holding the drugs. It must've been an angel on my shoulder. Then I remembered the sadness on the one cop's face as he peered at Dizzy and then back at me. I was almost seventeen, but I looked every bit of twelve. And I may have been hanging out with a thug, but I was about as square and innocent as they came. Perhaps that officer had a daughter of his own and I somehow reminded him of her, and he didn't want to see someone like me go to jail that night. I guess he was the angel on my shoulder.

The next day, Dizzy called to tell me it was quits, 'cause I was too much of a wimp. Basically, I wasn't his "ride-or-die kinda chick." Obviously, I was no Carmen.

I lost it...I cried...I pleaded...and I begged with all my might. Never mind that Dizzy had gotten Carmen pregnant, that he was now addicted to snorting heroin, and worse yet, had almost gotten me thrown into jail for heroin possession at only sixteen years old. I was still so terrified, so fearful, of this physically and emotionally abusive gangsta leaving me. Who would protect me now?

But after Dizzy made it crystal clear he was done with me, the reality of the horrible episode with the police finally sunk in and gave me the courage I needed to move on.

Right after Mom and Sam were married, we moved away from the McKinley Projects to a beautiful condo on the Grand Concourse, and I never saw Dizzy again. The roller-coaster ride of the year I'd spent with him was finally over.

I got a bit of a reprieve as I concentrated more on my acting career. I enrolled in an acting workshop, called The Players' Workshop. I was meeting exciting people doing theater, booking small TV film roles and commercials. It seemed my life might be taking a turn for the better.

Chapter 32

Riverdale, New York
Mid-1970s

"Mom, guess what??! My agent got me booked in a play that may be headed for Broadway. But first we're going for out-of-town tryouts!"

"Honey! That's wonderful!"

I had graduated high school and had started attending Manhattan Community College. I was also taking regular acting classes down in the East Village at both The Players' Workshop, taught by a man named Clay Stevens, and attending Woodie King's New Federal Theatre where classes were taught by the gifted Dick Anthony Williams.

My life was finally looking up. No longer did dope fiends and hustlers surround me, but young people, like myself, embarking on a hopeful acting career. I'd put the past behind me and moved into a brand-new world.

The play, *What the Wine-Sellers Buy,* was a coming-of-age story between two young lovers growing up in the inner city and written by a wonderful playwright named Ron Milner. Now that I was becoming part of the black theater circle, I was seeing lots of theater and auditioning for various stage productions. I'd already seen the original stage production of *Wine-Sellers* when it debuted with a small run at New Federal Theatre.

The lead actor would be Glynn Turman, who'd starred on the television series, *Peyton Place*. The female lead was a talented girl named Loretta Greene. My small role would be as one of Loretta's high school classmates.

I decided to take a leave of absence from college for the out-of-town tryouts. It'd be nice going out on the road for a while, but until that happened, I was also finally looking to have my own apartment. Living with Mom and Sam wasn't really my cup of tea anymore. So after meeting a delightful Afro-Asian girl named Arlene Quiyou in my acting class at The Players' Workshop, the two of us decided to get an apartment together. We moved into a three-story walk-up on Tenth Street and Avenue C, in the heart of the East Village.

The apartment was pretty rundown, with three rooms, a living room, kitchen, and bathroom, which only consisted of a toilet. There was a shower stall that stood off in a corner of the kitchen, and a loft bed, also in the kitchen. But Arlene and I were ecstatic to get it.

The village was a happening place, full of theater, local restaurants that offered up more than just a meal. There were poetry readings, music, serious talk and laughter about the craft of acting. Most of the community seemed to be saturated with artists and creativity. It was all so heady, and an environment I cherished being a part of.

Arlene was a struggling actress, working part time in her mother's boutique shop in the West Bronx. Arlene didn't have much left over after we'd pooled our monies to get the apartment, but that was fine by me. I was still booking commercials and print work, so I was able to afford a little makeover to our East Village flat all by myself.

I had the place painted a beautiful powder blue, with white ceilings and baseboards. The kitchen counter was stripped and stained a dark cherry. The tiny bathroom was painted a canary yellow with red baseboards, and I even found a red toilet seat! I bought a queen-sized mattress that would double as both a sofa and a bed for Arlene.

I found a pretty lavender quilted comforter to go over it, and filled it with bright pillows.

Sam offered to reconstruct the sinking platform bed in the kitchen, where I'd opted to sleep. I took him up on it because I'd not found anyone else to do it that wasn't going to charge an arm and a leg. Once I put everything together, it was darling...my first *happy* home.

When I'd lived with Mom and Sam on the Grand Concourse, it was in a very upscale area of the Bronx. It was large and airy with two bedrooms and two baths. According to Sam, he'd been searching for the perfect place for months. But Sam turned out to be a cleverly deceitful rogue. Eventually, we found out that Sam had moved my mother into the very apartment he'd shared with his ex-wife and infant daughter before he'd deserted them.

I was truly grateful to move into my own place. I tried not to dwell on Mom and Sam's relationship, hoping for the best. Instead, I went about preparing myself for my future.

After out-of-town tryouts, we'd have a successful run on Broadway at the prestigious Lincoln Center, in the Vivian Beaumont Theater. I'll never forget that first day of rehearsal, which was actually a read-through of the script, and a meet-and-greet with all the other actors.

So much excitement filled the air as we sat at a long table in the rehearsal hall. The director, Michael Schultz, had everyone go around the room and introduce themselves.

Glynn Turman (he was so black and fine with that deep, deep voice, but skinny as a toothpick), Loretta Greene, Dick Anthony Williams (Dick had been one of my acting teachers who would end up winning a Tony Award for *Wine-Sellers)*, Marilyn Coleman, Sonny Jim Gaines, Jean DuShon, (Jean was an older woman who would take me under her thumb; we'd end up being roommates on the road), Kirk Kirksey, Ray Vitte, Berlinda Tolbert (Berlinda and I would end up being great friends, and she'd go on to star in the popular sitcom, *The Jeffersons*), Debbi Morgan, Sheila Goldsmith.

All of us gave our names, and smiled and applauded each other. But I don't think anyone was smiling wider than me.

Rehearsals had been long, but so much fun. The early previews went extremely well. Word was out; we were a hit! But now everyone seemed filled with butterflies as we prepared for opening night—everyone except Mr. Turman, who seemed to radiate coolness.

Watching Glynn in rehearsals, I understood why. Everything he did was brilliant. I was in awe watching such a gifted talent who possessed such assurance and confidence with a tilt of his head.

It might be fair to say that along with Glynn's strong self-confidence came a bit of arrogance and cockiness, but I actually thought it was sexy. Glynn also had one of the brightest smiles I'd ever seen, absolutely infectious. His eyes would light up like they had miniature light bulbs in them. Glynn also possessed a wonderful sense of humor.

One day in rehearsal hall, a couple of the actors walked in dressed in their costumes. Ray Vitte, who was especially handsome, took off his shirt and handed it over to the costume designer. Apparently there was a tear in it. Looking at Ray's juicy biceps brought out an audible sigh from all the actresses.

Not to be undone, Glynn walked out and slowly strutted back in, but not with his shirt off. He had on a fedora, cocked down over one eye like *Mr. Slick*. But Glynn had rolled his pant legs up to his thighs. And when everyone took a look at those skinny-minny, chicken legs, we lost it! It was the funniest thing you ever wanted to see.

Glynn pranced around the room looking dead serious, saying, "What? What? What's so funny? What's everybody laughing at?"

Then he stood next to me. "Now come on, Debbi, you know these are some fine legs; go ahead, say it. These are some fine legs, Glynn."

I was hysterical.

"Come on; you can do it. Say it with me."

I sputtered, "Those...are...some...fine...legs...Glynn."

Then Glynn threw his arms around me. His embrace felt so good; as he held me, I was surrounded by a deep belly laugh.

After that, Glynn always seemed to make a point to stop and chat with me. On one of our off evenings, the producers got everyone tickets to the Negro Ensemble Company's production of *The Great McDaddy* starring a wonderful NEC actor named Charles Weldon.

Glynn managed to be seated right next to me. Berlinda and Jean Dushon started teasing, saying it was obvious Glynn had a thing for me. I wasn't completely sure about that, but secretly I hoped it was true.

The day before our opening, Glynn came up and asked if I were going to the opening night party. I said, "Yes." Glynn smiled, so self-assured, and asked if I'd like to go with him. I said, "Yes," with a thousand trumpets marching across my chest.

On opening night, after I'd finished my scene, I went up to a small room where a window looked out onto the stage. I pulled up a chair and watched the rest of the production, mesmerized with every move Glynn made, and every word he spoke. It was like a master class in acting.

After our curtain call brought down the house, erupting into a standing ovation, everyone ran back to the dressing rooms, hopping with joy.

We girls shared a huge changing room, and as we were buttoning each other up, sharing lipstick, hugging over our success, my head took it all in. It was one of the few times in my life I felt tears welling up from pure joy.

There was a big knock on the door.

"Who is it?" Shelia Goldsmith called, laughing as she went to the door in her panties with her large breasts swinging from side to side.

"Sheila, you'd better put a robe on!" scolded Loretta playfully.

"It's Mr. Turman."

"Shit!" Sheila whispered loudly. "I don't need to put on a damn thing!"

Everyone laughed, but I was suddenly very nervous knowing that Glynn was on the other side of that door.

"Is Miss Morgan in there? Tell her if she's going with me, she'd better hurry up."

"I'll be right out!" I shouted.

There was nothing but silence, as all eyes were on me. But now the girls decided to really let me have it.

Sheila, always the funny one, started right up. "Oh, Miss Morgan, it's for you. You'd better step to it!"

"That's right; you don't want to keep the star, Mr. Turman, waiting," said Starletta, who was cracking up. Starletta Dupar was an excellent actress, and so fun-loving.

"Don't do anything I *would do!*" someone else shouted out.

"You know they say Glynn's a black cowboy. He raises horses out in Malibu, California. And you know what they say about cowboys. They sure can ride!" Sheila started smacking her butt, and everyone in the room hollered.

Once I'd put on my coat, they all practically shoved me out the door, laughing frantically.

I walked out of the room; basically, I was thrown out. Glynn was standing in the middle of a circle, surrounded by Mom, Sam, Aunt Sport, Uncle Bill, Aunt Virginia, Terry, Carol, Denise, Vanessa, and Arlene; everyone was completely excited for me.

Glynn had been so sweet, taking his time to speak with my family and friends. It was easy to see how enamored they were by his charm.

Nobody wanted to go with us to the party, even though I wanted them to. I think once they saw Glynn put his arm around me and my face flushing, they decided not to tag along. But I could see the glee in their eyes, salivating to eventually get the 4-1-1.

The welcome mat had definitely been laid out for *Wine-Sellers,* and we all had an absolute ball! The party couldn't have been better.

Glynn took me home afterward and when we reached the door, I told him Arlene was probably in there sleeping.

Glynn grinned and said, "Lucky Arlene." Then he pulled me close and gave me the sweetest kiss.

One Monday evening, our day off, Glynn phoned to say he'd stop by. Arlene was staying over at her boyfriend's, so I had the apartment to myself. I took a quick shower and got casually dolled up, waiting for Glynn to arrive.

When I heard a whistle outside the window, I peeked my head out to see Glynn standing there in the freezing cold.

"Do you want anything from the store before I come up?"

I'd just started trying to smoke cigarettes because I thought it looked so sophisticated and cool.

"Yeah. Would you get me a pack of Tarringtons?"

Glynn hesitated for a moment, and then nodded his head.

When he got upstairs and I opened the door, he didn't say a word. He swept me up in his arms and we melted into a deep kiss. I think I'd seen him kiss the actress, Judy Pace, like that on *Peyton Place.* Now I knew first-hand how good it felt.

Glynn was a great conversationalist and storyteller. I loved hearing all his tales about growing up in the business, all the stars he'd hobnobbed with, and his time on the series Peyton Place.

One thing that still seemed to have left a sore spot was *A Raisin in the Sun.* Glynn had played the original role of young Travis in the Broadway stage production with Sidney Poitier. Glynn's mom had been a very close friend of Lorraine Hansberry, the extraordinary author of *Raisin*. Lorraine was the moving force in Glynn getting the role.

When Glynn found out the play was going to be made into a movie, he jumped for joy. He went to school and told all of his friends he was going to be in a big movie with Sidney Poitier. But when time came to shoot the movie, Glynn's height had spurted up quite a few inches, and the director felt he was now way too tall to play the young Travis. Glynn was understandably heartbroken.

As time came for me to start sharing some of my life, there was nothing I wanted to offer. Instead, I lit up a cigarette and took a long drag, knowing Glynn would think I looked cool and alluring.

Glynn smiled, and took the cigarette from my lips. "You think you're grown, huh?"

"What do you mean?"

Glynn laughed. Then he caressed the side of my face and stared at me very seriously, emphasizing each word. "I'll tell you what I mean. If you plan to be hanging out with me, you definitely won't be smoking these. They killed my mother, and I can't stand them."

Glynn's mother had died from lung cancer when he was only sixteen. Glynn crunched up my pack of cigarettes and threw them into the garbage. And thanks to Glynn, I never picked up a cigarette again.

I smiled to myself, thanking God for finally bringing such a gem into my life. Though I was about to find out I wasn't the only one who might think of him that way.

"Glynn, Sheila said you live on a ranch in California."

Glynn smiled. "Oh yeah? What else did big-mouth Sheila have to say?"

"That was it."

"Yeah, I do have a ranch. Kay and I have some beautiful horses, too."

Kay? Who the heck was Kay? "Who's Kay?"

"The woman I live with. She has a daughter who lives with us, too."

Glynn said this very matter-of-factly, like he was asking what I wanted to eat. I should've known it was too good to be true. Nonetheless, I was choked up. But I tried my best to cover it, and decided then and there, this would be the ending to something that had barely gotten started. The problem was, I didn't let Glynn in on it.

A few evenings later, Berlinda and I were on our way out of the dressing room, leaving the theater, when Glynn came up.

"Hey, you." Glynn put his arms around me and gave me a kiss. I couldn't resist. "Can I walk you ladies out?"

Berlinda and I each took an arm as we walked down the long corridor. Suddenly, Glynn dropped both our arms as a woman came around the bend.

"Okay, didn't know my woman was planning to show up," Glynn said softly. I was puzzled. A tall, white woman, smartly dressed in a cape coat and matching tam, who looked to be damn near in her fifties, was approaching us. *This could not be Kay!*

"Hi," the woman said to Glynn, exuding the same self-assurance as him. Maybe that was the attraction.

"Hi," Glynn responded, and then leaned in and kissed her. My heart sank.

"Kay, this is Berlinda and Debbi."

"Hello," Kay said, offering up a knowing smile.

Berlinda and I said, "Hi," at the same time, probably still sounding like Minnie Memphis, like we did in the play.

Then Berlinda took hold of my arm, leading me away. "Nice to meet you, Kay."

Glynn hadn't told me Kay was spending a few days in town. And Kay hadn't told Glynn she'd be meeting him after the show. She'd already caught one of the performances, so apparently Glynn wasn't thinking Kay would show up at the theater. But Kay obviously knew her man.

For the remainder of the week, I kept my distance from Glynn, but once Kay returned to Malibu, it was like all hell broke loose. Everyone seemed to be having a liaison with someone else involved with the play. Actors, actresses, producers, writer, director...we were all such an attractive bunch. And I was right in the mix, having a torrid affair with Glynn.

But it was more than sexual, so much more. Glynn was kind to me; he spoke to me in a loving way. It was so nice and easy being in his presence, and we always seemed to have fun together. Suddenly, I realized something was missing...fear! I had none!

However, once *What the Wine-Sellers Buy* came to an end, so did my affair with Glynn. I'd done my best to prepare myself, but my heart ached like hell. However, I didn't hate Glynn. How could I? Even though Glynn was involved with someone else, he was the first man I was ever involved with romantically, who had ever brought such ease and comfort into my life.

And it'd be a long time before one ever would again.

Chapter 33

Dean put an arm around me. "It's a nice night. You feel like walking?"

"Yeah, it's not too cold. I don't mind."

I'd met Dean Irby when he was starring in the Negro Ensemble Company's Broadway production of *The River Niger*. Another actor starring with him was Charles Weldon, whom I'd seen in the play, *The Great MacDaddy*.

It'd been a few months since *Wine-Sellers* had ended, and shortly thereafter, I'd begun having a brief fling with Dean.

Dean and I were walking down St. Mark's Place in the East Village, on our way to Dean's apartment. After a few blocks, we saw a man rushing into a building.

"Hey, Charles!"

It was Charles Weldon. Charles turned and saw Dean and me approaching.

Charles was an extremely handsome man, but I'd noticed that the first time I'd seen him at NEC. Charles was brown-skinned, about average height, and had a very chiseled bone structure. His eyes were the color of chestnuts, and they crinkled at the corners when he laughed. His big, hearty laugh invited everyone to join in. But the most important thing about Charles Weldon was that one day in the very near future, he'd become husband #1!

The following Saturday afternoon, Dean and I had a nice brunch together, and then I headed up to the Bronx to spend the weekend at Mom's.

During my short stay, I could tell things weren't quite right, though my mother was being mum. But Terry pulled me aside and said that a lot of women had been phoning the house for Sam. My sister told me about a big fight between Mom and Sam concerning an eighteen-year-old girl who'd kept calling.

I felt for my mother, for the cards she'd been dealt yet a second time around. In addition to abuse, she, and my grandmother before her, had also endured husbands who weren't faithful. I prayed she wouldn't be driven to the lengths she had taken before. A national tour of *Wine-Sellers* was underway and I was ecstatic when I was offered the female lead. Glynn would not be returning and neither would Loretta Green. She was pregnant with the director, Ron Milner's, child.

Before I could get my new apartment on West 96th Street completely set up, it was time to leave. But I invited Mom out to dinner one evening before I left.

I grilled my mother about her relationship with Sam. I could see how much she was hurting. Mom assured me she was going to ask Sam to leave. But my bigger concern was my mother's state of mind. Mom assured me I didn't have to worry. I prayed to God that was true.

Life on the road was not quite what it had been before on our out-of-town tryouts. Many of the original actors had elected not to be a part of the second tour. Missing Glynn was a no-brainer. I also missed Berlinda tremendously. She had hooked up with Ray Vitte and moved out to California. But I had to admit, playing one of the lead roles in a large part made up for the people I missed.

I started getting calls from my sister, however, that threw a wrench

My maternal grandparents, John Hammond and Willie Rose Smith
Courtesy of Debbi Morgan.

Great-Great-Aunt Minnie
Courtesy of Debbi Morgan.

Me as a baby Courtesy of Debbi Morgan.

Mom Courtesy of Debbi Morgan.

Daddy—See where I got my dimples?
Courtesy of Debbi Morgan.

Me—first grade Courtesy of Debbi Morgan.

Terry—We were often mistaken for twins Courtesy of Debbi Morgan.

Mom & Dad at prom Courtesy of Debbi Morgan.

My paternal grandparents—grandmother Cora and grandfather George. I always thought he looked like a black Clark Gable Courtesy of Debbi Morgan.

Aunt Margaret
Courtesy of Debbi Morgan.

Daddy's brother, Uncle Bill
Courtesy of Debbi Morgan.

Aunt Thelma
Courtesy of Debbi Morgan.

My beautiful mom
Courtesy of Debbi Morgan.

Mom and Aunt Sport Courtesy of Debbi Morgan.

Jim Mendenhall—I'm an actress today because of him. In my eyes he was FAMILY
Courtesy of Debbi Morgan.

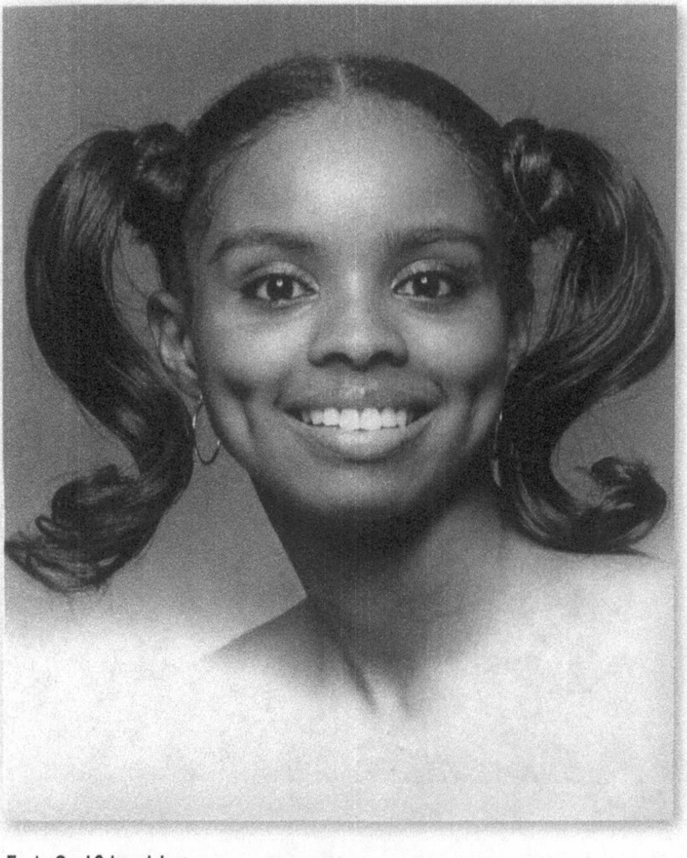

Early 8 x10 headshot Courtesy of Debbi Morgan.

Wedding Day 2009—Me, Jeff, Jaden (grandson), Terry, Darnell
© Kent Ballard.

Terry and me
Courtesy of Debbi Morgan.

Husband #4, Jeffrey Winston—Sexy, Hot, Forever!

into my excitement. Whenever I phoned home and spoke to Mom, she wasn't sounding at all like herself. A couple of times, she'd even sounded drunk. Her speech was slurred, and her sentences were non-sequiturs. Terry informed me that Mom was coming home at three and four o'clock in the morning because she'd been out trying to find Sam.

"Debbi, I'm so scared. Sometimes, I can't even sleep at night wondering where Mommy is. And I'm tired the next day when I have to go to school. I hate Sam! I hate him! Now he has Mommy drinking all the time because she's always mad at him. And, Debbi, I think she's on some kind of pills, too, because half the time I can't even make out what she's talking about."

I was extremely alarmed. "I know, Terry. When I spoke to her the other day, she seemed completely out of it. Listen, I'm going to fly you guys out here to Detroit for a visit. That way I can sit down and talk to Mom in person. In the meantime, I'm going to call Aunt Sport and ask her to keep a check on her."

"Mommy needs to leave Sam, period!" my sister stressed.

Terry was quite different from Mom and me. Thank God, the genetic dysfunction had bypassed one of us!

"Do you know Mom had to put a lock on my door, Debbi?!"

"Why?'

"Because I came in from a party the other night and found Sam in my room!"

"What was he doing in your room?"

"That's what I asked that fat jerk! I said, 'What are you doing in my room, Sam?!' He said he was looking for something. I told him there was nothing in my room he could be looking for and to get out! After he walked out, I slammed the door on him. And then I noticed that the drawer I keep my panties in was open. I could tell Sam had been going through it."

"Did you tell Mom?!"

"Yeah! I told her the next morning. And when Sam came home that night, she cursed him out. They had a big fight. And the next day Mom put a lock on my bedroom door. But I told her she should've called the police and had that pervert husband of hers locked up!"

Five days later, I flew Mom and Terry out to Detroit. I stood there waiting as all the passengers got off the plane, wondering if Mom and Terry had missed their flight. Finally, I saw them and ran to give them each a hug.

"Terry!" My sister and I gave each other a tight squeeze. "Mom! It's so good to see you."

"You too, Sweetheart! You look wonderful!"

"What took you guys so long? I thought maybe you'd missed the plane."

"Mom couldn't find where she'd put her hat. I told her she didn't bring it."

"All right...all right. *MOTHER*, can we forget about that now?" my mother said sarcastically to my sister. Then looking at me, she said, "You know your sister thinks she's *my* mother all of a sudden."

I watched Terry roll her eyes.

We got back to the hotel and after letting Mom and Terry unpack, I observed there was something very different about my mother. Her personality had changed. Her mood seemed to fluctuate between overly giddy and downright glum. Then she'd start a conversation talking loudly, and a mile a minute.

When I took them to lunch and my mother ordered a drink, I was taken aback. I'd never seen Mom drink liquor during the day. At one point, when she'd gotten up and gone to the bathroom, Terry grabbed my arm. "You see what I mean, Debbi? I don't know what Mom's on, but she's on something. She's started acting so crazy. And she keeps saying she's going to put Sam out. But all she ever does is sit in her room and cry when he doesn't come home. Or else she's out in the street at all hours trying to find him. I feel like I'm going to have a nervous breakdown."

I hugged my sister, wondering if I was equipped to handle what was going on with Mom. It sounded like she might need some professional help. I decided I'd sit and have a heart-to-heart with her after my evening's performance.

The show went really well that night, and I could see Mom and Terry standing up in the front row, applauding. Mom was jumping up and down, obviously thrilled to see me playing one of the starring roles.

After the show, the producer, Woodie King, took everyone out to dinner. I thought this would be a great way for Mom and Terry to meet a lot of the cast they hadn't met before.

Woodie had reserved the dining room at a very exclusive restaurant. We all sat at a long table, ordering all the delights we could eat. There were bottles of champagne and drinks all around, for those of us who indulged.

Everyone was laughing and talking, having a great time, when Mom began to get exceptionally loud and boisterous. Both Terry and I got a bit embarrassed, but especially me. I had to work with these people.

Dick Williams was another actor who'd opted not to return to the play in his role as the sly pimp, Rico. Gilbert Lewis was now playing the part. Gil was a wonderful actor, but Dick had put his stamp on the role, winning a Tony in the process. Someone was talking about a mishap that'd happened on stage when Mom rudely interrupted.

"Gilbert! Hey, Gilbert! You were wonderful as Rico! That's one of my favorite parts in the whole show, except for my daughter of course! You were really, really good, but not as good as Dick Williams! Nooo waaay! I...am...so...sorry! But can't nobody do 'Rico' like Dick Williams!"

You could hear a pin drop. Mom took another swig of her drink, obviously oblivious to the huge slight she'd made to Gilbert. I wanted to die. And then Gilbert broke the silence with a huge laugh. The others joined in, including Mom. Terry and I both excused ourselves to the bathroom.

When we returned to the hotel room, we were both furious with our mother.

"Mom, how could you say something like that to Gilbert?"

"Jesus Christ, Debbi! What did I say that was so wrong?! I told the man that he was good!"

Terry jumped in. "Yeah, and then you said he wasn't as good as Dick Williams!"

"Oh, God! Oh, God! What did I do?! Tell me, what did I do?!" Mom ran into the bathroom and slammed the door. She was screaming and crying as if she were being physically attacked.

"WHY?! WHY?! WHY ARE YOU TWO DOING THIS TO ME? WHY, GOD? WHY?"

Terry and I looked at each other with our mouths hanging open. I had no idea what to make of this. And neither did my poor mother.

Chapter 34

Hollywood, California
Late 1970s

"Mom, I'm going to Hollywood! Sonny Jim says I need to come out and give L.A. a shot." Sonny Jim Gaines had been in the original tour of *Wine-Sellers*, and was yet another person to take me under his wing. "I've spoken to Berlinda, too. She invited me to stay with her and Ray until I find a place."

"Debbi, I bet you'll make it out there, too. You just watch. Your mother has every confidence in the world in you, Sweetheart. But it breaks my heart you're not finishing college." Mom seemed somewhat more herself, though she was still with Sam.

Terry informed me that our mother could be quite sane and rational one minute, and the next she was flying off the deep end.

Clearly, my mother was sane and rational as she offered her encouragement and blessings.

I gave away what furniture I had to family and friends and bought a one-way ticket to California. This was where my career was taking me, although I carried concern for Mom along with me.

Berlinda and Ray lived in a small, quaint house in Altadena, California, a suburb of Los Angeles, about thirty minutes from the city. I was so happy for my friend. Berlinda was starring on *The Jeffersons*, and had become a bona-fide television star. I only hoped to be half as lucky.

I stayed with Berlinda for a few weeks before she helped me find an adorable, one-bedroom apartment in the Beachwood Canyon area. The apartment was huge, and would've cost twice as much in New York. It was filled with light, and had four large picture windows looking out onto a pretty, tree-lined street.

I immediately set out browsing all the shops and decorating my abode to perfection. But first, Sonny Jim helped me go out and find a used car. It was a 1972 gold Audi, and it ran flawlessly.

It took no time to find my way around L.A. Unlike New York, all the street numbers ran consecutively. I had no problem at all finding KTTV. Sonny Jim had gotten me an appointment to meet with Jane Murray, the casting agent for *Good Times*. As soon as I entered the room, Jane said, "She's perfect to play JJ's girlfriend." Two weeks later, I was doing my first-ever television guest spot, playing Jimmy Walker's girlfriend.

I was filled with jitters on tape day, especially when I had to kiss Jimmy. But he was sweet, although seemingly shy and quiet. Nothing like I would've expected from watching the character of JJ on television. Most of the rest of the cast was cordial, but I especially liked meeting the great actress, Esther Rolle. Bern Nadette Stanis, who played Thelma, seemed standoffish at the time, but it didn't matter because the week went by pretty quickly and then it was over.

About a month after I'd moved into Beachwood Canyon, I ran into an actress I knew only casually from New York. She happened to be living right across the street from me. Her name was Bebe Drake-Hooks. Bebe was a live wire, in every sense. She had a larger-than-life personality and a take-charge attitude.

Bebe turned me on to her agency for representation. Now I had an agent, an apartment, a car, and I'd done my first television show. My feet felt firmly planted in Hollywood.

One day, Bebe came over and said, "Do you know Charles Weldon?!"

"Uh...I've met him. Why, is he living out here?"

"Yeah, Girl! Everybody's out here now. Come on; we're going over to CW's right now," Bebe ordered.

We pulled up to Charles Weldon's rented house. It was rather unkempt, outside and in, and filled with a bunch of kids of mixed races, running wild.

"Charles!" one yelled out. "There's no more toilet tissue!"

"Hold on! I think there's some up here!"

"Hey, CW, I brought someone over here to see you!" yelled Bebe. There was an awful lot of yelling going on.

Charles came tearing down the stairs wearing a pair of jeans and cowboy boots, and carrying a half roll of toilet paper.

He took a look at me, and gave a hearty laugh. "Hey there, Debbi! I didn't know you were out here. Damn, girl, you look good! Where'd you find her, Bebe?"

"Shit! She livin' right across the street from me!"

"You lyin'? Well, how long you been out here, Debbi?"

"Charles, I need some toilet paper!"

"Hold on, I'm coming! Excuse me, Debbi. Let me go take this toilet paper to my kid."

I noted that Charles's son called him "Charles" instead of Daddy.

Later, Charles introduced all four of his young sons who happened to be visiting him. Two were white, one was Mexican, and one was of African American and Mexican descent. His name was Charles, too, but everyone called him Chucky. Chucky was Charles's only blood son. The others were by two women Charles had spent many years with. He'd raised the boys from toddlers. As far as Charles was concerned, they were all his sons.

After that brief visit at Charles's house, we became involved. But, oh, I wish it wasn't so. I guess you'd call Charles a free spirit, sort of a hippie; he was kind of out there with a devil-may-care kind of attitude.

Charles was a talented actor who'd been working quite a bit when I first came to Hollywood. And although he no longer made a living at it, Charles had a wonderful voice, with sort of a country twang. He'd been the lead singer of a singing group back in the late sixties, and they'd been a one-hit wonder with a song called "Diamonds and Pearls."

But Charles's two older sisters, Ann and Maxine, were the ones who actually made a living with their voices, singing at different supper clubs around town.

When I fell for Charles, I fell hard. He was sixteen years older than me, and once I was under his spell, all the old patterns returned with a vengeance. They'd probably never left; they were lying dormant, waiting to rear their ugly heads.

Though work had been coming pretty steadily for Charles, suddenly he was going through a dry spell. Charles told me he was going to have to let his place go and move in with a friend at the beach.

This so-called friend was a woman named Lauren. And I'm sure Lauren considered herself a lot more than a friend. But Charles, being the free spirit that he was, would dismiss any questions on the subject.

"Debbi, come on; what've I told you about that? Lauren's a cool lady; you're both cool ladies. She's a lot older than you. But if you two met, you'd really dig each other. She's helping me out, that's all. You trying to fault her for that?"

"Are you sleeping with her?"

"So what if I am? I'm sleeping with you, too. And sometimes I'm sleeping with Lauren and her friends. And that's cool, too."

What in the Sam Hill was he talking about? "What do you mean, Charles?"

"I mean, I need for you to stop being so uptight. I'm here with you, and you're my woman. And when I'm somewhere else, you're still my woman. But I want you to think about being a little freer. That's what our experience together needs to be, instead of putting energy into some kind of jealousy. That stuff doesn't even need to be discussed because it's irrelevant."

Charles didn't seem like he was on drugs, not yet anyway. But why was he acting like sleeping with other women should be of no concern to me? I wasn't quite sure about the rest of the stuff coming out of his mouth, but my instincts told me it wasn't good either.

However, the next time I brought up Charles living with Lauren, he kissed me softly on the lips.

"Now didn't I tell you about dwelling on that silly shit?" And Charles walked out the door. I didn't hear from him again for one whole month.

It felt like my right arm had been cut off. I couldn't eat or sleep. When Charles finally showed up again, I'd gone down to ninety-five pounds. Charles took one look at me and hit the roof. "What happened to you?!"

"I was upset and I couldn't eat," I cried. "I thought you weren't ever coming back."

"So you're going to kill yourself! That's fucking smart! I *should* leave and never come back! If you're going to be that stupid, I will too!"

I was so intimidated and afraid of losing Charles that I tried to go along with everything after that.

Charles had a sexual habit of being with more than one woman at the same time. That's what he'd been alluding to. And one night I actually went out to Hermosa Beach to be with him and Lauren.

Lauren was a real plain-Jane, white woman, about five feet tall, with straggly blonde hair. I had no idea what Charles saw in her. Then again, maybe I did. She acted friendly enough, but this was way out of my league. I heard myself in the midst of conversation, but had no idea what I was saying.

When it got late, and Charles suggested the three of us go to bed, those familiar pangs rocketed my insides. Lauren had two children, whom she'd introduced to me earlier. I wondered about all the things they saw going on in this house.

I followed Charles and Lauren into the bedroom. They took off every stitch. I left on my underwear.

Charles climbed into the middle of the king-sized bed with Lauren and me on either side. I was shaking so badly, Charles put an arm around me and whispered, "It's okay. We're not going to do anything."

In the morning, Lauren's daughter came bouncing into the room. "Mom, I need some money for school." The kid didn't seem the least bit thrown that another woman was in the bed with her mother and Charles. It was just too much.

I'd slept in the same spot all night, too shaken to move a muscle. When I got up, my back felt like it needed to be in traction.

I returned home while Charles stayed at Lauren's. And I cried a river all the way. I cried because I hated myself. I hated my weakness, hated my insecurity, hated that I couldn't go to the one person who loved me more than anything in the world. Why would I? What advice could she possibly give?

Chapter 35

"Miz Carrie, I cain't stay after school t'day. My mama says I's gots to hurry on home!"

"I'm sorry, Elizabeth. I was hoping we could go take a look at some of the new books I'd gotten for you."

"No, M'am. Not t'day. I gots to be hurryin' on along now. My mama's waitin'!"

"Okay, Elizabeth, maybe tomorrow we..."

I turned to run out, tripping over my two nervous feet. The director, John Erman, jumped out of his chair and ran over to help me up.

"Debbi, are you okay?"

"Yes, I'm okay."

"You sure are," the director said. "You're a lot more than okay." And everyone in the room nodded their heads, and applauded. Obviously, the audition had gone very well.

When I returned home, I sat by the phone, willing it to ring. When it finally did, I was too afraid to answer. "Charles, can you get it?"

Charles grabbed up the phone. "Hello. Yes, she's right here. It's your agent."

I took the phone from Charles and held it to my ear, now too afraid to speak. "Debbi, say something," Charles ordered.

"Hello."

"Hello... Is this Elizabeth Harvey?"

"Oh, my God! Oh, my God! Oh, my God! Oooo, MY GOOOOOD!" I was jumping up and down and screaming so loudly, I didn't realize I'd dropped the phone. Charles picked it up.

"Your agent said you can call back for all the details after you've calmed down."

Charles picked me up and spun me around in a circle; our laughter filled the room. "Congratulations, BABY!!!"

Once I'd gotten over the initial shock of landing one of the lead roles in *Roots: The Next Generations,* I called my agent back and got all of the particulars.

Because it was my first major television role, I'd only be paid a scale salary, which was minimal. But that didn't matter to me in the least. I'd be playing the role of a lifetime, Elizabeth Harvey, Alex Haley's great-aunt. My character would begin at sixteen, and I'd play her all the way up to eighty. Every actress in town had tried out for the part, and I'd gotten it!

Charles had been the one to help me nail the audition. He'd coached me long and hard, and it had paid off.

I stayed up half the night, calling everyone I knew, starting of course with my family. Mom sounded like she might faint from joy. Because of the huge critical success of the original *Roots,* everyone knew this was a big deal. They couldn't have been happier for me.

I called Carol, Vanessa, and Denise back in New York, and they were simply elated. But when I called my dear friend Berlinda, I was surprisingly disappointed.

"Berlinda, I got the part of Elizabeth in *Roots*!"

"*You* got that part?" Berlinda sounded surprised. "I auditioned for that part, too."

"I know you did, Berlinda. I'm sorry. But at least you're on a big, hit television series."

"So what? That's not all I want to do. I want to do dramatic roles, too."

I wasn't sure what else to say. I thought since Berlinda hadn't gotten the part, she'd at least be happy for me. It was an eye opener to the jealousy in this business. When great roles for black actresses were so few and far between, it tested friendships.

Sadly, Berlinda and I began to drift apart, and I realized how much I missed my home girls, my real friends, back in New York City. But at least I had Charles. Charles was a great guy with a big ole heart. In retrospect, given the age difference between us, Charles was kind of like the father I'd never had. Maybe that had been part of the attraction.

I wasn't sure what happened between him and Lauren, and I didn't ask. But he did end up moving out of her place and in with me. Thankfully, he didn't try to bring any of his fun-loving group antics up again. So when he asked me to marry him, I happily said, *Yes!*

We flew to New York and got married in Mom and Sam's living room. Terry was my maid of honor, and the gifted actor, Adolph Caesar, who was Charles's best friend, stood in as best man. Charles's sisters, Anne and Maxine were both in attendance, along with another Weldon sister, Jewel. The small ceremony concluded with a song from Maxine. Then Charles, *husband #1,* and I were back on a flight to Los Angeles. I was about to start production on *Roots: The Next Generations.*

Before shooting began, all the actors appearing in the first episode met at the home of our director, John Erman. When I walked in and saw the great Henry Fonda, and Olivia de Havilland, I had to touch myself to confirm that I was still alive.

I got up the nerve to walk over to an actress I'd seen on the television series, *That's My Mama.* Her name was Lynne Moody.

"Hi, my name is Debbi. I'm playing your daughter, Elizabeth."

"Hi, Debbi!" Lynne grabbed my hand and pulled me across the big living room. Lynne would become a lifelong friend.

"Georg! This is Debbi! She's playing our daughter. Isn't she a doll?"

I recognized Georg Stanford Brown from the television series, *The Rookies*.

Georg smiled, and extended his hand. "Hello, Daughter." And to this day, that's what he still calls me.

Once everyone had gathered, we were introduced to the great Alex Haley. A few of the actors, like Lynne and Georg, already knew Alex quite well from the first *Roots*.

Alex gave me a warm hug. "So, you're *Aunt Liz?*"

I smiled. "Yes, I am, Mr. Haley. Thank God!"

Alex laughed. "You can call me Alex, *Aunt Liz.*"

We sat down wherever we could. I chose to sit on the floor very near to the rocker Alex was sitting in.

Alex began telling stories about the relatives who hadn't been in *Roots 1.* Elizabeth Harvey, Alex Haley's great-aunt, never married after losing her first love. Elizabeth became an old maid after her father refused her permission to marry her half-white beau. This saddened me deeply.

I raised my hand to speak. "Alex, that must've been so awful for Elizabeth. Not to ever meet another man she wanted to marry."

Alex chuckled. "Not really. *Aunt Liz* had many suitors. But after a while, she said she was glad she'd not taken that step. Men were nothing but a headache." Everyone laughed.

There were other questions asked. And then Alex told us how important it was to keep our history alive by questioning older members of our family. We needed to probe, make discoveries about where we came from, see how that contributed to who we were, and process where that knowledge would take us both as individuals, and as a people.

Something stirred inside me, but I wasn't quite sure what to make of it. I'd never asked a lot of questions about Granddaddy Hammond, Grandma Rosie, or my mother's childhood. I hadn't needed to. I'd been hearing the stories all my life. Whenever my aunts and uncles gathered together, they would ultimately get around to talking about their daddy, and what it'd been like growing up in their household. The pictures were painted so clearly, I often felt as though I'd been right there with them.

Each of my aunts, except for Aunt Sport, had married dominant, abusive men. But in a weird way, though I feared and despised it, it almost seemed natural. After all, it'd been the only life I'd known, a life I still, albeit unconsciously, wasn't quite sure how to quit.

One day, after completing a particularly gut-wrenching scene, which had me taunting my father in a Jim Crow Dance sequence, members of the cast all applauded. I went back and fell into my chair, emotionally drained, when I heard a voice say, "Young Lady, you're quite the actress. That was superb."

I turned my head and looked into the face of Henry Fonda. A huge grin spread across my face. "Thank you, Mr. Fonda."

I would never forget that moment as long as I lived.

Roots would undoubtedly go on to be one of the major events of my life, but not merely in terms of career. Ultimately, it started the seed that one day would finally bring me to a better and securer sense of self.

I started to notice a shift in Charles. He was drinking more, and a few times I noticed him at parties snorting cocaine. But that seemed to be the rage in Hollywood. It invariably made me think of the ugly times with Dizzy. For now at least, Charles seemed to have it all under control, indulging only on a recreational basis.

Work had almost come to a standstill for my husband. I was working like crazy and I'd come home to find Charles still in his pajamas, waiting by the phone. Charles was only a few years from being almost old enough to be my father. So I found having to support us particularly unsettling.

When Charles landed a part in *Roots* as a character named Doxie Walker, a war buddy of Alex's father, it felt like the tide might be changing.

Charles had been quite vocal about the little interest producers had shown after the many parts he'd auditioned for. Now here was his chance, and I was so proud of him. But the night before he began shooting, Charles hung out with friends until quite late, even coming home drunk. The next day, he showed up on set with bloodshot eyes, and forgetting his lines. When he finally got through it, Charles was brilliant. A testament to the really good actor he was.

It looked like his career might be jumping back into gear. Next, Charles landed a pretty sizable role in the Richard Pryor movie *Stir Crazy*, along with Georg Stanford Brown. But it was only the beginning of the end for us.

When I visited Charles on location, I noticed an obvious difference. Charles was unusually hyper, his eyes dilated and wild-looking. He obviously wasn't drunk, and didn't exude the same kind of attitude as when he'd been snorting cocaine. I didn't know what to think. Charles said he'd been drinking large amounts of coffee to keep himself going, because they'd spent many nights partying in Richard Pryor's hotel room.

What Charles failed to mention was that most of those nights were spent on the pipe, freebasing cocaine.

Things had slowed down a bit when I got a part in a play at The Inner City Cultural Center in Los Angeles. The play was titled *When*

Hell Freezes Over, I'll Skate. The legendary Vinette Carol, who'd directed the Broadway smash, *Your Arms Too Short to Box With God*, would direct the piece.

My jaw dropped on the first day I walked into rehearsal. Standing in a corner talking to Ms. Carol was Glynn. When he looked over and saw me, his smile was so bright. I'd had no idea until then that Glynn would be in the play.

He rushed over and we gave each other a big squeeze. "Look at you. How you doin', Baby?'

"I'm fine, Glynn. What about you?"

"Can't complain... can't complain."

Glynn looked good and it was wonderful to see him again. He'd left Kay, and it'd been in all the press that he'd recently married Aretha Franklin.

"Congratulations, Glynn."

"Thank you, Baby. And it's been a while, but congratulations to you, too."

"Thanks." I felt a brief moment of sadness, wondering what might've been.

But Glynn didn't stick around too long. In fact, he left the play during rehearsals. I came to the conclusion that Vinette Carol was a tyrant and a real control-freak. Obviously Glynn wasn't putting up with any of it. None of the rest of us had the balls to go against Vinette, so we weathered the storm.

The best part about doing *Skate* was meeting a girl who'd become like a sister to me. Conni Marie Brazelton was as cute as a button. Brown-skinned, with large brown eyes, and a big, Jewish-looking nose, she was a dancer and an actress, and so much fun to be around. We took to each other like white on rice. Conni Marie was outgoing and a laugh-a-minute. But she rarely held her tongue. Whatever Conni thought about something, she'd usually comment on it; it was a quality not everyone appreciated. But I loved her, and knew we'd be friends and sisters forever.

After the play closed, work dried up again. But then I got a very important audition for a major movie.

I had my fingers, toes, and everything else I could cross crossed, as I waited anxiously to hear whether or not I'd gotten the part. The movie was *Cross Creek*, starring Mary Steenburgen, being directed by Martin Ritt. My audition with Mary Steenburgen had gone well and I was hopeful. I was up against two other actresses, my dear friend, Lynne Moody, and Alfre Woodard.

This time the phone call wouldn't be in my favor. I'd lost the role to Alfre Woodard, who'd go on to be nominated for a best supporting actress Oscar for her stellar performance.

I couldn't understand it, but the potential of great things happening after my dramatic turn in *Roots* didn't immediately come to fruition. I was getting frustrated about not working. What else would I do if my career went no further?

One day I was watching one of my favorite soap operas, *All My Children*. The show had brought on a new character named Jesse Hubbard. The actor, Darnell Williams, who was portraying Jesse, was easy to watch. He was not only gorgeous, but also wonderful as the street kid from the wrong side of the tracks who was sent to live with his upscale relatives. Each and every day I kept waiting to see whom the show would bring on as Jesse's love interest. And then it hit me!

I made an immediate call to my New York agent with what I thought was my bright idea. Certainly the show intended to bring on a girlfriend for Jesse down the line. As it turned out, the show was way ahead of me. They were already on their last round of call-backs for the role of Angie Baxter. ABC agreed to fly me to New York to test for the part.

When I arrived at the *All My Children* studio, I saw only one other girl waiting in the lobby. The casting agent, Joan D'Incecco, informed me that all the other actresses had been ruled out, except the stunning girl standing down the hall. Joan pointed and said, "That's your competition."

She was absolutely beautiful with a head full of golden curls. I wanted to get right back on the plane and head home. Then I noticed the guy my competition was talking to; it was *Jesse!* Well, really Darnell Williams. He was even more handsome in person.

I was called into the producer, Jorn Winther's office, to read two scenes with Darnell. "Debbi," Mr. Winther said, "This is Darnell. Darnell, this is Debbi Morgan."

Darnell and I said hello to each other and then sat down to read the scenes depicting when Jesse and Angie meet for the first time. I felt very comfortable with Darnell, as if I'd been playing Angie to his Jesse all my life. When we were done, I stood up to shake his hand. Darnell said it was a pleasure and left the room.

"When are you leaving for California?" Jorn asked.

"My flight is in two hours." I was due back for a big commercial audition. I wouldn't even get to see Mom and Terry.

"Can you be back here on Tuesday?" Today was Thursday. "Because the part is yours if you want it."

I couldn't believe it! Just like that! "Yes, Mr. Winther, I certainly can."

When I stepped out of Jorn's office, I saw Darnell talking to the girl who'd been my competition up until a few minutes ago. I called him over. "Darnell, may I speak to you for a minute?"

The other actress moved off down the hall.

"Yeah, what's up?"

"Yorn offered me the part of Angie! Isn't that great?! I'll be starting on Tuesday."

"Wow...uh...yeah. That's uh...that's great. Congratulations." And Darnell walked away.

Was I reading him right? Darnell didn't seem thrilled at all about my getting the role. I'd find out later that he hadn't been. Darnell had been pushing for the other actress, a good friend of his by the name of Kasi Lemmons.

In due time, Darnell and Kasi would become my lifelong friends. And one day, Kasi would become a gifted screenwriter and director, giving me my best screen role ever, in the haunting film, *Eve's Bayou.*

Chapter 36

New York City
1982

"Darnell? Kim? Are you guys going to be able to come to my opening?"

Darnell and Kim Delaney (she played Jenny and would garner much fame in the future as one of the stars of *NYPD Blue*) were sitting in the rehearsal room, running lines.

"Are you going, Darnell?"

"Yeah, I'm planning to."

"Well, why don't we go together?"

"Sounds like a plan. We'll be there, Deb. You'd better be good, too, or you gonna hear us in the back booing you off the stage!"

I snatched off the cap Darnell always wore backward as Jesse, and swatted him playfully.

I was delighted with my role on *All My Children*. When I was cast in *Roots*, the casting director, Reuben Cannon, sent me a lovely note. In it, he said that *Roots* would make me a household name. Actually, I'd have *All My Children* to thank for that.

Charles and I were doing an NEC play together called *Colored People's Time.* He'd been instrumental into my getting into the show because of his strong ties with the theater. We'd be doing a series of vignettes that encompassed the black experience in America over a span of forty years. There were about six other cast members in the show, one of whom was a talented actress and songstress named Jackée Harry. After moving on to unbelievable fame and fortune in the hit television series, *227*, she'd simply be known as Jackée. Jackée and I became immediate friends; she was, and still is, sassy and funny, funny...funny...funny.

New York had turned into a big, bright spot for me. I was appearing on a hit soap opera and was about to perform in a Negro Ensemble Company production.

But there were a few lows. Mom and Sam had moved out of the apartment on the Grand Concourse into a ritzy development in Riverdale. Charles and I had been living with them for the past two months. It'd been hard finding the time to look for an apartment with our tight schedules. As soon as the play went up and rehearsals were over, however, I knew we'd be able to find something.

Mom was not in a good place. She seemed to be upset when Sam was at home, and upset when he wasn't. But Sam didn't seem to be home much at all. Once Charles and I started running in the play, we wouldn't get home until way after midnight. Hours later, I'd often wake to the sound of Sam just coming in.

A few times we overheard my mother ranting and raving about the rent being late, and Sam not giving her enough money for food. Mom was rightfully angry, but her tirades were extraordinary. What made it worse was that Sam would be just as calm as she was irate, saying to my mother, "Why are you carrying on like that? I'll take care of the rent. I'll give you the money you need for food." I felt Sam was manipulating the situation, making Mom out to be this horrible shrew.

Charles and I were hardly there, and always ate out. But when I tried to offer Mom money, she flatly refused. "Sam makes tons of money! You don't need to give me anything. He's being an asshole! I'm getting fed up with his shit!"

But according to Terry, Sam would come home with expensive jewelry, along with alcohol and some pills for Mom to pop, and then it'd be lovey-dovey all over again.

Terry tried as best she could to get on with her life. She was attending Fordham University in the Bronx, and had begun dating Denzel Washington; yes, *the* Denzel Washington. My sister's relationship with the future superstar would last for two years, dissolving after Terry moved away to attend school in Tennessee, and Denzel subsequently moved off to Hollywood. Denzel would tell me many years later that my sister had broken his heart.

The play Charles and I had been doing at NEC got great reviews. I also managed to find us a beautiful loft-style apartment in a newly constructed building on Horatio Street in the West Village; it was a relief to have our own place.

After Charles and I closed in the play, he was back to being idle. He wasn't working and started keeping late nights, hanging out with some unsavory characters.

I'd been working pretty steadily on *All My Children*, but hadn't as yet been offered a contract. So when I got the television movie, *The Jesse Owens Story*, portraying Jesse's wife, *All My Children* had to figure a way to work around my movie schedule. I jetted back and forth between Louisiana and New York a number of times to tape episodes of the soap. I was making good money and it was being spent as quickly as I made it, but not by me.

When I wrapped the movie and came home, I was shocked to see that our thirty thousand dollars savings had dwindled down to five!

Charles wasn't giving me any straight answers about where the money had gone, and he was extremely nasty when I questioned him about it.

Whenever I was home, he seemed to be in a foul mood, or he'd come in during the wee hours, drunk. I was getting to the point where I didn't relish being around Charles at all. I finally opened a separate bank account.

It seemed like Mom and I were running a race to see who'd get to the finish line of their marriage first. After discovering that Sam was cheating yet again, Mom won the race, but only by a matter of months. As Charles's acting career continued to plunge, he'd taken an even deeper plunge into freebasing crack cocaine. Our marriage was all downhill from there, and then it was over. However, it gives me great joy and pleasure to know that Charles has left that lifestyle way behind, and has been completely free of drugs and alcohol for over twenty years. It also gives me great pleasure to be able to call Charles a friend today.

After Mom's marriage was over, she began to have very erratic behavior patterns: temper-tantrums, loud outbursts, and crying fits over many inconsequential things. Terry and I made a number of unsuccessful attempts to get Mom into therapy. It always backfired after she'd tell the therapist that the problem was my sister and me, and then go off the deep end when they tried to address her issues.

To this day, my mother is very much a product of the emotional traumas experienced throughout her life; we all are, however, our symptoms manifest in different ways.

Mom continued to have uncontrolled outbursts, going from loving and sweet one moment, to being downright nasty the next; her behavior often unpredictable and quite embarrassing.

Terry had a strong personality and was fearless. She refused to let anyone take advantage of her. But my sister was often distant; never the kissy, huggy, feely type that Mom and I were.

Of course, it's been clear what my symptoms continued to be, even though I didn't manifest in the almost bipolar sickness that had taken hold of my mother, or the emotionally detached attitude of my sister, I had my own demons to fight. But I was an actress, and had early on learned to wear the mask that hid my demons from the rest of the world.

Chapter 37

"How do you like living by yourself now that you and Charles are over?"

"You know, Darnell, I like it. I'm happier than I've been in a long time. My best friend, Conni Marie, is coming out from L.A. to spend a few months with me. I can't wait for you to meet her. She's a hoot."

"Cool. So are you still moving into that carriage house over on West Tenth Street?'

"Yeah, I am! D, it's great! It was built in 1836, has two stories, and there's even a fireplace! You know I'm going to need your help with the move."

"No problem."

"We'd better hurry up or we won't be able to find seats!"

Darnell and I were headed downtown to the Ziegfeld movie theater. We'd become so close as friends that we'd started hanging out together outside of work.

When we walked into the darkened theater, the coming attractions had already started. Luckily, we found two seats off the aisle in the middle section. About two hours later, Darnell and I slowly walked out of the theater with the rest of the crowd. We were talking about trying to find a place to eat when we began to hear a low murmur.

"Is that Jesse and Angie?" "Hey, that looks like Jesse and Angie." "I think that's Jesse; and look, I think that's Angie with him." "That is them! Oh my God! It's Jesse and Angie!!!!"

For all the time Darnell and I had been on *All My Children* together, we'd been pretty insulated. We had no idea of how huge we'd become as a black, daytime super couple. We were at the height of our popularity, and this was the first time we'd been out together in such a large crowd.

We were both stunned and a bit frightened as the pandemonium started to set in. Then things began to get downright scary. I mean, it's not like we were Michael and Janet Jackson, but the way the crowd began to descend on us, one might've thought we were.

People were grabbing at us and screaming our names. Not our real names—our character names. *"Jesse! Angie! Jesseeee!"* I thought the women were actually going to rip Darnell's clothes off. A couple of security guards ran over to investigate the commotion.

Darnell grabbed my hand. "Debbi, run!! Runnnn!!!!!!"

We bolted out of the theater, running as fast as we could. We heard what sounded like cattle stampeding behind us as we were chased down the street. *"Jesseeee! Angieee!"*

We kept on running I don't know how many blocks with our hands locked together. Darnell led us through an alleyway as we ran for our lives. Suddenly, we realized we were no longer being followed and finally stopped. We were panting and totally shocked by what we'd experienced. Darnell and I looked at each other and said, *"Oh...shit...!"* as we laughed breathlessly.

Not long after that incident of fan pandemonium, Darnell went on to win a Daytime Emmy Award as Jesse Hubbard. It would be one of three he'd garner during his six-year run on the show, more than any other African American male to date. I'd get my first nomination a year later, but wouldn't win...just yet.

Conni Marie and I sat in the Cort Theater on Broadway, as the curtain went up for the first act of *Ma Rainey's Black Bottom*. I hadn't heard much about this play, but she'd talked me into accompanying her on that Sunday afternoon.

The play opened with three older men who were supposed to be musicians getting ready for a recording session. I recognized two of the three actors. One was Conni Marie's friend, the talented Joe Seneca, and another actor named Leonard Jackson, who'd played the cantankerous father in the black comedy film, *Five on the Black Hand Side*. I wasn't familiar with the third actor, Robert Judd.

The three men burst onto the stage and then proceeded to get into an energetic conversation about a trumpeter named Levee who was decidedly late. They talked about the probability that Levee had probably stopped off to buy some new shoes. Apparently Levee always spent every dime he made on women or new shoes.

The way the musicians set up the character of Levee, I imagined some tall, handsome, slick-looking guy appearing onstage. But out hopped this chunky, kind of funny-looking guy of medium height. This was Levee, and according to the playbill, the actor portraying him was a man named Charles S. Dutton.

At first Conni Marie and I didn't know what to make of this actor. He skipped around the stage, and kept kicking his foot out, like he might be mentally challenged. At one point, I turned to Conni and whispered, "Where'd they get this guy from? He's awful."

But as the play went on, I was slowly swept up by the sheer brilliance of Charles S. Dutton. The character of Levee turned out to be a frightening human being. He'd carried around this tormented pain from a childhood trauma, which ultimately causes him to murder the musician, Toledo, in the final act of the play. But instead of playing Levee as this one-note, dangerous guy, Charles brought vulnerability, lovability, and an almost childlike quality to the role, which explained his constant kicking up of his foot and his skipping around the stage.

At the curtain call, Conni Marie and I jumped to our feet along with the rest of the audience, giving the cast and the play a resounding standing ovation. I clapped so hard my hands were stinging. Although the entire cast was no less than outstanding, my applause was mostly directed toward the magnificent Charles S. Dutton.

"Come on; let's go backstage so I can say hello to Joe."

I followed Conni down the alleyway to the stage door. "Conni, can you believe that guy who played Levee? He was incredible!"

"I know. He was a little scary, though. But he was funny the way he kept kicking his foot out."

The person at the stage door allowed Conni and I to go on up to the third floor to Joe Seneca's room. But when we got to the second landing, I saw Levee, or rather Charles S. Dutton, coming out of his dressing room. He looked directly at me with a big ole grin on his face.

"Hey, I know who you are; you're Angie!"

I was a bit taken aback. He didn't seem like the type of guy who sat in front of the TV watching soap operas. He was a big hunk of a guy, not my type at all. But his large carriage was in direct contradiction to his little boy charm. He proceeded to kick his leg out like he'd done onstage and he was swaying back and forth, rubbing his palms together. "So did you like the play?!"

"Yes! Of course! You were so great! I mean, absolutely wonderful! I loved you!"

Charles was looking at me with big, twinkling eyes draped with heavy bags under them, and a smile filled with vampire-looking teeth. He was the ugliest, cutest person I'd ever seen.

"I'm sorry; I didn't even introduce myself. My name is Debbi Morgan."

He smiled with those fangs called teeth. "I know your name. I called you Angie, but I knew who you were. I've seen you in lots of things.

You were great in *Roots*." He was grinning from ear-to-ear. "My name is Charles Dutton, but everyone calls me Roc."

I smiled. "Hi, Roc. Oh, and I'm sorry; this is my girlfriend, Conni Marie."

Conni laughed. "I thought I'd wait until you two finished appreciating each other."

Roc extended his hand. "Hey, Conni Marie. So you're the one who was sitting out there with that big red hat on?"

"What you doin' noticing my red hat? You were supposed to be in the moment."

He laughed. "True. True. But, Babe, that hat was so big and red it took me out of the moment, but just for a moment."

We all laughed and Conni excused herself to run up to Joe's room.

"This play was so wonderful. I'm going to tell the cast over at *All My Children* that they have to come and see it."

Roc smiled sweetly. He was so funny-looking to me. It actually made him adorable. "Do you think you'll come back again?" Now he seemed almost shy, which was also adorable, being that he was such a big hunk of a guy.

"Oh, I'm definitely coming back."

"That would be great! Let me give you my number and I'll make sure you get great house seats."

I brought Darnell, Kim, about six other cast mates, and also Carol and Vanessa. I took everyone backstage to meet Roc after the show. They all gushed at his stellar performance, just as I'd done.

Darnell and I had been the last to say goodbye when Roc stopped us by calling my name. Darnell didn't figure it was anything private, so he walked back with me.

Again, this big bear of a guy seemed shy as he asked softly, "Would you mind if I take you out to lunch?"

I was a little thrown. I mean Roc was incredible in the play, and he seemed so sweet, but I didn't necessarily want to go out anywhere with him.

Yet, I'd been so impressed by his performances, not to mention he'd gotten us great orchestra seats. "Uh...uh, when?"

"How about tomorrow? I don't have a matinee to do."

"Tomorrow? Uh...okay. Okay...I tell you what. I'm taping tomorrow, so why don't you come over to ABC at one o'clock? We're right at the corner of Sixty-Seventh and Columbus. We'll go somewhere near the studio."

"Deal. Deal. I'll be looking forward to it."

Darnell and I said goodbye again and left the theater.

"Debbi! I think he's trying to hit on you!"

"You think? I certainly hope not. Maybe he was simply being nice because I came back to the show and brought you guys."

"Deb! Come on. Did you see the way he was looking at you? Are you really going to have lunch with him?"

"I guess so, but that's about all I'll be having with him. I hope he doesn't get any bright ideas."

Roc showed up at the studio at one p.m. sharp, wearing jeans, a dark brown leather jacket, and a cap. His permed hair was sticking out of the sides of the cap, which looked rather comical. I assumed his hair was only permed for the role of Levee.

Roc stood by the door in the lobby as Kim DeLaney, Laurence Lau, Lisa Wilkinson, Kathleene Noone, Darnell and I walked out to meet him. When I saw Roc standing there with that huge grin on his face, looking like this big, lovable teddy bear, I felt a bit guilty. He'd been very sweet to invite me out to lunch, and here I'd felt the need to drag the others with me. If Roc were a bit perturbed by this gesture, I'd certainly understand.

"Hi, Roc. Listen, I hope you don't mind, but I've invited some of the cast to go to lunch with us."

"Of course not! That'd be great! How's everybody doing?"

The cast said hello and once again expressed their amazement at Roc's performance. What I found amazing was Roc's down-to-earthness. Sitting at the long table at BBQ's on Seventy-Ninth and Columbus, Roc shared snippets of his rough upbringing. I gathered that he'd been a mischievous kid who'd had a few minor run-ins with the law, but I focused on his current achievements and personality. He was a major splash on Broadway, and though I sensed Roc had a great deal of humility about his newfound success, I could tell he couldn't help but bask a tiny amount in the glory of his own personal praise. Why shouldn't he? I found him to be a real man for whom I could develop a deep respect.

Hanging on to Roc's every word, I hadn't eaten a morsel of food from my plate. He was quite talkative, but in a way that held his audience captive. He was extremely articulate and expressive, conveying his words with such warmth and a natural sense of humor. There was no mistaking Roc's intelligence, but what stood out even more was that undeniable, exuberant charm.

At one point, Roc turned his attention to me, and whispered, with no lure or come-on, "How are you doing, Pretty Girl?"

It was like I'd been whacked with a truckload of cement! And suddenly the cute ogre became the handsome prince. Of all the beautiful men I'd fallen for, I couldn't ever remember falling like this. It was so unexpected. I had sort of an out-of-body experience as I surveyed the faces around the table, staring at Roc with the same unmitigated awe. I realized I wasn't the only one caught in his spell.

I walked back to the studio quite light on my feet. "Roc is a pretty remarkable guy, Debbi," said Larry Lau, who played Greg on the show.

Everyone nodded their heads in agreement.

"Yeah, Larry, I think so, too," I managed to say.

The cast walked on ahead, but Darnell and I lagged behind. Putting my arm through his, I said, "D, I'm completely blown away by this guy."

"Yeah, I can see why. He's pretty cool and real interesting, too."

"I hope he calls me. He asked for my number."

Darnell started laughing. "First you were hoping the guy wouldn't get any bright ideas; now you're worrying about whether or not he's going to call. Believe me, I really don't think you have to worry about that."

Darnell was right. Roc called me later that same day in my dressing room, and every day after that. We'd talk for hours on the phone during the day, and then on the phone again into the wee hours after he got home from the theater. Both our schedules were a bit hectic. We got together as often as we could. Pretty much we ended up falling in love over the phone!

Roc had been fortunate to get a Broadway lead right out of Yale. But fortune had little to do with it. It was more the fact that Roc was simply so gifted.

We went out to dinner and a movie a few times, but it really didn't matter what we did, or where we went. Merely being in the man's presence was soooo exhilarating.

And then, on one of his dark nights from the theater, we were at my place when things began getting pretty hot and heavy. Roc and I were about to christen my trundle bed when Conni Marie bounced up the stairs. I hadn't expected Conni until much later, or I would've respectfully shown Roc to my bedroom.

"Hey! What in the hell is going on up in here?"

Roc and I scrambled for our clothes as we all started laughing at Conni Marie's jokingly authoritative tone.

But our love fest wouldn't continue in my bedroom. Roc said he was going to go ahead and leave because he needed to get home.

There was something in the way Roc said, "I need to get home." The feeling I had was visceral, and for the first time, it made me question whether or not he was seeing someone else. There was that familiar pang in the crevices of my belly.

Chapter 38

I was relaxing on a sofa in the green room eating a toasted bagel when I noticed a copy of *People* lying on the table. Imagine my surprise when I picked it up, and came face-to-face with a picture of Roc, smiling, with a white bird in his hand! Then I read the caption: *From Jail to Yale.*

What?

I sat back on the sofa, flipped through the magazine and immersed myself in the main article, reading it from start to finish. Roc talked about being born in Baltimore, Maryland, and his love for animals. I continued reading to discover he'd had much more than a few teenage run-ins with the law. He'd spent seven-and-a-half years in prison for armed bank robbery, and manslaughter...manslaughter?!!! I was floored! Roc had stabbed a guy to death in a street fight! But what really struck me was not the crimes he'd committed in his life, or the years he'd spent in prison, but the way he'd ultimately turned his life around.

I'd been in committed relationships with men who'd started out good, and then decided to wreck their lives. Here was a man who'd grown up in the inner city, lost his father as a young teenager, and then succumbed to the streets. But after spending years in prison, being a gang leader, starting revolts, and being shoved into solitary confinement, Roc did what only a very few would ever do. He completely turned his life around. Roc said he'd found his humanity. He studied and had gotten his GED, and then began taking college courses. There was a young woman allowed to teach acting to some of the inmates; she would point Roc toward his true calling.

Once released, he auditioned for and was accepted as an undergraduate into the Yale School of Drama under the tutelage of the renowned and respected Lloyd Richards. Roc graduated from Yale with honors. He'd made a big burst onto the *Great White Way*, starring on Broadway.

Since I already had such an appreciation for Roc's talent and had been charmed and wooed by his persona, instead of feeling afraid or ashamed, I was proud of him. How many people can say that they've come out of prison and completely turned their lives around?

I smiled as I read through the accolades declaring my new beau the toast of Hollywood. Until I read the part about his girlfriend. According to this very recent article, Roc had been living with his girl*friend*, a woman named Angela Bassett, who would one day be nominated for an Oscar in her breakout role as Tina Turner in *What's Love Got to Do With It.*

Damn! Damn! Damn!

I was too angry, embarrassed, and hurt to speak to Roc. I let the answering machine do the screening, avoiding Roc's phone calls for weeks.

I'd gotten an opportunity to flesh out even more of Roc's lies of omission in the following days. Tom Wright, who played Jesse's brother on *All My Children*, had been off for a while, and was not around when the cast went to see the play, or when we'd gone with Roc to lunch.

When I saw him in the studio hallway, I gladly welcomed him back.

"Hey, Deb. Yeah, I was wondering how long it was going to be before *All My Children* wrote me into another script."

"Hey, did you get that message I left you about all of us going to see *Ma Rainey's Black Bottom?*"

"Yeah, Debbi, I did. I'm sorry. I completely forgot to call you back on that. But I've seen *Ma Rainey* a couple of times. I saw it when it opened here on Broadway. And I'd already seen the production when it was up at Yale. Roc Dutton's a buddy of mine."

"Really, Tom?! I didn't know that."

"Yeah, I been knowing Roc and Angie since we all met up at Yale together."

Tom piqued my interest and I suddenly went fishing for more clues. "Angie is his girlfriend, right?"

"Yeah. Roc's ole lady."

"Oh." I smiled, sadly. "They live together, right?"

"Yea, they live together. Why?"

"Oh, nothin'."

"Uh... uh. What's that look on your face? Did you get to meet Roc when you went to the play?"

"Yeah, I did... I've been seeing Roc, and he never said anything to me about Angie. We talk on the phone all the time and she's never answered the phone when I've called."

"That's because she's been up at Yale all summer doing several productions. I believe she got back yesterday."

That explained why Roc *needed* to get home. I heard the telephone ringing in my dressing room, "Excuse me a minute, Tom." I ran into my room and grabbed up the phone.

"Hello."

"Hi, Pretty Girl."

I should've been telling him where he could go with his *Pretty Girl* bit. But now, anger was the furthest emotion from my heart. I was incredibly sad. If ever I thought someone was meant to be in my life, it was Roc. I needed answers.

"Are you there, Pretty Girl?"

"Yeah, Dutton. I'm here."

"Listen, I wanted to let you know that Angie's back in town."

"Angie?" I heard myself say, sounding like a robot. "Who's Angie?"

"This girl I'm living with. But listen, I don't want to get into it over the phone. Can I meet you at your house after the show? I want to explain to you what's going on."

"Sure, that's fine." My automated voice cracked.

"Hey, don't sound like that. It's all cool. I'll see you tonight."

But I chickened out. I couldn't bear to hear Roc tell me his woman was back in town, and that we'd have to sneak around or, even worse, call the whole thing off. No, the easiest thing was not to see him. I couldn't take confronting Roc in person.

I was glad we hadn't slept together; that would've made the closure even harder to take. But it also let me know how deeply I cared, and that my feelings were pure, untainted by sex.

I phoned the theater and left a message saying something unexpected had come up, and I had to cancel.

Conni Marie had left earlier that morning on a European tour that was starring a hilarious actress and comedienne named Jennifer Lewis.

So I sat alone, listening to the answering machine. Roc made five unsuccessful attempts to reach me...but he did reach me, showing up on my doorstep the following night.

"Listen, Pretty Girl," he started, before I had a chance to object. "Just let me say this, and if you decide you no longer want to continue us, I'll have to accept that. When I first laid eyes on you, I knew without one ounce of doubt that you were the future I had to have."

Good Lord, he had a way with expressing himself! My heart melted on the spot. I respectfully showed him to my bed. The love we made was sweet and passionate, hard and angry. I screamed from the joy and the pain. And I knew right then and there that whatever Roc offered, I'd accept.

"And for Outstanding Featured Actor in a play, the Tony Award goes to..." I squeezed Roc's hand and held my breath; waiting for the name I just knew they would say: *Charles S. Dutton*. But I saw the formation of her mouth as it rounded to say, *Ro...bert*. Everyone was on their feet clapping for the actor, Robert Morse, who'd won the Tony for his one-man show, *Tru*.

I tucked my hand back into Roc's and whispered, "You were robbed, Honey."

He leaned over and kissed my cheek. "It's all right, Pretty Girl."

Roc and I went to the after-party and I was in a bigger funk than he was. His losing made it somewhat difficult to join in the gaiety of the evening. But Roc smiled, shook hands, and extended his congratulations to the winners, including Robert Morse. I was so proud of him because I realized how much he'd wanted to win, but he handled the loss with such dignity.

I was also proud to be his lady, and happy that I no longer had to share him. Roc had broken up with Angie, and was now living with me. When I questioned him about what'd happened, Roc was brief and to the point.

"Like I told you, Pretty Girl, Angie and I kind of fell into a relationship. We'd been roommates and friends. But we both knew this thing wasn't going to last forever. I was honest with her. I told her that I'd met someone, and that I wanted to move on with my life. Angie was cool with that. She understood. But I'm glad that I waited until she got some work. She got this new gig on a soap opera, and she's really excited. I didn't want to feel like I was leaving her out there high and dry. And the most important thing was that I wanted to leave the relationship the same way I went in, as friends."

But I'd one day learn this story was far from the truth.

The actual fact was that Roc had told Angie he wanted to get his own place, but they'd still remain a couple. When Roc was nominated for his Tony Award for *Ma Rainey*, Angie had gone out and purchased a dress in anticipation of accompanying her man to the awards. However, Roc lied and told Angie he'd only been given one ticket, and that his mom would be disappointed if he didn't take her. Angie sucked it up and said she understood. On the night of the Tony Awards, she sat in front of the television with many of their friends from Yale, hoping to hear Roc's name called to the podium. But Angie looked on in horror and embarrassment as the camera closed in on me giving Roc a kiss on the cheek when his category was called.

Her exact words were, "Well, that damn sure ain't his mama!" I'd get this straight from the horse's mouth many years later when Angie and her husband, the talented Courtney B. Vance, wrote their autobiography. Angie and I sat up for hours filling each other in on all the lies we'd each been told while Courtney sat in a corner laughing his ass off about how we'd each been duped!

It was difficult to believe the kind of man Roc used to be. I'd never seen a hint of his former self, except through his character in *Ma Rainey*. But one night, Roc and I were walking down Eighth Street eating Häagen-Dazs ice cream cones. We were laughing and talking when someone yelled out, "Hey, Angie, come here! Where's Jesse?!"

A bunch of guys in a car were stopped at a light. Roc and I kept on walking.

"What? You can't speak to nobody, bitch?!"

I looked up and saw the ice-cold glaze in Roc's eyes. He didn't say a word; he ran over to the car and went to snatch open the door.

"Roc!" I yelled.

The light changed and as the idiots sped off, Roc threw the remainder of his cone through the window, smacking one boy in the head.

I was glad nothing more serious had happened that night. However, I did feel a tinge of excitement knowing I had a man who could and would protect me in any situation. That same sense of protection had also drawn me to Butch and Dizzy.

Yet, somehow, it was different with Roc. Of course if he were still a criminal, I'd have wanted no part of him. But he wasn't. And thank God he wasn't a drug addict either. Finally, I'd gotten rid of that association in my life. Like me, Roc didn't smoke or do drugs. He drank, but only on occasion.

As the relationship grew, I began to sense something else with Roc. He possessed what no other man I'd ever been with had had—a controlled, dangerous sense of power, lying right beneath the surface. I found this aura even more of a turn-on than being with a man who might've been very physically handsome.

Roc was *from* the streets and *of* the streets. I was *from* the streets, too, so being with someone like Roc wasn't completely foreign to me. But the fact that Roc had risen above all that, yet still had that edge, that quiet danger, was so talented, so intelligent, and had people falling at his feet in their praise of him, became like a drug to me, extremely hypnotic and sexual.

My mother, on the other hand, was not the least bit misled. She didn't find Roc's metamorphosis at all endearing. Shortly after the

People article was released, she called me in hysterics. "Debbi! You didn't tell me this guy you've been seeing spent ten years in prison! I swear, after all these bums you've been with, now you want to end up with some jailbird?!"

"Where did you get your information, Mom?"

"Carmelita read about him in some magazine." Carmelita was one of Mom's best friends, *also the bearer of hot topics.*

"First of all, Dutton was in prison for seven-and-a-half years, not ten."

"Oh, well, that makes a big difference."

I ignored my mother's sarcasm. "And secondly, did Carmelita mention how the article talked about him turning his life around? Or did you simply take the fact that he'd spent time in prison and run with it?"

"Listen, I'll tell you this. You need to take the time and find out about these men before you go getting involved with them! When are you going to learn, Debbi?!"

"How can you, of all people, tell me about my choices in men?" I fumed.

"That's why I can tell you, because of my own experiences!"

"I don't see where *experience* has done you any good, Mom!"

"It's taught me a lot, thank you very much. That's why I'm trying to teach you. I mean, come on, Debbi! This guy killed somebody! That scares the hell out of me! Anyone who's capable of doing that once can certainly do it again! What if he gets mad at you one day and decides to kill you, too?"

"Will you stop it?! That's not even a remote possibility!"

"How the hell do you know?"

"I'm not listening to any more of this. I'm hanging up."

"Let me say one more thing. You're so convinced this man has turned his life around. Even if that's so, I'd like to know something. How serious are you getting with him?"

"Very serious."

"I certainly hope you don't plan on marrying him. If you do, I hope to God you don't plan on having any children. Because if those kids end up looking anything like him, they're going to be *messed* up!"

I slammed the phone down and began to hyperventilate; I was so angry. The phone rang about seven times, but I refused to answer.

I'd been involved with two drug addicts who'd caused me a wealth of pain, but Mom had never reacted so adversely to either one of them.

After that nightmarish phone conversation with my mother, which was always in the back of my head, I went about trying to enjoy my growing relationship with Roc.

Roc was a big lover of animals. Not long after he moved in, we got a huge German Shepherd we named Rocco; after his loving master. Having a large dog, having a dog, period, especially in the small carriage house, took some getting used to. But it was sweet watching Roc care for him.

Rocco got sick one night and had severe diarrhea. The floor and the rug in the parlor were a mess. But Roc became a doting nursemaid as he tended to Rocco and got him all cleaned up, whispering gently, "It's all right, Champ. You're going to be okay. First thing tomorrow, I'm going to get you to the vet and have you all fixed up." Then Roc cleaned and disinfected the parlor floor from top to bottom.

But poor Rocco ended up having severe hip dysplasia. It became impossible for him to walk up and down the stairs. Sadly, we ended up sending Rocco off to a dog farm. Dutton wanted to get another dog, immediately. But since we were saving to buy a house in New Jersey, I convinced him to wait.

I saw how much Dutton loved animals (along the way, I'd begun calling him Dutton instead of Roc. This amused him because he said it's what his father had been called.) I also saw how much he cared for his family, especially his mom. Dutton took me to Baltimore to meet Gloria Dutton. I saw at once where he'd gotten his physical appearance. His mother was also short and round, jovial and warm, like her son. It was quite clear how proud Gloria was of Dutton, and how much she adored him. I also learned what a saving grace Dutton was to his mother. Her other two children, Jackie, Dutton's baby sister, and Vernon, Dutton's older brother, were both heroin addicts. If Dutton hadn't chosen to turn his life around, Gloria would've lost every one of her precious children to the streets. It was quite clear that Dutton was her Golden Child.

Gloria and I hit it off immediately, and from the start, I began calling her Mom Gloria. I also hit it off with Dutton's Aunt Gwendolyn, his mother's older sister. You could tell Gwendolyn had been quite a beauty in her day, and was still an attractive woman. Gloria and Gwendolyn had one other sister who was the baby girl, Anne. Dutton's grandmother had been a prostitute, and her three daughters had been fathered by three different johns. Gloria was the only one whose father had been black.

Dutton's older brother, Vernon, was nice enough. But he always seemed to be slipping in and out of places. Because of my own experience around heroin addicts, I could see Vernon's addiction immediately. But in Dutton's younger sister, Jackie, I saw a deep sadness that seemed to go far beyond her addiction. Jackie was a very large woman, and as far as I could tell, not at all comfortable in her body. Her addiction seemed to go hand-in-hand with her deep sense of insecurity and low self-esteem. She spoke very little whenever I was around her, and never seemed to look me directly in the eye.

Mom Gloria called our house many nights in tears and frustration, telling Dutton about the loud screaming in her basement. Jackie and Vernon would get into some pretty heated confrontations over drugs. Gloria would ask Dutton to intervene. At times, Dutton would threaten that his brother and sister better not return to their mother's home. Other times, he'd hop a plane and rush back to Baltimore trying to get one of them out of jail or into rehab.

The depth of Dutton's love for his brother and sister was quite apparent, and I saw how much his inability to change their lives pained him.

Dutton's love for his nephew, Jackie's young son, was especially heartfelt. Dutton made sure that he sent his mother money to help take care of her grandson. It was a curse for the young boy to see both mother and uncle so often in the throes of their addiction.

Trips home to Baltimore were made as often as possible. Dutton always made sure to spend ample time with his nephew. He was determined his nephew would not follow in the footsteps of his mother and uncle.

After getting to know Dutton's family, I got to know a few of his Yale friends. One of Dutton's very best friends, a young actor by the name of Reggie Cathy, was a natural comedian. Another one of Dutton's good friends was D. Dwight, as Dutton referred to him. He was a musician studying to go into the ministry. He was warm and affable, and anyone who met Dwight liked him right off the bat. I was no exception. I became immersed in Dutton's life with his friends and his family, namely his mom and his aunt, whom I adored and who seemed to adore me. I only wished my family had given Dutton the same reception.

Recently, I'd gotten a call from Terry. It'd been a while since we'd spoken, so I was excited to hear from her. But my excitement quickly waned as she brought up her concern about Dutton.

"Debbi, Mommy told me about this guy you're seeing. She said he'd been in prison for a long time, and that he'd actually murdered somebody! Mommy's really scared for you."

I could hear the fret in my sister's voice, and at that moment, felt like murdering my mother. But at least Terry was open to reason and listened to what I had to say.

I told my sister that once Dutton was out of prison, he never looked back. And then I read her Dutton's *People* magazine interview.

Terry admitted that my mother had put her own spin on the situation. By the end of our conversation, my sister said she and her husband, Charles, would try to make a trip to New York over the next month or two. Terry wanted to meet Dutton for herself, and see *Ma Rainey* before it closed.

Dutton wanted to know when my mother was coming to the play. It'd be closing in two months and he wondered why she hadn't been to see it. Embarrassed, I admitted, "My mother heard about the *People* interview. We got into an argument because of how she felt about my being with someone who'd been in prison. I'm not speaking to her right now."

My man put his arms around me. "Hey, Pretty Girl, that's your mom. I don't want you not speaking to her because of me."

"But her attitude is totally unfair! She doesn't even know you."

He looked at me with a stern expression on his face. "Pretty Girl, if you were my daughter, I wouldn't want you seeing me either."

"You wouldn't?"

"No, I wouldn't. Your mother loves you, and I understand very well how she feels. It's okay. You need to give her some time. But don't expect she's going to jump on my bandwagon anytime soon. I'm going to have to show her how much I love you, and how well I'm going to take care of you."

"You said you love me." Dutton's affirmation made me teary-eyed.

"That's right, Pretty Girl. I do love you."

"I love you, too, more than anything."

"I want you to promise me that you're going to ease up on your mom, okay?" I nodded my head. "In fact, I want you to give her a call. There's no reason you shouldn't be talking to your mother. That's not good, Babe."

I nodded my head again, like an obedient child. And then Dutton swooped me up, and carried me up the stairs. I didn't feel like a child after what happened upstairs; I felt like a woman, a sensuous, erotic woman. And that *was* good.

The next day, I sat down and called my mother. Any other man might've been incensed knowing how Mom had jumped the gun, instead of at least giving him a chance, but not Dutton. Not only wasn't he mad, but he insisted I should be more understanding of my mother's feelings. Christ! I had a gem of a guy and Mom didn't have a clue.

"Hi, Mom. It's me."

"Hello, Debbi," she said dryly. Apparently, she wasn't going to make this easy.

"I want to apologize for the way I spoke to you, Mom. But I was very upset by the things you said."

"And I was upset by the things you said as well. No matter what, I'm still the mother here, and I deserve respect."

"You're the mother, but I'm a grown woman. I'm not a child. I deserve some respect, too. The things you were saying were not—"

"Listen, did you call to apologize, or to start in again telling me what I should or shouldn't have said?"

This wasn't going well. She was getting testy, and so was I.

"Look, Mom, I called to apologize. That's why I called."

"Your apology is accepted."

If I thought for one moment my mother would offer an apology for some of the nasty things she'd said, I had another thing coming. Mom never apologized because she was always right.

"Honey, would you like to come up and have dinner this weekend?"

Reluctantly, I agreed. "Uh...yeah, I guess so."

When I arrived at my mother's that Saturday night, her friend, Carmelita, answered the door.

"Hi, Debbi! Ooo, girl, you look great! Give me a kiss."

Carmelita planted a huge kiss on my cheek. As far as I was concerned, she'd been the one to start this whole blow-up between Mom and me. But I tried not to let my irritation show.

"Hi, Carmelita. I didn't know you'd be here. Is Mom having a dinner party or something?" If she was, why was Carmelita standing here in a pair of jeans and a sweatshirt?

Carmelita ignored my question. "Debbi, it's good to see you! I haven't seen you in ages, Girl!" Carmelita was always so effusive. "Lora is in the bathroom."

I followed Carmelita into the living room. Immediately I noticed the absence of any food aroma. So I went into the kitchen with Carmelita trailing behind me. I opened the fridge to get some juice, and observed there were no pots or pans on the stove.

"So, Debbi, what have you been doing? I've been watching you on the show. You and Jesse are the best things on there, if you ask—"

"I thought Mom was cooking dinner, Carmelita. But I don't see..."

"Don't worry; don't you worry. You'll be having a very nice dinner tonight. In fact, your entire night should be quite wonderful."

At that moment, my mother breezed into the kitchen wearing a long robe. Something didn't feel right.

Carmelita was talking a mile a minute, and Mom joined in the endless chatter. Between the two of them, I couldn't get a word in.

"Mom, I thought you said you were cooking dinner tonight. Where's the food?"

My mother and Carmelita shot conspiratorial glances at each other, and then started giggling. I was not in the mood for Mom's off-the-wall drama.

"I didn't say I was cooking, Debbi. I asked if you wanted to have dinner tonight."

Mom and Carmelita cracked up laughing. I was sick of them both.

I stomped out of the kitchen and headed for the front door. My mother ran behind me and grabbed my arm.

"Listen, young lady, you come back in here and sit down. Goodness gracious! You can't even allow your mom to do something nice for you."

My mother led me back to the living room and gently pulled me down on the sofa. Then she took a deep sigh, for dramatic effect. "Sweetheart...Carmelita and I have set you up with this really wonderful guy. He's going to be here any minute to take you out."

"What?!" I was immediately on my feet. "Who gave you the right to do that?! I'm living with someone!"

"Living with someone?" Now it was Mom's turn to jump to her feet. "I thought you were just seeing that guy! You didn't tell me you were living with him!"

"Why should I, after all the nasty things you said about him? Why do you feel the need to try and control my life, Mom?! You've got some nerve, setting me up on a blind date, and getting Carmelita involved, too!"

"You haven't even met the damn guy yet, Debbi! He works at NBC, and he's rich!"

Now Carmelita joined in. "Yeah, Debbi, he has a great job. He's an executive at NBC, and he's a real nice guy. I think..."

"I don't care what you think, Carmelita! Don't you and my mother understand? I'm involved with someone...we're living together... I'm in love with him. We're actually getting ready to buy a house together."

"Lord, have mercy! You have lost your mind?! The least you can do is go out with this guy tonight. Then maybe you'll come to your senses. He's really handsome, too!"

My mother was a piece of work! I wondered if she'd been popping her pills all day.

"I'm leaving."

The doorman rang the intercom and said there was a gentleman downstairs. Mom said, "Oh great! Send him right up!"

"If you wish to be rude, Debbi, after the guy has driven all the way up here to Riverdale, then you should be the one to tell him."

"Why?! Why should I be the one to tell him anything?! This is all your and Carmelita's doing."

"There's no reason for you to be acting like this! It's not like I knew you'd moved this guy into your house. Perhaps if you'd told me, I wouldn't have tried setting you up with anyone."

By the time I realized my mother was keeping me engaged with her excuses so I wouldn't leave, the doorbell rang.

"Coming! Coming!" Mom gleefully bounced off to the door, leaving me standing there, seething!

Carmelita looked at me sheepishly. "Debbi, he really is a nice guy. I've known him quite a while."

"Then why don't you hook up with him?!"

"Debbi, you know I'm with Paul."

"Carmelita, you know I'm with Dutton!"

Mom walked backed into the living room with a very, very, attractive chocolate man. He was wearing an expensive beige suit with an open-collared, crisp white shirt. And he reeked of money as he stood there holding a colorful bouquet of flowers. I hated flowers, except for exotic ones. They always reminded me of a funeral parlor.

Carmelita threw her arms around the man. "Hey, Carl; howya doin'?"

"Hi, Carmelita; good to see you."

"Honey, this is Carl." My mother's smile was a mile long. "Carl, this is my beautiful, beautiful daughter, Debbi." Mom was dripping saccharine and it was making me sick.

"Hello, Debbi. It's a pleasure to meet you. These are for you." Carl handed over the flowers with his manicured hands.

"Oh, Sweetheart, let me take those and put them in some water. You can pick them up when you get back."

Who the heck said I was going *anywhere* with Carl? I'd never been more livid with my mother. But Carl was standing here, looking like the perfect gentleman. I didn't have the heart to be rude. Certainly none of this was his fault. I gave my mother another slightly disgusted look, and then turned a smile to Carl.

"So, Carl, where are you taking me?"

Mom and Carmelita immediately erupted with these big, stupid grins on their faces.

"I got us tickets to *Saturday Night Live*. And then I made dinner reservations at this new restaurant over on the East Side. The food is supposed to be exquisite. I hope that sounds okay to you."

"Ooo, that sounds wonderful, Carl," my mother gushed.

I stared daggers at her. Wasn't Carl speaking to *me?!* "Yeah, Carl, sounds like fun. I've never been to a taping of *Saturday Night*. Let's get going then; I can't be out too late tonight."

"Oh, Honey, don't worry about anything. Let Carl show you a good time."

I didn't respond to my mother. Carl said a polite good evening to the two meddlesome women; I just walked out the door.

When we got down to the parking lot, Carl opened the passenger's door...to his cream-colored Bentley. Then he jumped in on the driver's side, started the car and turned up the volume on some soft jazz.

I quickly let go of my anger. Carl was soft-spoken but with a very deep voice, and seemed genuinely sweet. The first impression about a man such as himself might've been possession of a colossal ego. But Carl spoke very little about himself. It wasn't that he wasn't forthcoming with answers to any of my questions, but he seemed genuinely interested in talking about me.

So I was just as forthcoming. I told Carl I was involved in a serious relationship, and that we were living together. I also told him how my mother and Carmelita had set me up.

Carl couldn't help but be embarrassed and said he didn't mind taking me home. He said he was also going to have a good talk with his friend, Carmelita. But I told Carl I had no problem going ahead with our plans for the evening. Instead of a romantic date, we'd consider it a friendly date.

Saturday Night Live and Eddie Murphy were hilarious. I also enjoyed the wonderful restaurant Carl took me to. The ambiance was quite inviting, but I found myself wishing I'd been there with Dutton.

As promised, my sister and brother-in-law came into town for a quick visit. I took them to see *Ma Rainey*, and afterward, we all went out to a late dinner. There was no denying how charmed my sister and her husband, Charles, were by Dutton. And of course they loved his performance and the play immensely. We had so much fun that evening. We ended up closing the restaurant and had to be kicked out.

I'd refused to speak to my mother and hadn't returned any of her calls. Terry must've spoken to her, though, because Mom called again the next day. This time, I answered.

"Okay, Honey, I've been thinking about this. Maybe I have been a little unfair. So if it's okay, I was wondering if you'd take me to see Dutton's play."

"It's a date, Mom."

Her whole attitude changed. I'd had no doubt that it would if she gave it a chance. My mother was absolutely blown away by Dutton's talent, and equally so by his charming personality. Mom sat across from Dutton and me in Joe Allen's restaurant, completely enthused and bubbling with laughter. She listened with rapt attention while Dutton breezed from topic to topic. Quite surprisingly, Mom didn't even jump in and interrupt as she usually did.

Finally, she was on Dutton's bandwagon. Mom talked about him to all the family and all her friends, adamantly instructing them each to go down to see *Ma Rainey* before it closed. My aunts came; Mom's friends came; and Gloria came back in from Baltimore. We all enjoyed a wonderful night together.

Soon there were only six performances left. I attended all six. Mom was by my side for four.

Chapter 39

Englewood, New Jersey

We'd found a small, two-story Cape Cod house, right across the George Washington Bridge. It needed a bit of work. But as always, because of my passion for designing and decorating, I'd jumped right in to restoring it to its original charm. Dutton loved my decorating skills. He was always as excited as I was to see how I'd transform a place.

It felt really good to be lying in a bed in a house we owned. This was a first for both of us, and a feeling of real accomplishment. In moments like these, Dutton and I seemed to bare our souls to one another. Snuggled up, talking about the past, grateful to be where we were now, and especially grateful to have each other.

"Honey, how is it that you never ended up like Vernon and Jackie, addicted to drugs?"

Our noses almost touched as we lay only inches apart, inhaling each other's breath. Dutton had his huge arms wrapped around me. I'd never, in all my life, felt so secure or so unafraid.

"Well, Pretty Girl, it's not like I never tried it. But I had a rep to protect. See, the first time me and my boys got us some heroin, we immediately went to shoot up. But none of us knew what the hell we were doing. Since I was always the leader, I was going to be the first one to try it. But I took too much. All of a sudden, I started going into convulsions and foaming at the mouth."

"Oh God!"

"Yeah, Babe, I was about to OD. One of my boys knew enough to get some ice to put on my balls. It brought me around. If it wasn't for him, I wouldn't be snuggled up here with you right now, Pretty Girl. That would've really pissed me off."

I chuckled.

"Then a few days later, I tried it again."

"You mean you almost OD'd, and you were trying it again?"

"Yeah, you know, young and stupid. I figured this time I knew not to shoot too much. So I took a hit and the high felt good as shit. That's why it's such a hard drug to kick. I was feeling like I didn't have a care in the world. I left the apartment and went wobbling through this alley. I heard somebody yelling. 'Hey, there's that nigga right there! It's Roc! He looks like he's fucked up, too! Let's tighten his ass up!'

"I was in such a dream-like state I didn't have my guard up. And I was so high, I couldn't have fought back anyway. These two guys jumped me because we'd all had a beef with each other. They ran up and started kicking my ass. Some guys I used to hang with from time to time happened to come up on us in the alley. When they saw me, they jumped in before I got my ass killed; that was an awakening.

"Wasn't nobody in the neighborhood who felt they could take me in a fair fight. That's the rep I had. But I realized if I got hooked on heroin, my rep was going right out the window. I'd be getting my ass kicked all the time for all the shit I'd done to folks, and I wasn't about to let that happen. It was a no-brainer that I wasn't ever touching dope again.

"When I got busted and went to the joint, it broke my heart when

Vernon would come to see me. I could tell he'd started using. And then it really fucked me up when I found out Jackie was hooked, too. It made me mad because I felt like if I'd been around, I could've prevented that shit from taking hold of my brother and sister."

Dutton brushed a tiny tear from his eye. "You know, by the time I got out of prison, Pretty Girl, it seemed like everyone from fourteen to forty was hooked on that shit." *I could definitely relate. I'd grown up seeing the very same thing living in the projects.*

We breathed in silence for a moment. Then I continued...

"Honey, did you ever imagine your life would turn out so different?"

"You know, Baltimore is the only city that has a prison right in the middle of a neighborhood. When I was a kid, I'd look right out my window and see that big, black building looming down at the end of the street. I knew one day I'd end up in there. We all knew it. We kind of aspired to it, like a rite of passage. If it weren't for this young white woman who came to the prison and got me interested in acting, I might've died in the penitentiary. She was fine, too, for a white woman."

I laughed. "Oh, that's probably what got you interested in acting. You were interested in the teacher."

"Oh no, not at all. She was pretty, but I ain't ever been interested in no white woman, ever. A sister is the only thing that could ever do it for me. Anyway, acting is what saved me. Before then, I was always startin' shit in prison, always getting into a beef with somebody. I remember one day, we were sitting down watching a basketball game, and this guy named Chilly came up and switched the channel to *Cotton Comes to Harlem.*"

Dutton climbed out of bed to reenact the scene that had taken place. "So I got up and switched the channel back. I said, '*What the fuck you doin', Nigga? We watchin' the basketball game.*' He switched the channel back again, and said he was watching *Cotton Comes to*

Harlem. I changed the TV back to the game, and said,*'Nigga, if you touch that television one more time, yo' ass gon' have to go pick some muthafuckin' cotton!'* Everybody cracked up laughing.

"The next day, I was sitting in the rec room playing cards. I went to lift my arm to make a play, but I couldn't. Then I saw these shocked looks on everybody's faces. Their eyes were wide and I couldn't really make out what they were saying. It was like they were talking in slow motion. Then I started feeling a pain in my neck. I stumbled up from the table, and turned around. Chilly was standing there with an icepick and a big old grin on his face. He'd stabbed me in the neck. *'Got you, muthfucka...got yo' ass!'*"

"Oh God!"

"Before I passed out, I remembered thinking to myself, *'Shit! This nigga done stabbed me, and my ass gon' die right here in prison. Fuck!'* I was thinking about my obituary and the headstone on my grave saying, *'The Nigga Died In Prison!'*"

I tried not to laugh because Dutton's story wasn't at all funny. But he was so dramatic. No matter what Dutton ever told me about his past, his stories were always fueled with humor.

"After that shit happened, I'd kind of already gotten to a point where I was ready to stop being a knucklehead. Soon after, the acting teacher came into the new prison I'd been sent to. That changed everything for me. She took a special interest, and urged me to get as much education as I could. I got my GED and then started taking some college courses. When I was finally released, I started attending Towson State University in Baltimore. Most of the cats that I loved had either been killed, or were strung out."

He'd pour his life out to me in many sweet, tender hours. Once, I finally got the courage to ask, "Honey, what did it feel like when you stabbed that boy to death? I mean, knowing that you'd actually taken someone's life?"

Dutton was silent for a moment, seeming to choose his words carefully. "The two of us had been enemies for years. I think we both knew things would come to a head one day. We were at a party, and ended up getting into a fight over this girl. The fight started in the club and we fought all the way out to the street. I was getting the best of him, and that's when he pulled out a knife. Man, I didn't even know he had it on him. He slashed me across the stomach...I wrestled the knife from him...and stabbed him in the chest.

"When the cops and the ambulance arrived, they took us both to the same hospital. We were on the same floor, our rooms down the hall from each other.

"At first, I was thinking to myself, *I got that muthfucka!* Then I heard these screams from the hallway, these blood-curdling screams. Jackie went out to check. She came back in and said it was the guy's mother and grandmother who were screaming like that. The guy had just died."

Dutton had this faraway look in his eyes, as if he were right back in that moment. We both lay there in silence, feeling the gravity of his action. Dutton was aware that it could've just as easily been his mother screaming in that hospital corridor. But I looked into his face, and could see the magnitude of guilt he still felt for taking a human life.

Chapter 40

Dutton was in his early thirties, but looked every bit of forty-five because of the bags under his eyes, and the deep folds of skin over his eyelids. I'd tentatively mentioned us taking a visit to a plastic surgeon, but Dutton didn't seem too comfortable with that suggestion.

When he'd been cast in the television movie *The Murder of Mary Phagan* with Jack Lemmon, I'd gone to visit him on location.

One day, we were in the hotel swimming pool when two little girls swam over to us. One said to me, "Would your daddy mind if you played with us?"

Of course, I giggled out loud. Dutton rolled his eyes and said jokingly, "Get on outta here, li'l girls."

He'd grinned with that boyish grin of his. "You already know I'm fine, but it wouldn't hurt to see if the doctor could make me finer."

Dutton and I started laughing. "That's right," I said. "I got the finest man in the world! So maybe I'd better not let the doctor mess with you. I don't wanna be beating the women off with a stick!"

We had three consultations with three different plastic surgeons, but I'll never forget the first one. He kept stretching up the skin of Dutton's forehead, demonstrating a particular procedure he'd do. "Knock ten years off your age. Because your eyes make you look really old."

I don't remember what the doctor had been saying next, but I heard the word, *Neanderthal*. I just about lost it. I was laughing so hard I started choking.

The doctor was totally embarrassed. "I'm sorry. I wasn't trying to make fun. I'm trying to define for you the structure of—"

Dutton cut the doctor off. "See, can you believe her, Doc? She's supposed to be bringing me here so you can help me, and she's standing up here laughing at me." But Dutton was trying hard not to laugh himself. He was so good-natured about the whole thing, and not embarrassed in the least by what the doctor was saying.

I tried to pull myself together, for the doctor's sake. "I'm sorry, Doctor. Now what were you saying about my boyfriend? That he's a descendant from the Neanderthals?" I couldn't help myself...

After having his eyelids done as well as dental work, Dutton underwent a transformation.

"Uh oh, Honey." There was that boyish grin again. "You'd better watch out!"

I'd thrown my arms around Dutton. He looked beautiful to me. But he'd already been beautiful to me for a long time, inside and out.

Dutton had been traveling back and forth to New Haven for a period of time, while playing the title role in the Yale production of *Othello*. He eventually decided to take a temporary apartment while there.

I really missed having him at home and had been feeling a bit sexually frustrated. Wasn't quite sure why, but our sex life had seemed to wane somewhat. Dutton had often been the initiator; lately, I'd found myself being more the aggressor. And if my instincts were correct, Dutton wasn't as turned on by my forwardness as he'd been in the past.

I tried to put it off to exhaustion. Dutton had immersed himself fully into his role as Othello. But the situation still gave me concern. I'd gone up to New Haven a number of times. Dutton and I had only made love on one occasion, when I'd initiated it.

One weekend, I was rushing out to jet back to New York. I had an afternoon commercial audition. It was a rarity that I didn't make the bed before leaving. But on this particular morning, Dutton told me not to worry. He'd make it up later. So I left the covers hanging off the foot of the bed, dragging the floor.

It was three days before I came back up to New Haven to stay with Dutton. I'd been a little peeved because I'd been calling him late in the night, and had been unsuccessful in reaching him. Each time I called, it was well after when he should've been home from the theater. Dutton said some friends had come up from Baltimore, and they'd been hanging out after the play every night. I didn't seem to remember the bars staying open that late in New Haven.

When I walked back into the New Haven apartment, I took my small suitcase into the bedroom, and let out an audible gasp.

Dutton came in behind me. "What's the matter, Pretty Girl?"

"Dutton, where have you slept for the last three days?"

"What are you talking about? I slept here."

I looked at the covers down at the foot of the bed, dragging the floor, exactly as they'd been when I'd left. Then I looked at Dutton, who was looking back at me with a straight face. I knew with every bone in my body he'd not slept in that bed since I was there. He was standing there, boldly lying to my face. It just about broke my heart. Before that moment, I would've sworn before God that was impossible for Dutton to ever do.

"The covers are exactly the way they were when I left here the other morning. How could you have slept in this bed, and the covers be in exactly the same place?"

"Do you know how ridiculous you sound? Who remembers how

they left covers lying on a bed for three days? I've slept in this apartment every night since you've been gone. This is stupid. I'm not even going to discuss it with you anymore."

Dutton walked out of the room. I stood there staring down at the bed.

The next time I came back to New Haven, I brought my friend, Kasi Lemmons. She'd been dying to see Dutton's play. I'd also mentioned the incident to Kasi about how I'd found the bed covers.

"Debbi, you think the man spent the night with someone else for three whole nights?"

"I don't know about that, Kasi. But I do know Dutton didn't sleep in that bed. He couldn't have."

An hour later, Kasi and I sat in the theater, watching Dutton's electric performance as Othello. And then I noticed something. The actress who was playing Desdemona had thrown her arms around Dutton's neck, burying her head deep in his chest. She was pleading with him to believe in her innocence, that she'd not betrayed him with Iago.

As the actress rubbed her head across Dutton's chest, I felt there was too much of a familiarity in the way he gently stroked her hair.

It was to me a defining moment, a moment in which you could tell when actors had crossed that line with their characters.

I turned to Kasi and whispered, "He's fucking her."

Kasi looked at me and then back at the two of them. She said nothing. It was probably too difficult to refute at the time. So my friend would wait until later to try and convince me I was most likely hallucinating.

We went backstage and Kasi waited for me outside Dutton's dressing room door. He was changing and preparing for us to take the drive back to the city. The following day was Monday, his day off.

"Dutton, are you sleeping with your Desdemona?"

I hadn't meant to blurt it out like that. But my suspicions were overwhelming.

"What did you say?" Dutton spoke quietly, but I saw fury in his eyes.

Suddenly, I felt like the biggest fool. What on earth was I thinking? Dutton became whatever character he played. Everybody in the theater was supposed to believe the relationship between Othello and Desdemona, including me. I was an actress, after all. I should know better. And I did.

"That girl is engaged to be married, and I happen to be friends with her fiancé. Why don't you walk on over to the parking lot and wait for me. I'll be out to the car in a minute."

I left the dressing room feeling like an ass. Kasi and I walked the long block to the parking lot and sat in the car. I told Kasi what'd I'd said, and what Dutton's reaction had been.

"Debbi, you shouldn't have said anything! And I didn't get what you were feeling at all. Roc loves you, Girl. Plus, he doesn't seem like he's into white women anyway."

For a moment, I felt uplifted. "You're probably right, Kas. Dutton has even said that to me before, that no one but a sister could ever do anything for him."

"You see. Deb, you're worrying for nothing."

But the situation with the bed still nagged at me, and so did the picture in my memory of Desdemona's head buried deeply into Othello's chest as Dutton gently stroked her hair.

"Dutton is taking a long time. I'll drive around to the theater."

When I pulled up in front of the historical, red brick building, there was no parking space. So I pulled into a space across the street. Kasi and I both looked as the stage door opened. Dutton walked out with the actress who played Desdemona. He reached up and caressed her face. She placed her hand over his and smiled. Were they still going for their character's believability out here on the street?!

"I told you, Kasi! I told you!"

Kasi grabbed my hand and squeezed as it trembled inside hers.

I made a U-turn and pulled parallel to a car in front of the stage door. It was hard not to miss the surprise in Dutton's eyes. He'd assumed Kasi and I were still parked in the parking lot.

Desdemona said goodbye to him and quickly walked off. Kasi went to jump out of the front seat.

"That's okay, Kasi. Stay there. I'll hop in the back."

"Roc, you were great in the play! The whole production was wonderful. I loved it."

"Thanks, Kasi. I'm glad you made it up here."

Kasi and Dutton talked back and forth for the two-and-a-half-hour drive home. I said not one word. I couldn't speak; all I could do was feel, and the feelings were excruciating.

As soon as we dropped Kasi off, Dutton lit into me. "What the fuck is your problem?! First you accuse me of sleeping somewhere else, and then you accuse me of fucking somebody I'm working with who's engaged to be married! And I'll bet you told Kasi that stupid nonsense, too, didn't you?"

He'd never spoken to me that way before. But the first time always happened. History should've prepared me.

"Is it nonsense, Dutton? I saw you rubbing her face when the two of you walked out."

"So what?! That has to mean I'm fucking her?! She had a big fight with the director earlier, and she was upset. I was talking to her about it after the show. I reached up and rubbed her face, and told her not to worry. It would all work out. And you're going to sit here and make some big shit out of that? *And* try to make me out to be a liar?"

There was something I definitely couldn't lie about: the familiar, burning lava erupting in my insides and settling at the base of my stomach. Call it my friend, because it was always a warning, or call it my enemy, because it always meant doom was a stone's throw away.

Chapter 41

With the addition of a pit bull named Hawkeye to our household, our place had gotten too small for us. Between the times I was working on the soap, looking for a new house, and trying to sell the one we were in, I was kept quite busy. Dutton was busy as well, rehearsing for a new one-man show he'd be performing in the city at The American Place Theater. Woodie King, who'd produced *Wine-Sellers*, would be directing Dutton's theater event.

But in the midst of all the things going on in our daily lives, I was feeling a deep sense of rejection. There was a real problem brewing in our relationship.

On the surface, everything seemed normal. In our spare time, Dutton and I got together with friends in the city, or people would come out and see us. But our romantic relationship, at least our sexual one, had dwindled quite a bit. Whenever I tried to seduce Dutton, many times he'd say, "Why don't you go on upstairs and wait for me, Babe. I'll be up in a minute." It got to be a joke because either I'd fall asleep, or I'd come back downstairs and find Dutton asleep on the sofa.

Dutton always told me how much he loved me, and I believed him. We still kissed and hugged, and laughed, but I couldn't figure out why we weren't still banging the walls down.

It was hard to broach the subject with him. Dutton was quite versed on many topics. He had no problem offering an opinion or debating in depth any matter at-hand. But when it came to discussing the seriousness of what was happening in our sex life, he'd completely clam up.

I buried myself in work and house stuff, naively hoping that our problem would go away.

Our new, yellow-and-white, three-story colonial sat at the end of a long road on Hillside Avenue in Englewood. We were right down the hill from Bubble Hill, the palatial estate that'd recently been purchased by Eddie Murphy.

I was quite adept at handling the renovation and design of our new home, but at almost 4,000 square feet, it'd be a bit of an undertaking to do it alone. So I sought out an interior designer to work with.

It took a mere six months for the total top-to-bottom transformation. And it turned out to be my first dream house. The living room had a huge, brick fireplace and was surrounded by French doors looking onto a beautiful garden. Dutton even had a gorgeous fishpond constructed, and bought expensive, exotic fish to live therein. Our kitchen had the old tin ceiling, which I loved, and a large island where we could gather with our friends and family to eat.

Our bedroom was enormous, with a sitting area and a large bay window that looked out to a pretty, tree-lined street. There was a beautiful, wood-mantled fireplace, which sat about six feet from our bed. Our bed was a king-sized, cherry four-poster that'd I'd purchased from an antique show.

The home was so special, so beautiful, I had no doubt that Dutton and I would be deliriously happy there.

And we were happy, in all aspects of our life except for one—our sex life. But I'd have to speak for myself. I really had no idea what was going on in Dutton's head. He seemed to be perfectly fine, and still tight-lipped in engaging in any conversation to the contrary. I was getting to the point that I was ready to pull my hair out. I was so frustrated. Masturbating only satisfied for so long, especially when I was lying next to someone I loved, and desperately needing him to touch me, to want me.

Night after night, I'd fall asleep deeply discouraged by the situation. I'd then go off to the studio the next morning, acting as if I were the happiest woman on the planet. I always tooted Dutton's horn to the heavens. I couldn't let him fall from his pedestal.

"Debbi, I haven't told anyone yet, but I'm leaving the show."

"Darnell, you're kidding! You can't leave!"

"Yeah, I am, Deb. I've been here for six years, and I don't want to be Jesse for the rest of my life."

For me, Darnell's leaving was almost as bad as a death in the family. I couldn't imagine being on *All My Children* without him. The network and producers, once they found out, weren't happy with Darnell's decision either. They decided to write Darnell out of the show by killing off the character of Jesse.

Normally, for a character as popular as Jesse, the show would've had him go off into the wild blue yonder, in case the actor ever wanted to return, as so many did. When a character was killed off, oftentimes it meant everyone was pissed at the actor for leaving. The higher-ups were pissed at Darnell because he'd waited until the very end of his contract to notify ABC. They'd written a big storyline for the two of us. Now it would have to be scrapped.

However, not all was dim. The storyline in which Jesse is killed would be a powerful one, one of the great moments in daytime history. It would give me the most heart-wrenching scenes to play. But it was our very last scene together that I will never forget.

Jesse was lying in bed, dying from a gunshot wound, and hanging on to life by a thread. The director had me sit in a chair next to Jesse's hospital bed as we said our final goodbyes. I was so torn up over Darnell's leaving; my emotions couldn't have been more honest or full.

I pushed away the chair and climbed up on the bed next to Darnell, crying my heart out.

I was told that the producer almost stopped the scene. "What is she doing?" But the director said, "Let her go," and had the cameraman follow my movement from the chair to the bed.

When Jesse breathed his last breath of air, gasps were heard around the country. No one believed Jesse would actually die. He was too integral to the show. Suffice it to say, there were lots of angry viewers who thought Darnell Williams had been fired, unaware it'd been his choice to leave.

At the end of the scene, Jesse closed his eyes while lying in my arms. My gut-wrenching tears couldn't have been more real.

Cast members were standing off to the side of the stage, weeping in silence. They were going to miss Darnell, too. He was so loved by all the actors. And then there was this thunderous burst of applause.

After the show aired, my phone kept ringing off the hook. People reacted like it had all been real life. I even got a call from my good friend Lynne Moody in California. Her message really choked me up.

"Debbi, I'm sooo upset." Lynne was actually crying over the phone. "I know this is stupid; it's a soap opera. But you guys made it seem so real. The performances you and Darnell gave were utterly amazing."

Apparently, a lot of people agreed with Lynne because I was nominated for my second Emmy Award.

By the time the Emmys rolled around, I was a nervous wreck. Everyone was so positive I'd walk off with the award. But a black actress had never been given the statuette.

Dutton looked especially handsome that night, wearing a navy suit with a burgundy tie. And he was smiling with his beautiful new set of teeth, and looking at everyone, with no bags under his eyes. I would've been so proud to have him by my side. But family members and friends had to sit in another section. I sat with the *All My Children* cast very close to the stage. I was seated right next to Susan Lucci. Susan was the first one on her feet, throwing her arms around me when my name was called.

"And for Best Supporting Actress, the Emmy goes to... Wow, it's a tie. The first winner is from All My Children...Debbi Morgan!"

Even though I ended up tying for best supporting actress with Nancy Lee Grahn from *General Hospital*, I was the first African American female who'd ever actually won, and to date that is still the case. Certainly not something I'd give daytime television a pat on the back for. However, on that evening, I was absolutely thrilled.

Oprah Winfrey, who'd been in attendance as a nominee and a winner, gave an intimate gathering in her hotel suite. Dutton and I were both invited. The only other person there from the show was Susan Lucci, accompanied by her husband, Helmut.

When we entered the suite, Oprah gave me a big hug. "I knew you were going to win, Debbi! I knew it!" Oprah had always been a very big fan of *All My Children*. She was also a fan of Dutton's. She'd seen *Ma Rainey* and gone back a second time, bringing along Stedman and some of her staff.

It turned out to be such a wonderful evening. We left Oprah's, and joined the rest of the cast and producers at a swank restaurant on the Upper East Side for dinner. It'd been my lucky night, and it got even luckier.

Dutton took me home and made love to me. I was like a sponge, soaking up everything he gave, and then begging for more. We fell asleep, entwined and dripping with love juice. The next morning, I woke to find Dutton staring at me with a sweet smile, and then he popped the question...

"Pretty Girl, will you marry me?"

Chapter 42

I should've been jumping from the ceiling with excitement about my upcoming wedding and the elaborate ceremony I was planning. The date was set for June. My maid of honor and my bridesmaids had been chosen. And we'd picked out our perfect place to have the nuptials—Edgewater, New Jersey, on the Binghamton, a large ferryboat with a restaurant that catered weddings and large events. We'd planned to sail up and down the Hudson River with a live band. Dutton's good friend, Dwight, now a minister, would be officiating the ceremony.

But Dutton and I still had a very serious issue concerning our sex life. We'd go weeks without making love, and I could barely get him to discuss it.

I loved the man more than anything in this world; that had not changed. I wanted more than anything to be his wife. But living a married life of near celibacy was not what I wanted.

Perhaps, some of this had to do with Dutton's time in prison. He'd told me dozens of stories about being incarcerated, but of course, he'd never delved into any sexual experiences. I'd no idea if he'd ever engaged in any homosexual activity or not. Oddly, it wasn't anything that'd ever even crossed my mind. But there had to be a reason this was happening. I certainly didn't feel like Dutton was no longer attracted to me. Maybe he was experiencing some degree of impotency, and was too embarrassed to discuss it. But how could we possibly get married under these circumstances?

Early one Sunday evening, I went upstairs and took a hot bath. I'd left Dutton downstairs in front of the TV as usual. I spent a half-hour in the tub trying to soak all my worries away. When I got out, I applied a delicately scented cream over my body, and slipped into a red teddy.

I pulled back the sheets on our bed, fluffed up the pillows, and lit a few candles around the room. Then I hurried back downstairs. Dutton was still watching television and playing with our dog, Hawkeye.

Hawkeye noticed me right away. He immediately ran up and started sniffing my leg. *Damn, even the dog knows what to do!* But Dutton just stood there, looking at me with trepidation. *What in the world was the problem?!*

I went over and grabbed his hand. "Come on, Honey. Let's go upstairs."

Dutton took my hand, but acted as if were going off to the gallows. When we got upstairs, Dutton allowed me to undress him, and I began to make love to him. Once we were in the throes of passion, he responded wholeheartedly. Everything was definitely in working order, so why the difficulty in getting to this place?

Then I got a cold chill. Since Dutton's mechanics seemed to be in working order, what if it was *me?* What if he'd somehow lost interest, and couldn't bring himself to tell me. I was literally terrified of that possibility. But it was a possibility I couldn't ignore.

One night after talking about the lack of sex yet again, I said, "Dutton, I don't think we're going to be able to work through this on our own. So I'm going to research finding a therapist for us to speak to."

Suddenly, I had Dutton's rapt attention. He'd not expressed any big emotion about our situation until now. "Are you crazy?! We're not going to any therapist!"

"Why not?"

"Because we're not!"

Dutton let go of his momentary fury, and went back to playing with Hawkeye. "I don't know why you're getting yourself all worked up like this, and for nothing."

Slowly, I rose from the sofa and went upstairs. There were calls I needed to make right away. Obviously, marriage wasn't in the cards for us.

And then a long-forgotten thought reentered my mind. Once, I'd questioned Dutton about his relationship with Angie. He'd said, "Ang and I really never even had sex that much." I didn't believe him at the time. But because of what I was now experiencing in our relationship, I tended to believe it was true.

So what did that mean? Did Dutton lose sexual interest in a lover once he'd had her for a while? Or maybe it wasn't that dire. Perhaps his career and his life were changing so quickly, sex was the last thing on his mind.

Whatever the reasons, I couldn't figure them out on my own; I felt I was left with only one solution.

After I'd taken care of all the necessary calls, I climbed into bed alone, sobbing into my pillow. I stayed alone for the rest of the night. Dutton stayed down in the den.

The next morning, before I left for work, I went into the kitchen and found Dutton making a bowl of cereal.

"Hey, Pretty Girl. Did you sleep all right?"

"Dutton, I've called everyone that I needed to, to cancel the wedding. The only one left is Dwight. And if you don't mind, I'd appreciate it if you called him."

I walked out of the kitchen, without one word of objection from Dutton.

I'd crossed the GW Bridge to New Jersey on my way home from the studio. It was nerve-racking driving through the torrential rainstorm. Blinded by the rain and the tears streaming down my face, I decided to pull over into a restaurant parking lot.

Leaning my head down on the steering wheel, I felt the horrible knot in the pit of my stomach. The knot that was constantly there, dormant at times, but always waiting to surface.

What would happen now? Would we sell our beautiful home and part ways? Would this be the end to a relationship I wanted more than anything? Was there no way to solve this? A hundred questions filled my head.

Sitting back against the leather seat, a smile erupted from my lips. I was thinking of the moment when I'd been sure, sure that I wanted to spend my life with Dutton.

He'd been invited to speak at Rikers Island prison, to a group of young convicts. When Dutton had asked if I wanted to go with him, I'd first said, no. Going to a prison, even for a visit, was not my idea of fun. But I changed my mind, only because I'd be going with Dutton.

I don't remember the bridge we crossed to get to the prison, but as our bus crossed over it, you could see the large, ominous-looking fortress ahead. And if that wasn't scary enough, the sound of the heavy, metal door clanging behind us, as we checked through security, was downright chilling.

What possessed anyone to do anything that would bring him or her to a place like this was far beyond me. Well, I guess it wasn't that far. Because of the relationships I'd been around in my own life, I could see how people got here. Actually, being inside these walls made that knowledge a little more difficult to digest.

"Hello, Mr. Dutton; I'm Ms. Stalwart. Welcome to Rikers Island."

Sounded like an odd choice of words to me. A middle-aged white woman with horn-rimmed glasses, a little Tweety-bird voice, wearing a gray tweed suit, walked up to us as we passed through the security check. Ms. Stalwart looked like the last person you'd expect to be running anything in a place like this. "I really appreciate you taking the time out of your busy schedule to come and speak to our inmates, Mr. Dutton."

She led us into the room where Dutton would be speaking and promptly introduced him to the restless youngsters.

"Now we have a delightful gentleman, who has taken the time out of his busy day to come here and speak with all of you. I'm sure you'll find that he can relate to a lot of your issues. His name is Charles Dutton, and he is a big Broadway actor."

Dutton rolled his eyes and ran the side of his hand across his neck, like he wanted to tell Ms. Stalwart to cut. The way Ms. Stalwart was going on about him, Dutton must have figured she was already turning these young guys off.

"I would appreciate it if you give him your full attention, and a round of applause, for Mr. Charles Dutton."

There was the sound of one isolated clap as I took a quick glimpse around the room and observed the sea of young men. They sat with cocky expressions, slouched down in their folding chairs. Almost immediately, I had the sense that the last thing they wanted was another damn lecture.

Dutton strode up to the podium. I sat in a folding chair against the wall, facing to the side of him.

"Oh, shit! That's *Angie!* Hey, *Angie*, Baby. Damn, Girl. You fiiine!!"

I squirmed in my chair a bit.

"Okay, okay. That's enough. That's my lady, and I don't want none of you knuckleheads yelling out at her, or I'll have to pop one of you."

A few chuckles were heard around the room, and then someone yelled out. "How you get to have someone like *Angie* for your lady?!"

"Because I'm smart," Dutton replied. "You could have a lady like this too if you stopped acting like an idiot, and got your head into some books and learned something."

I glanced over at some of the faces. Smirks, frowns, boredom was mostly what I saw. A few even looked like they'd dozed off. Who cared about hearing some kind of pep talk from a stage actor?

But then Dutton began to share stories of his life. "See, fifteen years ago, I was you, sitting right where you're sitting, except I was in a prison in Baltimore, Maryland. I'd robbed banks; I was carrying guns; and I'd even stabbed someone to death..."

It was a defining moment as I watched the young men, almost in unison, shift their bodies to an upright position, Dutton captivating their attention. It was a defining moment for me as well. I'd seen the ability Dutton had to capture lots of people's attention, but this was more profound. Our young black men were drug-addicted, selling drugs, robbing and committing murder, and losing their lives every day because they'd gone astray, for one reason or another. At that very moment I recognized the power in Dutton to make a difference.

After sharing his experiences, Dutton gave raw, unadulterated advice. I looked around the room once again at many of the young faces who'd already lived far beyond their years. Who knew how many Dutton had reached, if any? But even if it was only one, it was a victory. And he'd certainly reached me, inside my heart, claiming it. I wanted to spend my life with this extraordinary creature, and that I'd be willing to cross any hurdles that arose.

That confirmation brought me back to the present, as I sat in my car with the rain splattering across my windshield...

And here, six months later, on December 30, 1989, holding on to the idea that this man was somehow more than just a man, I walked down the aisle to marry Charles S. Dutton, *Husband #2!*

Draped in my liquid gold, metallic gown, with the twelve-foot train, I floated on the arm of my Uncle Bill, Daddy's dear brother.

Whatever crown of glory I'd decided to place upon Dutton's large head, a certain fact still remained. The problem we faced had only gotten *somewhat* better. But it was also a fact that it'd been great once...so it could be again, couldn't it?

Now here we were in front of all our family, friends, and God, reciting our own written vows. I began by saying, "Dutton, you take my breath away." And he did. At least the idea I had of him took my breath away.

We didn't even make love on our wedding night. Dutton had had quite a bit to drink and fallen asleep. I was wide-awake lying beside him, waiting for the morning, in the hopes that we'd remedy the situation. But as the sun rose, I involuntarily drifted off. When I awoke, I found a note on the nightstand in our hotel suite at the Ritz-Carlton.

Good morning, my beautiful wife. You looked so sweet lying there, I didn't have the heart to wake you. I'm making a quick drive to New Jersey to take Mom and Aunt Gwendolyn food shopping for our New Year's Eve party. You just sleep. I know you're exhausted. I'll be back to pick you up in a few hours.

I love you

Your husband!

The morning after my wedding, and I was alone again, crying in my pillow.

I had an idea in my head of what this marriage would truly be... heavenly, fulfilling, totally rewarding, and lasting a lifetime. It was my fantasy, but it would not come to fruition anytime soon.

Chapter 43

"Hello."

'Hello, may I please speak with Debbi Morgan?'

"This is Debbi. Who's calling?"

'One moment, I have Jorn Winther on the line for you.'

'Hello, hello, my darlin',' Jorn said in his thick Polish accent.

"Jorn! How are you?!"

'I'm fine. How are you, my darlin'?'

"Oh, I'm great!" That wasn't exactly the truth, but I'd certainly not be sharing any of that with Jorn.

I hadn't spoken to Jorn since ABC fired him as executive producer from *All My Children* five years earlier. His departure had been personally devastating because I'd always had a special place in my heart for Jorn. He'd hired me as Angie, a role that turned out to be one of the highlights of my career. Now Jorn was over at NBC, as executive producer of a new soap, *Generations*. The show was being taped in Los Angeles and was also struggling in the ratings. It'd been created by a woman named Sally Sussman, and had one of the first black head writers, Judi Ann Mason.

Generations was the only soap to fairly represent our multicultural society. The ratio of white cast to black was about 60/30. A few black actors in the industry said we'd probably never see a soap opera like that again. To this day, that's been true.

'Listen, I'm curious, Debbi, when is your contract up at All My Children?'

"Actually, it's up in about six weeks."

'So I guess you're in the middle of negotiations now?'

"Well, the show hasn't approached me about my contract yet."

'They haven't?!'

Jorn was no more surprised than me. Usually, the network and producers approached an actor many months before the end of their contract to start renegotiations, unless, of course, they were planning to let the actor go. I was still very popular on the show, even with Darnell gone, so I didn't necessarily feel ABC had plans to drop me.

However, I did feel a bit taken for granted. Did the show assume I wouldn't have any plans of moving on? Therefore, they could come to me at the last minute and offer peanuts? I'd brought home a Daytime Emmy, for Christ's sake! I thought this would've been a big motivation for them to come to me much earlier.

'I can't believe ABC hasn't approached you by now. Well, hopefully, it'll be their loss and our gain, because I would love to have you on Generations. *You'd be a big boost to the show.'*

I was delighted to hear those words from Jorn. It'd be wonderful to be on a show that had more than a handful of people who looked like me. Though I adored my fellow actors and actresses and the team at *All My Children*, I was keenly aware of the fact that Darnell and I had never graced the cover of *Soap Opera Digest*. Darnell had actually been told by the editor that they wouldn't sell as many magazines with us on the cover.

We weren't included in promotional photo shoots. We were always in the background. Perhaps Generations would give me an opportunity to share in the spotlight with co-stars of every race.

But the biggest plus was a selfish one. Dutton was already in Los Angeles opening in *The Piano Lesson* before the show moved on to Broadway. We'd actually had conversations in the past about us one day moving out there together. I'd always preferred the California lifestyle.

Everything took on quite a momentum after I accepted Jorn's offer to join *Generations.* Yorn explained that he'd go back to Sally Sussman and the network with the great news, and then call my agent the following day with an offer. Of course, when *All My Children* found out, they were none too happy.

At first, they didn't want to accept any of the responsibility for losing me to another show. But after a rather awkward meeting with executive producer Felicia Behr and Agnes Nixon, the creator of *All My Children,* we all came to an understanding that it was time for me to spread my wings elsewhere. The parting was bittersweet on both sides.

I'd already called and spoken to Dutton in L.A., who was all for my decision. Dutton said that once he'd finished doing *Piano Lesson* on Broadway, he'd be more than ready to give L.A. a shot.

I was still hoping he'd give me some more shots—in the bedroom, that is. While we both had exciting professional changes up ahead, things in the bedroom were not improving. I could count on one hand the number of times we'd made love since our marriage.

When I got out to Los Angeles, Dutton and I rented a small apartment in the Oakwood Garden Apartments in Burbank. Conni Marie was happy to have me back in California, and the feeling was mutual. Still, I missed my childhood friends, Carol and Vanessa, tremendously. Denise and I had lost touch long ago after she'd divorced Pecky, and moved to North Carolina with their daughter.

It was exciting starting on a new show, where I'd be one of the stars, with lots of great stories to play. Joan Pringle, whom I'd known since guest-starring on the *White Shadow* back in the day, where she'd played the principal, would be playing my mother on *Generations.* It wasn't like Joan was old enough to be my mother in real life, but of course this was TV. Jonelle Allen, Kristoff St. John, who'd be playing my brother, and Vivica A. Fox, were also part of the cast.

In the beginning, I was taping the show almost five days a week. Dutton was starring in *The Piano Lesson* at The Doolittle Theater in Hollywood, six nights a week. That left us very little togetherness, not to mention any time to see Ron Bush, the sex therapist.

Our home back in New Jersey was still on the market. Once it sold, and Dutton was on Broadway again, he planned to rent a place in the city while the play was running.

A lot of angst started building up for me. I was working twelve- to fourteen-hour days, dealing with my real estate agent back east and potential buyers via phone, while looking for a more permanent place to live in L.A. Added to that the pressure, trying to work out an appointment with Ron Bush, who had been recommended by Dutton's friend, Dwight, Dutton didn't appear nearly as frustrated as I with our unsuccessful attempts in keeping our appointments. We'd had to cancel four times! Whenever it looked like we'd secured a time that suited all parties, Dutton's publicist would call with some huge interview he had to do.

'Sorry, Babe. You know I really wanted to make the appointment. But I have to do this interview. It's important.'

Sorry just about summed up our marriage and our sex life as other priorities took precedence. Dutton was riding high in Los Angeles with his rave reviews in *Piano Lesson*. He'd even been approached about the possibility of starring in a sitcom. Dutton was the talk of the town; I was quite proud, but not in the way he was treating us. I was becoming more and more disillusioned. The commitment we'd made wasn't being honored.

Before I knew it, the time had come for Dutton to fly back to New York and back to Broadway. We'd finally purchased a house in Sherman Oaks that we wanted to do extensive work on. It'd take several months before the home would be move-in ready. In the meantime, I lived with Conni Marie.

My husband and I were sexually intimate exactly two times in those two months, but managed to have at least five fights over the issue. When it was time for Dutton to leave, I thought we both had an understanding that upon his return, we'd fit in a few sessions with Ron Bush.

It was obvious how anxious Dutton was to get away from my nagging. But I was just as anxious and exhausted with the never-ending quarrel.

So I took it upon myself to begin having a few sessions with Ron, alone. At first, Mr. Bush said he preferred Dutton and I come in together. But when I insisted and told him how difficult this had all been for me, Ron acquiesced.

Ron Bush's office was in a tall red structure right off the 134 Freeway in Pasadena. Once inside the office, instead of being greeted by a secretary, Ron Bush greeted me himself.

He was a dark-skinned man of average height and looks. Ron wore gray pants, a white shirt, and a red tie. His face was adorned with glasses that made him look studious and a bit intimidating, until he opened his mouth and spoke in a soft, reassuring manner.

"Hello, Debbi, it's nice to finally meet you. I've been a fan for years. Dwight speaks very highly of both you and your husband."

After our exchange of pleasantries, he led me to a comfortable, green leather chair. I wondered where the black couch was.

"Initially, I like to see both partners. Later, I'll have a few sessions with them individually. So we're doing this a bit backward. But that's fine. I can understand the kind of schedule your husband must have. By the way, I saw his play. He was very good."

"Yes, he was. He's very talented. I'm really proud of him, and I love him so much."

Ron looked at me with warm understanding. "I believe you. I'm sure you wouldn't have married him otherwise."

"No, I wouldn't have. But I don't know if a lot of other women would have, not if he wasn't making love to them."

"So is that why you're here to see me? Your husband isn't making love to you?"

"Well...it kind of seems that way. Although, I don't think he does it purposely."

"What do you think?"

"I'm not sure. I know he loves me. I mean, why else would he marry me?"

"How often would you say the two of you are intimate?"

"You mean when we're under the same roof?"

Ron smiled. "Yes, that would be the time I'm speaking of."

"Maybe once or twice a month...if I'm lucky."

"And how long into the marriage has this been going on?" Ron probed.

"We haven't been married that long. This started way before our actual marriage. But since our marriage, sex has been on a steady decline."

"Was sexual intimacy a very important part of the relationship for you?"

"Definitely!"

"Then why did you marry Charles?"

I sat staring off into space for the longest time, not quite sure how to answer Ron's valid question. Ron remained silent.

"Maybe because he wasn't a drug addict." *I didn't know where that came from.*

"Had you been with a drug addict in the past?"

"Oh yeah, two! Married one of them. But that wasn't it, although I certainly never wanted to go down that road again. I guess...I guess...

I don't know. I was so in awe of Dutton, what he'd accomplished in his life, how much people respect him."

"Do you respect him?"

"Yes, I do. I have a great deal of respect for him. He...he...he makes me feel so safe. I feel like no one can ever hurt me."

"Do you feel your husband can hurt you?"

"Well...he has...but I don't think he realizes it. I mean, he might realize it, but I don't think he's trying to hurt me."

"What was it like when you first met? How was the sex then?"

"It was great! We had a very strong sexual chemistry. Somewhere in the back of my head, I kept thinking if we had it once, we could get it back again. If the sex had been horrible to begin with, I wouldn't have fallen for him the way I did. Even though there were a lot of other reasons I fell in love with him...Ron, I don't know whether you know this or not, but my husband spent a number of years in prison."

"Yes, I remember seeing his *60 Minutes* interview."

Of course, the whole country had probably seen that interview. Dutton had done it a few years after we'd started living together. He'd been very forthcoming in exposing everything about his criminal past, his prison life, and his subsequent road to success.

"I often wonder if maybe something happened with Dutton in prison that's affected him somehow."

We both heard a door open and close in the outer office, and Ron Bush glanced down at his watch.

"We're going to have to stop now. Do you have any idea when Charles will be coming back to California?"

"Not exactly. But he promised it'd be soon. When I know, I'll call and schedule an appointment. I'm actually flying back to New York tomorrow."

"Oh, you are?"

"Yes, I'm flying in for Dutton's opening night on Broadway."

"That's great. Debbi, let me make a suggestion. Until I can see you and your husband together, I don't want you to push the sex thing, okay? If it happens naturally, fine. But if it doesn't, I don't want you getting upset or trying to get into any discussion about it. Deal?"

I sighed. "Deal, Ron. I won't."

I left Ron's office feeling like maybe he'd have the ability to help Dutton and me. I wasn't sure, but I was hopeful.

Chapter 44

Opening night of *Piano Lesson* was a magnificent ride. All the actors, including Rocky Carroll, S. Epatha Merkerson, Carl Gordon, Tommy Hicks, Lou Meyers, and of course the always brilliant Charles S. Dutton, were downright amazing. Apparently the critics thought so, too.

At the opening night party, the *Times* review was read aloud. It hailed the play and the cast, and referred to the compelling Charles S. Dutton as a force of nature on stage.

I was only in town for five days, and barely got to see my husband. He was bombarded with press interviews, photo sessions, an appearance on David Letterman, and starring every night in a hit Broadway show. Dutton had the gift of gab, but I could tell my husband was getting pretty rundown with this fast-paced lifestyle. He'd even started losing his voice.

"Babe, I can't handle all this. I need to get an assistant. Every time I turn around, I'm getting some appointment screwed up. And you should see my dressing room; it looks like a tornado hit it. I write important stuff down and put it on my dressing table, and then I have to tear the place apart trying to find it."

"Can't your agent or publicist recommend someone?"

"This casting agent, friend of mine, knows a woman who might be able to help me out. She's coming to the play tomorrow and meeting with me afterward. Why don't you come to the show and give me your opinion?"

We hadn't slept together once. But I heeded what Ron told me, and didn't complain. Besides, I felt for my husband. This was an extremely hectic time for Dutton. And along with everything else going on, he was dealing with family issues.

Dutton had sent for Vernon to come and stay with him after I'd moved to California. Dutton felt if he could keep Vernon in a healthier environment, he might also be able to keep him off heroin. For a while it seemed to be working.

The night I was flying back to California, I attended Dutton's Sunday matinee. I was sitting in the theater with Mom, who'd come along with me. Just before the curtain went up, someone tapped me on the back of the shoulder. "Hi, are you Debbi?"

"Yes," I said, looking into the eyes of the most stunning woman. She had big brown eyes and a winsome smile.

"Hi, Debbi. I'm Yolanda."

"Yolanda...? Oh, yes, Yolanda!"

She was absolutely stunning! This was who Dutton wanted to hire as his personal assistant? Oh, hell no!

But then I noticed the man sitting there with his arm around her.

"This is my husband, and these are our kids."

I introduced Mom, and then Yolanda went down the row introducing all six of her children! There were so many I forgot their names as soon as their mother said them. The youngest looked to be about four. And the woman looked like she hadn't given birth to a one.

Though Yolanda was sitting, I could tell she was in very good shape. But who in the world had six children in this day and age!

That evening, Dutton and I raced through the worst traffic to get to Newark Airport. I was so sure I'd miss my flight, but we made it, and with fifteen minutes to spare.

"Give me a kiss, Pretty Girl."

Dutton pulled me to him, gently ran his lips along the side of my neck, and kissed me so passionately it made my toes curl. My God, it felt like the old days!

"Guess what, Babe? I'm coming to L.A., in two weeks to meet with these producers from FOX. They definitely want to develop a family comedy around me. They like a lot of my ideas. And I'm going to make sure I get them to hire Reggie to play my brother."

"Oh, Honey, that's fabulous!" I hesitated. "And...uh..."

"What, Babe? What is it?"

"Do you think we'll have time to see...Ron Bush, the therapist?"

"I'll make the time, Pretty Girl. That's a promise."

Dutton kissed me again—a long, deep kiss. When we broke apart, I looked down and saw his temperature rising. Lord have mercy, and I had to get on a damn flight!

Two weeks quickly flew by. It'd been difficult to contain my excitement about what lay ahead for Dutton and me. If our last moment together was any indication, things were definitely *a-changing!* I'd spoken to Dutton about his available time and had scheduled our appointment with Ron accordingly. We'd have an hour after I picked Dutton up from the airport to make the meeting.

My husband would be in town for only two short days. His fellow castmates weren't excited about being on stage with the understudy much longer than that. I'd booked us a cottage at the Bel-Air Hotel. Everything had to be special, and I felt this was going to be a new beginning.

That night, I called Dutton to see if he wanted a wake-up call. His flight was at 6:00 a.m. Vernon answered the phone and informed me that Dutton hadn't made it back from the theater yet. A few hours later, I called back and got the same story. I called back forty-five minutes later, ditto. Vernon was beginning to sound a little nervous speaking to me, as if he might have to start making up excuses. After that, I called back every fifteen minutes until five-thirty, East Coast time. Vernon never picked up the phone again.

Later that morning, I arrived at LAX, not knowing whether Dutton had even made his flight. He ended up being the third one off the plane as he walked toward me with a big smile, and outstretched arms.

"Hey, Babe. I missed you!"

Dutton lifted me up in the air and planted a quick kiss on my lips. "Man, it was so hard catching that six o'clock flight. But at least I got some serious shut-eye on the plane."

"I knew making a six o'clock flight would be tough. What time did you get to bed?"

"Oh, I crashed as soon as I got home from the theater. I was too tired to even pack. So I had to hurry and throw some things together before I left this morning."

"So what time did you get to bed?'

"I told you, Babe, as soon as I got home from the theater. I guess about midnight."

It was another big one...the knot in my stomach...I felt like I'd bowl over from the intensity.

Dutton didn't have any luggage at the baggage claim; he was carrying a large garment bag, and a large duffel bag.

"Did you have to park far away?"

"No."

Dutton took my hand and led me through the terminal, out to the curb.

We walked across the street to the first parking structure where my BMW convertible was parked. I got into the driver's seat, and Dutton hopped into the passenger side.

"So how long does it take to get to this place, Babe?"

I didn't answer. I kept driving out of the airport. "Debbi, how long does it take to get to this guy's office?"

"Why? Do you think maybe we shouldn't go?"

"What are you talking about? I thought you wanted to go."

"Let's forget about me for a moment. What about you? Do you want to go? Or do you want to sit there lying to me?"

"What the hell are you talking about?!"

"You know damn well what I'm talking about! You're a liar, Dutton. You're a big, fat liar!" I raged.

"I have no idea what the hell you're talking about!"

"You didn't come home from the theater and go to bed at any midnight! You didn't come home at all! I called you at one-thirty and Vernon said you hadn't come in. Then I called back at three-thirty, then forty-five minutes later! I kept calling every fifteen minutes after that until five-thirty this morning, and you never came home! Where the hell were you all night?!"

At first, Dutton mumbled something under his breath, which I didn't catch.

"What did you say?!"

"Will you stop all that screaming? I went to a club, okay? I should've told you. But that's where I was all night, at this club."

"You were at a club *all* night?!"

"Yes, I was."

"When did you pack?!"

"I came home and threw a few things together before I went back out."

"Dutton, what are you telling me?! Vernon said you never came home! And what did you do, go to a club carrying a garment bag, and a duffel bag?!"

"Vernon wasn't home when I came in, and, yes, I went right back out. I took my things with me to the club. It's not like I had that much. The owner knows me. I put my stuff in his office."

Dutton spoke very calmly, which only incensed me more.

"You're a liar! You are a liar, Dutton! What's happened to you?! I can't believe you would do something like this!!"

"I'm telling you for the last time, I'm not lying...and hey!! Will you watch where you're going?! You're acting like a crazy person!"

Tears streamed down my face. I was so wound up I'd almost run into a pole after I'd exited the freeway.

"Maybe you don't care about killing yourself, but don't try killing me in the process! If you can't get it together, we need to cancel this meeting. I'm telling you where I was, and that's the truth. I don't know what else you want me to say."

Dutton looked into my face without batting an eye. His expression was so earnest, and so guiltless. He'd probably come off really good in a lineup; it's not like he didn't have the experience.

"Hello, Charles. I'm Ron Bush."

"Hello, Ron, a real pleasure to meet you, Man. My wife has told me some really great things about you, and of course my good buddy, Dwight, has as well."

"By the way, Dwight sends hello. He happened to call me yesterday. We hadn't spoken in about six months. I told him you two were coming in."

I sat full to the brim, watching Dutton carry on a perfectly friendly conversation with Ron Bush. Ron turned to me at one point. I could tell he noticed something was wrong. And I hadn't said a word since we'd entered the office.

"So, Charles, tell me a little bit about what you think might be going on with you and your wife."

Dutton clasped his hands, seeming to ponder the question. Then he shrugged his shoulders as if he didn't have an inkling.

"I'm not sure what's going on with her. At times I feel like she thinks I don't love her. I have no idea what would ever make her think that. I love her the most in this world."

"Well, is there anything that you're having a problem with? Besides trying to get your wife to believe how much you love her?"

"Not at all; I want to make her happy."

"What is this bull you're saying, Dutton?! Why are we even here if you're going to be so dishonest?! You know the problem in our marriage revolves around sex! But now we have a bigger problem!"

I turned to Ron. "He stayed out all night, and lied to me about where he was?! I called the house all night. He never came home! First he said he'd gone to sleep, and then he said he was at a club! He's sitting here with a straight face professing his great love for me. How do you help a couple when one turns out to be such a flagrant liar?!"

Both Dutton and Ron were looking at me like I was the crazy person Dutton had accused me of being earlier.

"I think it's best if we end our session for today. It'll be better when you're not so upset." Ron and Dutton both stood. "Charles, any chance we might get together alone before you jet back to New York?"

"Sorry, Ron, I wish I could. I'm only here for two days, and it's going to be nonstop. But how about if I give you a call?'

"Sure thing; we can certainly do that. Let me give you my card."

"Ron, I'm sorry about my outburst." I quickly fled the office.

Dutton came out a few seconds later. I stood trembling, with my back to him. The last thing I wanted was to hear any more of his lies, or any phony apology. Dutton tapped me, and it felt like a flame sizzling on my shoulder. I spun around to see venom in his dark eyes. He spoke so low I could barely hear him and we were only inches apart.

"That's the last time you will ever try to humiliate me in front of anyone. A-N-Y-O-N-E. If you ever do, I promise...*you will regret it.*"

We rode home in silence. The knot in my stomach, which had a tendency to lay dormant but never quite disappear, came alive again.

Chapter 45

"Debbi, all the guys are here. Are you ready?"

"Yeah, I have to make a quick run to the bathroom. I'll be right there."

The stage manager on *Generations* nodded her head and hurried off toward the stage. I made my quick run to the restroom. Just before I walked out of my dressing room, there was a knock on the door. I opened it to find Conni Marie.

"Conni, you made it."

"Did they start the auditions yet?"

"The stage manager just called me; let's go."

Generations was holding auditions to find a love interest for me on the show. Conni Marie had come to the studio to watch. She was always so outspoken about everything, it'd be fun to hear her input.

Conni and I ran down the hall to the stage, passing several actors running their lines. I didn't really take a look at their faces. I wanted to wait until I was actually on stage doing the scene with them. However, there was one actor I already knew. His name was Randy Brooks. Randy and I had done a small, independent film together, years ago, when I'd first moved to California. It was a teenage comedy akin to *Cooley High*, but nowhere near as successful called *The Monkey Hustle*. I'd not seen Randy since then.

My character, Chantal, who was a lawyer on the show, would be prosecuting a superstar athlete named Eric Royal. Eric would be accused of drunk driving and running down an elderly bag lady.

The scene we were auditioning was very intense, escalating into a heated argument, where Chantal fights to maintain her professionalism. Smoldering beneath the anger, however, was a deep, mutual attraction.

Most of the guys played the scene too over the top, shouting loudly, and in my face. At one point, out of the corner of my eye, I caught Conni Marie vigorously shaking her head, like she was saying, *'I hope to God they don't pick him!'* I tried not to laugh.

The last actor who walked in was Randy, dressed in black from head to toe. I couldn't believe my eyes when I saw him. The first time we'd met, Randy had been a kind of cute, young guy, with a gap in his front teeth. But now he was strikingly handsome. About five feet ten with chocolate brown skin, large dark eyes with sweeping lashes, and sexy-looking as all get out. I heard a voice quietly yell out, *Damn!* I hoped no one other than me heard Conni Marie's enthusiasm.

Randy's self-assuredness could not be mistaken. During the scene, instead of screaming out his anger, he kept it contained. But *then* Randy did what no other actor had dared to do. He slid his hand softly around my neck, and kissed me. It took a moment for Chantal to gather her wits about her, and slap Eric for his presumptuousness. It took Debbi a moment to gather her wits about her, too.

At the end of the scene, applause could be heard coming from the control booth off the stage. A few of the show's actresses stood off on the side, also watching Randy's audition. There probably wasn't a single person not rooting for Randy to get the part of the spoiled, rich, superstar football player, Eric Royal.

Randy gave me a quick hug. "Debbi, it's so great to see you after all this time, and to work with you again. Hopefully, we'll get to continue."

Well, if I had anything to say about it, we'd definitely be working together again. There was no question in my mind that Randy was the best actor for the job.

After Randy left the stage, I ran into the control booth. Jonelle Allen and Joan Pringle were already putting in their two cents about Randy's great audition.

"Debbi, the way he kissed you like that, at the end of the scene, was just too hot, Girl! He'd be a great addition to the show, Jorn!"

Jonelle's big eyes almost popped out of her head. If she were speaking personally, Jonelle probably figured Randy would be a great addition in more ways than one.

"Debbi, what did you think?" Jorn asked.

"Jorn, hands down, Randy was the best Eric."

Sally Sussman nodded in agreement. "You two had immediate chemistry, and you look beautiful together!"

Yorn said, "Well, we all seem to like him. But we still have to get all the screen tests to the network and hear what they have to say."

Conni Marie was waiting for me in my dressing room. She jumped up when I walked in.

"Are they going with Randy?!"

"I'm thinking they will. But no final decision will be made until the network looks at all of the screen tests."

"Well, if they go with any of those other bozos, they're crazy. Did you see that first guy? He looked like Big Foot. You wouldn't want to have to be kissing his butt every day."

Conni and I cracked up.

That evening, I got a call from Dutton. He said it looked like the closing on our house might take a little longer. The couple that was purchasing it was about to get married, and suddenly the man wanted the woman to sign a prenup. The woman was refusing.

Our real estate agent said they couldn't back out of the deal, but things might get delayed a bit.

It'd been very awkward having a conversation with Dutton, even one that wasn't personal. After the scene outside Ron Bush's office, I wasn't quite sure what to make of my husband, who seemed like he was changing before my eyes. Dutton's reaction had definitely rattled me, and we'd spoken very little for the duration of his stay. But once he was back in New York, he'd called to apologize.

"Babe, I'm sorry. I didn't mean to get that upset with you. But it made me so angry that you wouldn't believe me when I told you I'd been at a club all night. I was telling you the truth. It pissed me off the way you kept calling me a liar. Then when you blurted it all out to that guy, it really pissed me off. The reason I didn't get into anything with him is because once we got there, I realized, I was not about to tell some strange man our business. Now if you're comfortable doing that, go ahead. But I'm sorry, Babe, I can't do it."

Then Dutton went on like all was right with the world. Obviously, in his world, it was. Dutton's meeting with FOX had been fantastic. The studio announced it would be shooting the pilot for my husband's own television series. Also if Dutton agreed, the producers wanted to call the show, *Roc*.

As if his career couldn't get any hotter, Dutton would also be co-starring with Sigourney Weaver in a sequel to *Aliens*. But as happy as I was for the success of my husband's career, I was as sad, frustrated, and scared for where our marriage was obviously headed.

The whole thing was wearing me down.

"Are you going right home?"

"I was planning to. Why?"

"You want to stop by my place first, and run that big scene we have for tomorrow?"

"Where do you live?'

"Not too far. Right over here in Studio City."

"Okay. I guess we can do that."

I got in my car and followed behind Randy's blue Jaguar out of the NBC parking lot. We'd been working together for over a month, and the chemistry we had on camera was electric. We'd gotten compliments from everyone about how great our scenes were together. But as I stopped behind Randy at a red light, I wasn't so sure this was a good idea. Maybe we should've stayed behind at the studio, and worked on the scene there.

Randy pulled into the driveway of a small, hunter-green cottage house off of Laurel Terrace. I pulled in beside him.

"Cute house, Randy."

"You think so? You'd better wait 'til you get inside. But it's not mine. I moved in here with my manager until I find a place. I needed to get out of where I was living."

"Oh, I see."

When we walked into the house, I could see what Randy meant. There wasn't a lot of light in the lifeless living room. The furniture was sparse, and what little there was, looked old and worn.

"Come on; we'll go on back to my room."

"Is your manager here?"

"She's probably out at meetings; otherwise, she'd be sitting in here at her desk with a cup of coffee."

We walked by a cramped-looking office that at one time might've been pink, but now looked a murky tan. I caught a glimpse of stacked papers on a wooden desk, and a small sofa piled with scripts. The office was even darker than the living area.

But when we entered Randy's room, it was in stark contrast to what I'd seen of the rest of the home. It was light, bright, and airy. There was a huge window with a beautiful magnolia tree sitting outside. I was glad because I was about to suggest going somewhere else to rehearse.

"This is a nice room, Randy."

"Yeah, the rest of the place looks like vampires live here."

I laughed.

"My manager's cool, but not much for decorating. I can't wait to find a place." Randy stared down at me for a moment and then switched gears. "You know I'm having a great time working with you on the show, but I wonder if *Generations* is going to make it."

"I don't know, Randy. I wish the ratings would stay up. Every time they jump up, they fall back down the very next week."

Randy said, "Maybe that scene we have coming up next week will keep 'em watching."

"You mean our love scene?"

"Yeah, have you read it?"

"Oh, yeah. It's pretty steamy. I'm sure a lot of it will have to be cut. It's probably way too risqué."

Randy smiled sexily. "I hope they don't have to cut a thing."

Suddenly, the room felt really small, and really warm. I looked away, pulling my script out of my bag.

"Well, we should get to work on this scene."

A car groaned up the driveway and Randy peeked out the window. "That's Louise. Come on; let me introduce you."

We walked out to the kitchen, which was a lot brighter than the living room. There were a few dirty dishes in the sink, and a crack in one of the tiles on the floor. But other than Randy's room, it looked to be the most pleasant room in the house.

A short, Jewish woman, probably in her mid-fifties, with shoulder-length, bleach-blonde hair, entered through the kitchen door. She had a cigarette dangling from her lips, while bangled arms held on to two large grocery bags.

"Oh, hi, Debbi; such a pleasure to finally meet you!"

"Hi, Louise; nice to meet you, too."

"I've been watching you every day on the show since Randy's been on."

"Debbi and I are getting ready to work on a big scene we're shooting tomorrow."

"Great! Don't let me stop you. If you guys need me to run lines with you afterward, I'll be happy to."

Randy and I went back to his room and started working on our big courtroom scene. My character, Chantal, had really started to fall for Eric, and it was getting in the way of her prosecuting him. She was supposed to get angry and start attacking him on the witness stand. But underneath, there was this sexual tension she was trying desperately to hide.

Randy had a gleam in his eyes as if we both knew where this could really go, which was way beyond our characters.

I pulled back and said, "Let's start the scene again." We rehearsed it a few different ways, and then I suggested we run our lines with Louise.

When we were done, Louise sat staring at us. "Wow! That was excellent. You guys got that word for word, too. That's not *all* you have, either." Louise smiled. "But we won't discuss that."

The following day, when Randy and I actually shot our scene, we got it in one take. It was exhilarating to get through such a great scene without a hitch. We gave each other a big hug, and were walking off stage when the stage manager came running up to us.

"Hey, guys. Jorn wants to see the two of you up in his office."

The way things had been going, hopefully it wasn't any bad news.

We entered Jorn's spacious office, and sat on the opposite side of his desk, adorned with family photos.

"I was watching the monitor up here with the scene you two just did. It was marvelous."

Randy and I looked at each other and smiled.

"You know we've been dropping in the ratings, but now with all this courtroom stuff between you guys, we've been picking up again. We want to keep it that way."

Randy and I nodded.

"Now that first love scene you two have next week, Tony Morina is going to direct. He wants it to be hot, and I'm all for it. The audience has been waiting for this. So we're going to try pushing the envelope as far as the network will allow.

"You guys seem to be good friends now, and pretty comfortable with one another. But I don't want you getting together and discussing anything about the scene. I want it to be spontaneous. Tony has some good ideas, but he's not going to share them with you until the day of shooting."

When Randy and I left Jorn's office, we couldn't help but wonder what Tony had in mind, but we agreed not to discuss it. Tony was one of our best directors, so at least we had that going for us. Randy and I had only one small scene together the following day. After that, we had no more scenes together until the end of the following week, the day of our big love scene.

'I didn't know you could play.'

'I can't. I just kind of peck around on the keys for fun.'

'Playing like that? Yeah... right.'

Eric is at the piano tinkering on the keys in his expensive penthouse apartment. He and Chantal are making small talk and joking with each other.

It turns out that Eric had not been drunk at all the night he'd run down the bag lady, but on medication that he'd mistakenly taken too much of. Between Eric's great attorney and a little help from the sidelines, plus Eric's superstardom, he's gotten off with just community service.

Eric begins playing something romantic on the piano. Then he starts to sing.

Randy had quite a lovely voice. I'd never had anyone sing to me before even while acting.

Eric stops playing, staring deeply into Chantal's eyes. She nervously rises from the piano, and crosses over to the middle of the room. She looks back at Eric, and urges him to continue playing the beautiful song. But Eric gets up from the piano and crosses over to her. Now he's just standing there, watching her, and undressing her with his eyes.

Randy had been directed to start unbuttoning my blouse. The costume designer had put me in a very sexy bra, which exposed my ample cleavage. Then Randy was supposed to start taking off my boots while I unbuckled my belt. But instead, Randy buried his mouth delicately into my bosom.

I let out an audible moan; I mean Chantal let out an audible moan; I mean Debbi did; no, I mean Chantal. Well, who cared? At that point, we were pretty much one and the same.

It had been so long since I'd been made to feel so wanted. I went through the rest of the scene hoping some of the shots got screwed up, so we'd have to repeat the scene over and over.

Randy and I were completely in sync with one another, and Tony was definitely pushing the envelope. The scene was broken up into a series of vignettes. *Now I was wearing nothing but panties, and a long man's shirt. I'd straddled Randy, or rather Eric, on the sofa, while our bodies gyrated up and down. Again, real life and make-believe became interchangeable.*

We tongue-kissed and caressed, and then Tony directed Randy to lift me up and carry me over to the piano.

I was gently placed on top of the piano, when I felt the weight of a warm body, bearing down on top of me. I think I finally heard,

"Cut." Randy and I both ignored it until we heard, *"Cut!"* once again.

After we'd finished shooting the scene, Randy walked me back to my dressing room and asked, "Do you want to follow me home?"

I said nothing. I simply nodded my head. We drove to Randy's house and an hour later, there was no *"Cut"* to be heard...for hours.

Chapter 46

Saturday morning, when I walked into our Englewood, New Jersey, home, it was a little after 9:00 a.m. I saw Dutton asleep on the sofa in the family room. I continued toward the staircase, but his voice stopped me.

"Babe, is that you?"

My guts were playing chopsticks as I turned back toward the den. *How do I tell Dutton? Do* I *tell him?* "Yeah...it's me."

I slowly walked into the fuchsia and white room with the pretty cranberry tiles. Dutton rose up from our large, comfy sofa to a sitting position. I sat down beside him. He leaned in for a kiss, and responding was one of the hardest things I ever had to do.

"Hey, Pretty Girl. It's so good to see you. Oh, listen, Vernon and I found a pretty nice place on the Upper East Side in the mid-nineties. We have to be out of here by Tuesday when those people take ownership. What's the matter?!"

Tears were streaming down my face as I tried to find the words. "Dutton...it...is...it's so hard for me to...to say this...to...to you."

"Say what?"

"I... I...I want a divorce," tumbled out of my mouth.

He looked at me with total shock, waiting for an explanation.

"I just... I can't live like this anymore."

"Live like what?"

"In a sexless marriage. I don't want to. And I can't anymore. It's not fair. I'm tired of all the promises you've made that you haven't kept, and I'm tired of being married to a husband who seems to have only an occasional desire for me."

"That's not true."

"Dutton! Please don't start that again. We both know the reality, and you refuse to want to do anything about it. Then you threaten me, scaring me half to death when I try to do something about it."

"What are you talking about, threaten you?"

"You know what I'm talking about, when we were outside of Ron Bush's office."

"You need to stop that. I wasn't threatening you. I was upset about the way you acted. I told you that. But I would never threaten you... I love you... Jesus, Babe, I can't believe you want to divorce me."

I watched the tears well up in Dutton's eyes, and I didn't know what to think, or what more to say. Staying married to Dutton while I was sleeping with another man was the last thing I wanted to do. The only other alternative was to end it with Randy, immediately, and continue having a sexless marriage with my husband. But that's what I'd been doing all these years; I simply couldn't bear it any longer. Maybe it was still no excuse for my infidelity, but it had been almost unavoidable, like a volcano waiting to erupt.

It tore me up to look at Dutton. He seemed completely crushed like he'd never in a million years thought I'd do something like this. But who knows how he'd be looking if he knew I'd been fucking Randy. I shivered, thinking about that. At the same time, I thought about the big lie he'd told, about being at a club all night. Who knew what his ass had been doing while I was in Los Angeles, but then again, maybe not much. Since Dutton didn't appear to have that much interest in lovemaking, maybe he was more into self-gratification—an uncontrollable, residual habit from his prison days.

Dutton rubbed his forehead and then stared down at the floor. It had to be at least two minutes before he spoke. "Okay...Okay. If that's what you want to do, I won't try and stop you."

"I'll have the contractors finish the house in L.A. and then we'll put it back on the market. I'll call a storage company for all the furniture here. Does that all sound okay with you, Dutton?"

"There was a message from our realtor, Bernadette, late last night when I got in. You'd already left L.A. to come here. She said there was a call from the buyer's agent, saying that now they wanted to make an offer to buy all the furniture. Is that okay with you?"

"Under these circumstances...I guess so."

Dutton got up from the couch and walked a few steps toward the living room. He turned back with sadness so deep, it was all I could do not to change my mind.

"I'm sorry you want to take such a big step, Pretty Girl. I really am."

Dutton went upstairs, and I looked around at what'd been our first dream home. Then I called a cab to take me back to Newark Airport.

We'd been married for only a year at that point, physically and sexually separated for months, emotionally and sexually separated for longer than that, probably. Yet, somehow, there was a deep regret to this official nail in the coffin of our six-year relationship.

In the beginning, I'd convinced myself that I might be falling in love with Randy. Perhaps, partially to justify what I was doing. But I wasn't in love with Randy. I was still in love with Dutton, despite rumors that he was sleeping with his casting agent, Kelley Sharp. Even Randy had heard the rumors.

Why had Dutton seemed so devastated about us divorcing? Was he only pretending? And if this was all true, then shouldn't I be happy? I was getting out, free of guilt for what I'd been doing. But the end hadn't justified the means. I was completely distraught.

After an abrupt end to an evening with Randy, I trudged back to the duplex I shared with Conni Marie. I felt like a ninety-year-old woman trying to ascend the stairs. Each foot felt like a hundred-pound weight.

I walked in the door and found Conni Marie in front of the tube watching *Jeopardy*, her favorite game show. But she took one look at me and immediately turned down the sound.

"Deb, what's wrong?!"

It was too much of a burden to sit, so I stood there. "I heard Dutton's been fucking Kelley Sharp."

Conni's big eyes seemed to flutter. "Well..."

"Well, what, Conni?"

I could tell it was difficult for her to say. "I've...been...uh...hearing that for a while now."

"And you didn't tell me?!"

"Girl, I wasn't going to bring something like that to you. It's not like I'd actually seen them myself. Plus, I didn't want to believe it. But after you finally told me what's been going on in you all's relationship all this time, and then you started seeing Randy, I was like, well, I don't need to say anything."

It had to be way after midnight when I heard the phone ringing next to my bed. I grabbed for it in the dark, knocking over a bottle of juice I'd not finished drinking

"Damn! Hel-hello?"

"Who are you talking to?"

"Hi, Dutton. Nobody. I knocked over a bottle of juice."

"So, are you alone?'

"Yes, why?"

"Are you sure about that?" he probed further.

I got a bit nervous. "Yes, I'm sure."

"So why did you come home telling me some bogus story about why you wanted a divorce, when the real story is that you're fucking that guy on your show?"

"What are you talking about?" I tried to deny.

"Don't give me that shit! You know very well what I'm talking about. People have been seeing you guys at the movies, at restaurants, holding hands and shit!"

"That's funny. I've been hearing people say the same thing about you and Kelley Sharp. Someone said they've seen you two leaving the theater together almost every night."

"First of all, Kelley is the one who hooked me up with Yolanda for an assistant. I'm also talking to her about some projects I want to do."

"That's supposed to mean you're not sleeping with her?"

"It means my relationship with Kelley is strictly business. Whoever said I'm fucking her is telling a fucking lie!"

"My relationship with Randy is business, too. Although we did go to one movie together. We weren't holding hands. And whoever said I was fucking him is telling a fucking lie!"

I figured if Dutton could tell more than a little white lie, so could I.

Chapter 47

In my head, I justified sleeping with another man by the fact that my husband denied me my rights as a wife. To hear that he'd been seeing another woman all along only complicated things. *Why?* Why would he be sleeping with another woman when he hadn't even touched his wife? It didn't make sense. And if he was no longer attracted to me, then why be so devastated about losing me?

Randy said it'd probably all been an act. But Randy didn't know Dutton, and had no clue how Dutton really felt about me.

I couldn't believe things had happened this way. It wasn't apparent to anyone but me that I still longed to be with my husband. I wanted the fairytale. I wanted Dutton as my husband, and my lover. And no matter how I tried to tell myself it was too late for that, that things would never change, that Dutton had been equally deceptive, I couldn't let go of my secret wish.

What did become apparent was that Randy was getting on my last nerve. That's what happens when you mix business with pleasure. We kept having little mini fights and disagreements, probably a lot of it having to do with residual stuff from my marriage.

One night, we doubled with Conni Marie and her new beau, Michael George. The four of us followed the waitress with the hillbilly accent and jet-black hair teased to the heavens. She sat us at a small table near the front of the stage. "I'll be right back for your drink orders."

We were in a club at the Aladdin hotel in Las Vegas. A couple of friends had told Conni and I not to miss an incredible singer named Ellis Horne.

"And now, Ladies and Gentlemen, coming to the stage for his last night here at the Aladdin, Las Vegas's own, the soulful Ellis Horne!"

A light brown-skinned man of medium height strutted out onto the stage singing Otis Redding's "Dock of the Bay." From the first note he sang, it was clear that Ellis Horne should have hit records instead of performing in some small club in a Las Vegas hotel. His sexy, husky voice, along with his incredible stage presence, had everyone up on their feet, dancing in the small aisle for almost the entire show.

After Ellis's ninety minutes were up, we were all shouting for him to sing one more song.

"Come on; let's go. I've heard enough of Doughboy!" Randy shouted.

Conni Marie and I both looked at Randy like he had a problem. But then Ellis began singing Babyface's "Whip Appeal." All the women in the room, including Conni and myself, started screaming.

"I'm going out to take a smoke!"

I ignored Randy. I also couldn't stand his cigarette breath anymore.

You've got that whip appeal, so come on and whip it on me...

Ellis's dynamic voice and sensual presence whipped it on every woman in that room, including me. And his rendition of "Whip Appeal" far surpassed Babyface's any day!

We were all our feet clapping, and wanting more, but that was the last of Ellis's set. Michael had walked off to join Randy for a smoke when the drummer from Ellis's band walked over.

"Hi, you're Debbi Morgan, aren't you?"

"Hi, yes, I am. And this is my friend, Conni Marie."

"Nice to meet you, Conni Marie. My name is Alex. Listen, Ellis wanted to know if you could wait for a second. He would love to meet you."

"Tell him we'll think about it, if he sings one more song...no, no, no. I'm just kidding." Conni was such a nut!

Alex looked at Conni and chuckled as he walked off. I started putting on my jacket. Now that we weren't jumping around anymore, it was freezing in the place.

Ellis Horne finally came over to us, wearing a white jacket, with a towel wrapped around his neck.

"Hi, I'm Ellis." He extended his hand with a strong grip. "You probably get tired of hearing this, but I'm a huge fan."

"After hearing you sing tonight, I'm a huge fan of yours as well."

"Thank you very much." Ellis extended his hand out to Conni. "Hello, and what's your name?"

"Conni Marie. You gave a great show."

"Thanks, Conni Marie. Did you all come down from L.A.?"

"Yeah, we did," I said. "And I have to tell you, I am in love with your rendition of 'Whip Appeal.'"

"Really? Would you like a copy of it?"

"Definitely!"

"That's no problem. Lily, come here a minute." A petite white woman with cropped, dark hair left the group to whom she was speaking and walked over to us.

"Lily, this is Debbi Morgan, and Conni Marie. This is my wife, Lily."

"Hi, Conni Marie."

"Hi, Lily."

"Nice to meet you, Debbi. My husband is such a fan of yours. He couldn't believe it when he saw you sitting out in the audience."

"Can you get all of Debbi's information, Honey? I want to send her a copy of 'Whip Appeal.'"

"Sure can." Ellis's wife fished through her purse and pulled out a small pad. Then she wrote down my address and phone number. "Debbi, let me give you our number, too."

After we'd exchanged information, someone called out to Lily.

"Debbi, Conni Marie, it was a pleasure meeting you."

We said goodbye and Lily darted off. Ellis was looking at me and shaking his head.

"I can't believe I've really gotten a chance to meet you. Hopefully, you guys will make it back down again. I'm usually here at the Aladdin or the Rio. But in the meantime, Debbi, I'll make sure Lily gets that tape to you."

"Thanks so much, Ellis."

Michael and Randy walked up. I introduced them both to Ellis.

"Michael, Randy, how you doin'?"

Michael shook Ellis's hand. "Enjoyed your show, Man."

"Oh, thank you. Thanks a lot."

Randy turned around and walked off. An awkward moment felt by everyone.

The three of us said goodbye to Ellis, and I told him I'd look forward to getting the tape.

In the car on the way back to L.A., Randy barely joined in any of the conversation, until Conni Marie brought up Ellis's show.

"That Ellis is a singing something. I wonder why he doesn't have a hit record."

"Ain't nobody gonna give Doughboy no hit record."

"What are you trying to say, Randy, that the guy is fat? He's hardly fat," I said.

"He might not be fat, but he's a chubbo!" Randy laughed.

Conni said, "That guy ain't even chubby, Randy."

"He isn't," I said. "And, Randy, why were you so rude? When we introduced you and Michael, you hardly said hello, and then you just walked off."

"I said hello to Doughboy. What, you mad because I wasn't falling all over him like you and Conni? Did you see the way they were acting over that guy, Mike?"

"Aw, Man, they seemed to be having a good time like everybody else."

Randy must not have cared for Michael's response. He said nothing further for the remainder of the ride. Hours later, when we pulled up to Randy's house, he finally spoke. "Are you staying over?"

"No, I'm not. I'm going home."

"Fine!" Randy got out and slammed the door, barely saying goodbye to anyone.

"Damn! What the hell is his problem? He acted like he was jealous of Ellis or something. Debbi, you might want to rethink your relationship with him, 'cause he's starting to act a bit on the nutty side if you ask me."

I thought to myself that Conni was quite right.

After the Las Vegas trip, I only stayed over at Randy's maybe once or twice again. I wasn't feeling the same about him, and began pulling back. That posture began interfering with our work. Randy would blow lines during our scenes together, and throw temper-tantrums when given directions. I began to dread the days we had to work together. But it wouldn't be for much longer.

Word came down from the network that *Generations* was being cancelled. The network had given us only three more months. I'd given Randy only three weeks before I officially told him it was over.

"Deb, I'm running out for a commercial audition. I put your mail in your room."

"Thanks, Conni. Good luck on your audition!" Conni Marie was already out the door.

I sat on my bed, and absently began sifting through my mail. I was terribly disheartened by our cancellation news. *Generations* had gotten to be a really good show, and if only given more time, I knew we'd get the ratings.

There I was sulking in this funk when I came across a small manila envelope with the name, *E. Horne* on the return address label. Who could that be? At first glance of the cassette tape, I was confused. Then I saw the bold, black letters, on white tape, staring me in the face, *Whip Appeal (copy for Debbi Morgan).* As much as I'd wanted the tape, I'd forgotten all about it. I pulled out the folded note.

Hi, Debbi. Sorry it took a little longer to get the tape to you. I've been in the studio working on some material. In any event, here it is. Hope you enjoy it as much as the real thing. And again, it was so great meeting you in person. You seem like a terrific young lady. I really do hope you'll come to another show.

Ellis

I ran over to my cassette player, and popped in the tape. It was *just* as good as the real thing. I played that song over and over and over.

One day, Conni said, "Damn! Can't you call that guy and ask him to send you another song?"

Suddenly, I remembered I'd not called Ellis at all to even thank him. How rude was that? I ran right into my room to look for his number.

"Hello?"

"Hello? May I please speak to Ellis?"

"Why hello, Ms. Morgan."

"How did you recognize my voice?"

"Because it's very sweet, and very recognizable."

I'd recognized Ellis's husky, sexy voice, too, as soon as he'd picked up, but thought it more proper to ask for him first.

"Ellis, I'm calling to apologize for not letting you know I'd received the tape almost a month ago, and to thank you for it."

"I was giving you three more days, and then I was going to come to L.A. and hunt you down. I was like, what's up with that woman, acting like she wanted a copy of the tape so much, and then I don't hear a

word from her. I was going to start spreading the news about you, Girl."

Ellis and I started laughing. Not only was he a great singer, but he also had a great sense of humor.

"You know I'm just playing with you. So have you enjoyed listening to the tape?"

"Are you kidding? I play it so much, my friend you met, Conni Marie, said, 'Girl, can you please call Ellis and tell him to send you another song?'"

"I most certainly can. As a matter of fact, I'll send you a tape of the show."

"Would you really do that?!"

"Of course I would, but under one condition."

"What's that?"

"You have to promise to come back to Vegas to see another one of my shows."

"Our girlfriend, Roxanne Reese, is doing her comedy show in Vegas in three weeks."

"I know Roxanne. I've caught her show a couple of times. She's pretty funny. Well, I'll be over at the Rio in three weeks. So will you and your friends come by?"

"You don't even have to ask. I wouldn't miss it."

"Great. And maybe I'll give you a call just to say hello in a couple of days."

"Okay, Ellis. That's fine. I'll talk to you later then."

Ellis called me the following day, and almost every other day after that. And then it was time for our trip back to Las Vegas. Our conversations had been light and fun, and I'd found him easy to talk to.

A small group of us went down to see Roxanne's show, and then we all went and caught Ellis's midnight show at the Rio. He was even better than I'd remembered. And Ellis's sexiness on stage was quite substantial. It was fun sitting back, and having my innocent fantasies that no one would ever know about. I wouldn't have been surprised if every other woman in the room was having her fantasy, too.

At the end of Ellis's set, we all waited to say hello. He was glad we'd come and asked what our plans were. We were going off to a club to dance. Ellis asked if he could join us.

Conni said, "All that shakin' and grindin' you been doing up on that stage, and you still have energy to dance?"

Ellis looked at me and laughed. "Where'd you get her from?"

Later, at the club, we all danced to fast-paced jams. Then the DJ started playing some oldies. He put on Luther Vandross's "A House is Not a Home."

"May I have this dance?"

"You may."

Ellis held me in his arms as we swayed to Luther's sensual tone. I had to admit I'd had fantasies about Ellis since the first night I'd seen him on stage. My thoughts had been like those of an innocent schoolgirl. But dancing in Ellis's arms right now, the feelings piercing through my body were not those of a child. I felt my body stiffen, slightly, for fear of being exposed.

When we left the club, Ellis offered to drive us all back to our hotel. He walked us into the lobby, where a message for Conni Marie was waiting at the front desk. Her agent had been trying to reach her. She had a big callback for a national commercial the following morning. Since planes left almost every half-hour out of Vegas, Conni thought it best to take the next flight she could get back to L.A., wanting to be fresh by morning.

Ellis offered to drive Conni Marie, and I said I'd go with them. After grabbing her few things from the room, we sped out to the Vegas Airport. After we dropped her off, he drove me back to the hotel. He asked the valet to leave his car close by because he'd be right back down.

When we got up to my room, Ellis asked, "Can I come in for a minute?"

I said, *'No'* in my head, as I opened the door wide for Ellis to step in. He took my hand and led me over to the bed, gently pushing me down against the pillows.

"Do you like chocolate?" he whispered.

"It's my downfall."

Ellis opened the wrapper of the chocolate candy that had been left on the pillow. He put it to my lips, and I took a small bite. Ellis ate the rest. Then he gently brushed the softest lips I'd ever felt along my neck, across my cheeks, the sides of my face, and then he stared down at me. Time seemed to literally stand still.

"You are so very, very beautiful. You take my breath away. And I truly hope I'll see you again."

Ellis got up and left the room. I lay there in a trance, and then I thought of the words Ellis had said: *you take my breath away.* Remembering the first words from the vows I'd made to Dutton quickly brought me out of my reverie.

Now I was filled with guilt. Of course, I was separated from Dutton. I'd told Ellis I was separated from my husband, and had in fact filed for divorce. And I was smart enough to know Dutton wasn't spending many of his nights alone. But even though I'd already had an affair with Randy, this was quite different. It was far worse, actually, because Ellis was very much married. Later I'd even learn he and Lily had a five-year-old son, and Ellis also had a thirteen-year-old son from a previous marriage.

What had just happened was not right, not at all. But what *had* happened? Ellis and I hadn't had sex. We hadn't even kissed. But it'd been in our heads nonetheless. That's where it would remain because this was truly dangerous territory. My life was in enough shambles as it was. I would not be making any more trips to Las Vegas.

And then I caressed my neck, my cheeks, and the sides of my face, remembering his touch. I promised myself that tomorrow I would go home and throw away his tape. I'd change my phone number. This man had gotten so under my skin; I'd not trust myself to hear even the sound of his voice.

But how could I block out the memory? That would prove impossible.

Chapter 48

To my surprise, Dutton invited me to stay in his hotel room while he was visiting L.A. on business. He was staying on the penthouse floor of the Beverly Hills Hotel. Apparently, the network was already giving Dutton the star treatment. I was nervous as I rang the buzzer. Suppose this was all a trick, and Dutton was waiting to get to me in person, about what he'd heard about Randy and me? What on earth was I thinking coming here? For a brief second, I thought about turning around and fleeing.

"Hey, Pretty Girl. Come in." He opened the door wearing a luxurious robe, and smiling. "I just got out of the shower."

So this was it. Once I stepped into the room, he'd have my head.

I entered the large, sea foam-colored room, with the beautiful antique furnishings, expecting the axe to drop.

"Do you feel like going out for dinner?" he asked.

"As long as it's not too fancy. I didn't dress for dinner." *Well, at least we'll have witnesses.*

"You look beautiful. Let me throw some clothes on."

Forty-five minutes later, Dutton and I were seated at an outside garden table at the Moustache Café on Melrose Avenue. He ordered the steak. I was picking at my seafood crepe.

"I couldn't wait to tell you all the good news about the pilot."

"It sounds really wonderful, Dutton."

"I have a thousand things to do before I leave for London. Luckily, I've still been able to hold on to Yolanda. She's kept all my shit in some semblance of order for me."

I wondered if Dutton was still having a relationship with Kelley Sharp. But I didn't want to bring the subject up. Surprisingly, Dutton didn't mention Randy either.

Once I figured I was safe, I sat back, relaxed, and took him in. Dutton was jovial and in great spirits. I found myself missing the old days, when we'd first met. Maybe it was those memories that led me to delay our divorce upon the advice of our business manager.

"I'm glad you decided to hold off on the divorce," Dutton said.

"You are?"

"Yes, I am. And I wanted to ask you. Let's not do anything until I get back from London. We'll both have enough time apart to see if this is what we really want to do. I'm going places, Babe. And I want you to be right there with me."

"Dutton, I'd love nothing more than to always be by your side. But we can't pretend we don't have problems and think they're going to go away on their own."

"I know that. Believe me, I know that. And I'm going to have to take a stand as far as my responsibility is concerned. But I have a feeling that in the end, it's all going to work out. I'm convinced it will. So will you promise that you won't do anything until I get back from London? Will you?"

"All right, I promise."

Dutton rose and leaned across the table to give me a kiss. "I love you, Pretty Girl." Then he sat back down and called the waitress to order two chocolate soufflés.

"You know what I'm thinking? It would be great for you to come over to London for a visit," he invited.

"Yeah, maybe I can. I've never been to Europe."

Dutton talked a good game. He had a gift. But wouldn't you know it, when we got back to the hotel, he didn't even attempt to make love to me. And I had no desire to initiate it. However, I'd given him my word. So I wouldn't be going through with the divorce...at least for now.

Rain was splattering against the windowpane so hard, I barely heard the phone. I picked it up and heard him speak.

"I'd really like to see you again." Ellis's voice caressed my heart through the phone.

Of course, this wouldn't have been possible if I'd changed the number like I told myself I would. I wanted to see Ellis again, too, but I didn't dare. There was no way to fool myself. Going back to Vegas would be nothing short of destructive.

"I don't think that's a good idea."

"Can I call you again?"

"Okay." At least we weren't in the same city, so what real harm could there be in talking to the man? But then I went and played his tape, the tape that I'd told myself I'd discard.

The next time Ellis called, it was after his last show, when his voice had dropped another octave, and I'd been playing his tape all night. The rich huskiness in his tone was enough to make me climb the walls. So when Ellis asked again to see me, I told him I'd take a flight out the very next morning.

I tried keeping my mind on other things, as I got ready to drive to the airport the following morning. If I allowed myself to think sensibly about it, I wouldn't do it. And I wanted to do it.

I told Conni Marie that I was going out of town for two days.

"Where're you going? You're going to Las Vegas to see that Ellis, aren't you?"

"No, Conni!" How weak did that lie sound?

Conni Marie burst out laughing. "Girl, yes you are. You'd better be careful, Debbi."

My friend's warning should've been enough. But the sound of Ellis's voice in my head, and the memory of his touch, threw *all* my caution to the wind.

I arrived at the check-in desk at the Rio hotel and picked up the key Ellis had left for me. When I entered the bright, sun-filled room, the light almost blinded me. And then I saw a huge vase of exotic flowers sitting on the dresser. How could Ellis know these were the only flowers I actually liked?

I read the note attached to one of the stems, tied with a red ribbon.

Thinking of you is like the scent of an exotic flower. I'll see you shortly.
Ellis

I drew the curtains and lay on the bed for a moment. This was so wrong, and I knew it. It wasn't too late. I could leave Ellis a note explaining that I'd changed my mind about all this. Thank him for the flowers, and get the hell out of this room. Instead, I drifted off to sleep.

My eyes slowly opened at the sound of a key in the door. But I didn't move. Ellis walked in. "Shh, shh. It's okay. Stay there."

He walked to the bed and looked down at me. "Well, looka here." He smiled. "There's an angel in my bed."

My heart was racing a thousand beats per second.

Sitting down beside me, Ellis was still smiling as he slowly unbuttoned, and pulled off my blouse. He reached behind my back and unhooked my bra, then seductively slid down my pants, slowly lifting me out of my lace panties, never once moving his eyes away from mine, until he stood.

Now Ellis was taking in every inch of me, while stepping out of his own clothes. First, his shirt, exposing a beautiful-toned chest—*and Randy had called him Doughboy!*—now his pants, and finally, his silk briefs.

Lord Jesus! Have mercy on my sinful soul!! I took one look at that huge hunk of love between Ellis's legs, and just about lost my mind!

Like the last time, Ellis brushed his soft lips across my body. Only this time, he took in my toes, the inside of my arms, and turning me over, ran his moist tongue down the center of my back, and then he turned me back to him, methodically placing each aching nipple into his hungry mouth.

Finally, and for the first time, Ellis covered my lips with his. Christ! Even his kiss was enough to bring me to an orgasm.

And when I did reach one, it was like no other experience I'd ever had in life. Ellis filled every inch of me. And with each powerful thrust, it was like I'd died and gone to hell, because anything this good could not be righteous, and righteous it wasn't!

Now I had a deeper understanding of the plight of a drug addict. A feeling of such ecstasy, such immeasurable longing for another dose, that whatever the cost, you'd cringe at the thought of being without it.

Dutton had been in London for a little over a month. So far we'd only spoken twice, and each time he'd called, neither one of us had brought up my coming for a visit.

One evening, I tried giving Dutton a call. The phone rang several times and finally someone answered, but it wasn't my husband. The woman spoke in a clipped Cockney accent. *'Hello, who's calling, please?'*

"I'm sorry. I must have the wrong number. I was looking for Charles Dutton."

'Roc's not home at the moment. Who shall I say was calling?'

What would be his excuse this time—that it was the maid who'd answered his phone?

"Tell him his wife called. Thank you."

I didn't wait for the woman's response, nor did I care to ask who she was. However, I couldn't say another woman answering my husband's phone even necessarily upset me. How could it when I was having my own lustful affair with another woman's husband?

But it was so much more than that. I was falling deeply in love with Ellis, and he with me. I was going down to Las Vegas almost every other weekend, and it still wasn't enough. I wanted to be with Ellis twenty-four hours a day.

Yet the last time I'd gone to Vegas, things began to get messy.

Ellis had taken me with him to a recording studio. While there, an old girlfriend of one of the band members stopped by. The woman knew Lily. Ellis was a bit concerned, and rightfully so. A few weeks later, the woman mentioned to Lily about seeing me at the recording studio with Ellis.

Ellis told me that he'd tried to pass it off as my being in town with friends, and stopped by to catch his show. Lily apparently accepted that story until she was in Ellis's dressing room a few nights later and found a note that said: *Debbi called.* Then she found an eight-by-ten photo I'd sent Ellis, signed: *I'm so glad we met. I hope we're part of each other's lives forever.*

Naturally, Lily was livid as she began hurling accusations at Ellis. At first he'd tried to cover, but his wife didn't fall for it. So Ellis finally confessed to a one-night mishap, but not to our ongoing affair. Lily was still devastated, and then Ellis lied yet again, swearing to his wife he'd never see me anymore.

I'd been devastated, too, because this meant the end, and putting myself in Lily's shoes, I could only imagine how much pain we'd caused her.

But Ellis insisted we'd have to think of another way because he couldn't let me go. And truth be told, I didn't know where I'd summon the strength to let go of him either. So we began talking about the possibility of a future together.

Months earlier, I'd been introduced to a fabulous gay designer named Tony Steele. Other than Conni Marie, Tony became one of my closest confidantes. He was always there with a shoulder for me to lean or cry on. Tony knew all about my relationship with Ellis. I'd shared many of the details with him. Once I told Tony that Lily knew Ellis and I had slept together, Tony became a go-between in making sure Ellis and I were always able to connect. We knew the relationship had to be dealt with much more carefully now. Often, Tony would be the one to call Ellis at home, and arrange a time that the two of us could speak.

When Ellis flew to Dallas, Texas, to perform at a large hotel, our arrangements had been carefully orchestrated, with Tony's help, for me to fly there and be with Ellis. And though the relationship would've certainly been viewed as scandalous, when we were together, it felt every bit right, like we were somehow entitled.

"Being with you is like coming home."

"What do you mean?"

Ellis and I were soaking in a huge spa tub filled with jasmine crystals in his hotel suite, surrounded by scented candles. I felt like I was on an island paradise lying back on Ellis's chest in the warm water.

"Lily was the first white woman I'd ever been with. I'd never had any attraction for white women. But we ended up hitting it off. She's been a great mother, not only to our young son, but also to my older son. I won't lie to you and pretend that my marriage was in ruins when we met, as an excuse for being with you. I do love Lily... but I love you, too. And being with you makes me realize how much I miss being with the spirit and soul of a black woman, a woman who understands everything about our struggles on a much deeper level."

Ellis sniffed the side of my neck. "Your scent is even different. That's what I meant when I said being with you is like coming home."

I turned around to face him. "I'm glad you're being honest with me."

Ellis averted his eyes.

"What's wrong?" I asked.

"That's ironic because I'm not being honest with Lily."

And was I being honest with myself? Internally, I struggled to reconcile the fact that I was still legally married and involved with another man who was also married.

My relationship with Ellis was different from the crazy fling I'd had with Randy. I'd be ready to call my attorney immediately and tell him to push my divorce through, if it meant spending the rest of my life with Ellis. But was that even an option?

It was a little after eleven when Ellis's second show ended. I stood near the entrance at the back of the stage, where I'd previously waited for him to exit. But this time, instead of giving me a squeeze and a peck on the lips, he darted right past me without a word.

By the look on Ellis's face, it was obvious that he was extremely upset about something. I wondered if I should follow him back to the room, or perhaps give him some time to deal with whatever had upset him.

I waited in the hotel lobby for about fifteen minutes, and then I slowly made my way back to the room. As I neared the door, I could hear Ellis yelling. It was obvious he was screaming at someone on the telephone. Then I realized it was Lily.

"You're not taking my son anywhere! If you want to leave, fine!

But you're not going anywhere with my child! I told you that she was down here visiting a friend. She heard I was appearing here at the hotel, and decided to come to the show. Now make all the threats you want, but you're not taking him out of Vegas, or else there is gonna be some shit!!"

Somehow Lily had found out I was in Dallas with Ellis and everything had exploded. This was not going according to plan. Ellis was supposed to sit down with his wife and carefully explain that he wanted out of the marriage. Now it seemed to have all gone awry.

Reality set in. I slowly entered the room averting Ellis's eyes. I could tell he knew I'd heard everything outside the door. Placing my suitcase on the bed, I began packing, all the while feeling the deepest pain in my heart.

Ellis put his arms around me. He held me to him like his life depended on it.

"I still want to be with you, Baby. Fuck! I don't want to ever let you go. But I have to tell Lily the truth now, all of it. And I need you to give me some time to work all this shit out."

I pulled away and stared at him. Ellis brushed the tears away from my eyes, but there was nothing else to be said. I'd have to be patient, and let the chips fall where they may.

Three weeks went by without one word from him. It was a living hell. I woke up every morning feeling as nauseous as a pregnant woman. And then, one morning at 2:00 a.m., the phone rang. I immediately grabbed it.

"Hello!"

"Hey, there." He sounded desperate.

"Hello, Ellis."

And then there was silence, both of us terrified of what had to come next.

"I can't leave blood in the street, Baby. We gotta end it, now."

My heart sank, but I said nothing. All I could do was listen as the tears flowed freely from my eyes.

He continued, "Lily took a flight to Dallas and got to the hotel after you'd left that night. She brought our son with her. After I was sure my boy was asleep, I told Lily that I'd fallen in love with you, and wanted to be with you. She didn't scream, yell, or make any more threats, like she'd done on the phone. She looked at me with this terrible hurt and shock in her eyes.

"It wasn't until we got back home to Vegas that Lily finally confronted me. *'Are you really going to rip apart our family to be with that woman? She means so much to you that you're willing to give up all we've invested, willing to take away our child's security of growing up with both his mother and father? Well, if that's what you really want, I won't stop you. I can get a free apartment in one of the rental buildings I'm managing. You don't have to move out; we will.'*

"And as much as what she was saying tore me up inside, all I kept thinking was how much I wanted to be with you. So I watched Lily every day, packing up boxes and preparing to move out. Then one afternoon when she was out of the house, my son walked up to me and said, *'Daddy, why is Mommy crying all the time? Why is she so sad, Daddy? I don't want Mommy to be sad.'* I just about lost it, Debbi. The severity of what I was about to do hit me hard in the chest. I swear before God, I love you like I've never loved another woman. If only God had let me meet you first. But for whatever reason, He didn't. And now I have to be unselfish and think about someone other than myself. As much as I'd like to ride off in the sunset with you, I cannot leave Lily and my son. I cannot leave a trail of blood behind me in the destruction of two loving, innocent lives. I'm sorry, Debbi. I am so sorry."

And then we said our final goodbye. I cried so much my eyes were practically swollen shut for days.

Why had *God cursed our union by not allowing us to meet first? Why did I have to end up marrying a man who didn't desire me the way I needed to be desired?*

Why in the end, couldn't Ellis have chosen to be with me, no matter what?

I suppose because neither one of us could've ever been happy living with that kind of guilt. And as distraught as I was, I honored Ellis for making the right choice.

Ellis would go on with his life, and I'd go on with mine. But I would never, ever, forget him, nor would I ever, ever, regret my time with him. And if I never had it again, I could look back and say, *'At least once in my life, I had a passion and a love that utterly, and completely, fulfilled me.'*

Chapter 49

Hollywood, California
1990s

"Okay, let's hear it for Carl Gordon, Rocky Carroll, Ella Joyce, and the star of the show, Charles S. Dutton! Come on, everybody, let's give it up for the cast of *Roc!*"

We all stood and applauded the cast for what had been a hilarious first show. The new series smelled like a hit. Dutton wore a grin on his face and a gleam in his eye. And I, too, was hopeful. Dutton had come back home and talked me into a reconciliation, with the promise of us going to couples therapy. Now that the door was closed with Ellis, I thought it might be best to give my marriage to Dutton one more shot.

We headed over to a nearby restaurant close to the studio after he'd gotten changed out of his costume. They were having a small party for the cast. I sat at a table with Dutton's assistant, Yolanda. I watched Dutton shaking hands, smiling, and being touted as the next breakthrough sitcom star.

The producers had given Dutton his own office on the studio lot. Yolanda had flown out for a few weeks to help him get everything set up, and to interview potential assistants for him in California.

I looked across the room, and saw Kelley Sharp, the casting director, talking to a small group of people. Kelley had been hired to cast *Roc*. I wondered if Dutton had had anything to do with her hiring. I'd chosen not to read for the part of his wife on the show. I had a feeling things might become a little intense working that close together every day, and being married. But I also would've felt very uncomfortable auditioning for Kelley, especially if all the rumors had been true. I expected they had been.

I continued to stare over at Kelley as she kept moving her head around the room in the midst of her conversation. She didn't appear engaged in the conversation; it was as if she were biding time. And then her eyes caught the back of Dutton's head, staying glued there five seconds too long.

As people began drifting out of the party, Kelley would find someone else to chat with, still staring after Dutton. Suddenly, I realized Yolanda was sitting there watching me, watch Kelley. And then I thought about the fact that Yolanda and Kelley were friends. Kelley had been the one to refer Yolanda to Dutton as an assistant.

I tried to find the right words to say, and then I came out with it. "Yolanda, Kelley is a friend of yours, so you don't have to say anything. But I know about the relationship she had with Dutton in New York when we were separated. We're back together now, but she's standing over there like she's hoping and waiting for him to take her home."

I could see Yolanda was uncomfortable as she clasped her hands, and lowered her eyes to the table. But then she looked directly at me.

"Debbi, I work for Charles, and really don't want to get into any of his personal business. But Kelley is my friend, and Charles never told her that you two were back together."

No wonder Kelley seemed to be waiting around with her hopes up. But then I watched Dutton walk over to her, and shake her hand in a very professional way. He seemed to be thanking her for her contribution to the show. Then he said good night and crossed over to the table where I sat with Yolanda. Kelley looked after him for a couple of seconds and walked out.

"Hey, Pretty Girl!" Dutton placed a big kiss on my lips. "You ready to go."

"Yeah, if you are."

"So, Yolanda, how many people are you interviewing tomorrow?"

"Four."

"I am sure I won't like any of them." Dutton pretended to pout. "Babe, I've been trying to talk Yolanda into moving out here for a while, at least until we see how things go with the show. I can't stand having to get used to someone else. They won't be as on the ball as Yolanda."

"Debbi, forgive me, but your husband is crazy. He'd better be glad my husband let me come out here for a few weeks. My six-year-old is going to be starting school. There's no way I'll be able to stay here any longer than I've planned." Then Yolanda looked up at Dutton. "Charles, I can promise you, you'll be very happy with the assistant I hire for you. Believe me."

Dutton chuckled. "Yeah, if you say so. Come on, Debbi, let's drive Yolanda back to her hotel."

After we'd dropped Yolanda off, Dutton and I headed back over the canyon toward the hills of Sherman Oaks. I'd held on to the small house we'd bought when Dutton was in L.A. doing *Piano Lesson*, and my friend, Tony Steele, had come in and taken over my job as decorator. I'd paid the contractors to complete some of the less major details on the house, and then Tony came and turned the two-bedroom bungalow into a charming and luscious dwelling.

At first, after the break-up with Ellis I didn't know what to do, or which way to turn. For a while, I was completely despondent. But slowly, Tony managed to get my spirits up, talking about all the possibilities for the house. And shopping for furniture always brought me joy.

Initially, Tony had a hard time getting me out of my funk. He kept trying to tell me not to worry, that before long, a great catch would be turning the corner. When I told Tony that Dutton would soon be on his way to L.A. and really wanted us to give our marriage another try, Tony was a bit skeptical. But his tune quickly changed after meeting Dutton in person.

Tony, who was usually less than impressed by most things, was quite impressed by Dutton. The two hit it off immediately. And once Dutton saw what Tony had done with the house, he'd eventually hired Tony to decorate his studio office. Soon Tony was strongly urging me to give both my marriage and Dutton another chance. "Debbi, when I'm over there at that office, all Roc talks about is you. I really think he's going to do everything he can to make your marriage work. So you need to hang in there."

When Dutton had first arrived in L.A., there were a few awkward moments. Even though we'd technically been separated, feelings of betrayal still loomed over me. But when my husband sat me down, so full of joy and determination about the future, and a strong willingness to make things better, I got caught up in the high. I'd already been married and divorced once. If Dutton was really ready to give a strong commitment to our relationship, I was completely willing to put all the past behind us, and forego another divorce.

The first time we made love again, it reminded me a lot of our first time. We clung to each other afterward with a satisfaction that we were where we belonged, and wanted to be. But it'd be a while before I could stop thinking of the enormous passion and erotic intensity I'd shared with Ellis.

For a while, Dutton and I had phone consultations with another therapist we'd been referred to. Dutton's schedule was way too busy to incorporate office meetings. But he did keep up with all of his scheduled phone consults.

Things were much more on an even keel. And neither Dutton nor I ever brought up anything that'd happened in our personal lives during our separation.

We began having a more active sex life. We weren't swinging from the ceiling or anything, but our intimacy had grown dramatically. We were laughing and enjoying each other, and slowly but surely, I found myself falling deeply in love with my husband all over again. It was during this period that work began to dry up for me. I was still going on auditions, but wasn't booking any jobs. I'd get discouraged from time to time, but Dutton was always supportive. "Don't worry, Babe. You'll get a job. But it's not like you have to worry about money."

This was true. For the first time in my life, I didn't have to be afraid about not working. When Dutton and I'd first met, I carried most of the bills. The salary from his performances on Broadway didn't compare to what I brought home from *All My Children*. With the first house we bought, Dutton was only able to contribute a very small amount to the down payment. And with the second house, still not that much. But now things had totally shifted. Dutton was being paid a huge salary for starring in his own show, and he'd also done quite well financially from costarring in *Aliens*. We both began spending a lot more money, and when it came to having a fabulous home, Dutton never once barked at what I spent on decorating.

By the end of the first season of *Roc*, it was clear that the show was a hit, but with that, came other issues. I began to see a lot of Dutton's controlling nature coming out. Dutton was coming home constantly in an uproar about the producers trying to make the show too ignorant. He'd always bring up the comedy, *Martin*, starring Martin Lawrence. *Martin* was hugely successful and in competition with *Roc*. Dutton hated *Martin*, and made no bones about it. When Dutton won the NAACP Image Award for Best Comedic Actor but the show lost as Best Comedy to *Martin*, Dutton was incensed. His attitude alluded to his distaste of how he felt Blacks were represented on *Martin*. I personally thought he went too far, and so did a lot of other people. But my husband's new success seemed to be turning him into a tyrant and egomaniac with little care for what anyone else thought.

After sitting down and talking with both Yolanda and her husband, and with a hefty salary offer, Dutton eventually persuaded Yolanda to move out to L.A. for one year. He promised to fly her home as often as possible. Yolanda had a large family, and I knew they weren't rich off of her husband's salary. It'd probably been a difficult decision for her to make. Yolanda had interviewed many people for the job, but Dutton always managed to find something wrong with them.

On one of *Roc*'s tape days, I decided to go over and watch the show. I didn't go to all the tapings, but I went to a lot of them. Seated in the mid-section, the comedian, Jay Anthony, who hosted the show, yelled out my name. "Let's give a round of applause to the wife of Charles S. Dutton, the talented actress, Debbi Morgan!"

I stood up and waved, and then quickly sat back down. It was common practice to introduce the star's family at the beginning of each taping. But I felt a bit shy about it. Eventually, I ended up asking Jay not to introduce me anymore.

After the taping, I stayed in my seat to wait for Dutton. When he finally came out, hordes of people rushed over to him for autographs. Then I saw Yolanda walk over and introduce him to a man she was with. I realized right away that it had to be Yolanda's husband. They were dressed in almost identical, blue silk pantsuits.

I walked down the steps and crossed over to them. Yolanda turned to me with a bright smile on her face. "Debbi, you remember my husband, James."

"Hi, James. So nice to see you again."

James extended his hand. "It's nice to see you, too, Debbi."

"Yolanda, do you and James want to go out somewhere to eat?"

"Thanks, Debbi, but we have plans."

Yolanda gave me a sly grin, and I could only imagine the plans she and her hubby had. They said good night, and walked off holding hands.

"Listen, Babe, I have a meeting upstairs with the writers and producers. I've got some real problems with this next script coming up."

"Okay, Honey. That's cool. I'll drive on home."

"Give me a kiss, Pretty Girl. And wait up for me, okay?"

I liked the sound of that. But by one o'clock, Dutton still wasn't home. I could only imagine the hell he was giving the writers and producers about the new script. Dutton wanted the show to have more drama. And the powers that be were resistant to the show getting too heavy, especially week after week.

A few days later, I dropped by my husband's office on the studio lot.

Dutton's office was filled with sophisticated furniture, paintings, and a beautiful, wall-to-wall leopard rug. Tony had joked upon its completion, "I don't know what those producers are going to think when they see this place. It's the best-looking office on the lot."

Yolanda had just finished giving a young assistant she'd hired some papers to fax. "Hi, Debbi!"

"Hi, Yolanda. I stopped by to speak to Dutton for a moment. Is he in his office?" Then I heard his booming voice...

"This is some ignorant-ass shit! I'm not doing this buffoonery! This ain't *Martin*!"

I locked eyes with Yolanda. "Who is he talking to?"

Yolanda shook her head. "The writers...and one of the producers."

"Does he always speak to them like that?"

"Whenever he's mad, which seems to be about every day lately."

I wondered if the producers now regretted giving Dutton his own show.

Then these two girls walked into the office with their skirts damn near up to their navels, grinning over at Yolanda. "Is he in?" said the one with the big booty about to protrude through the back of her skirt.

Yolanda squinted her eyes, looking quite annoyed. "He...is...in...a meeting."

Big booty girl squinted right back. "Well, tell him that he need to call *Sha'ron.*"

I was sure the little witch's real name was *SHARON!*

"Who *are* you?" I asked.

She gave me a disgusted look. "Who are *you?*"

"I'm Mr. Dutton's wife."

"Oh...well, could you please ask him to call Sha'ron?" Then the two twits sashayed out of the office.

I could tell that Yolanda seemed about as embarrassed as I was. "Why would she be looking for Dutton?"

"Debbi, now that he's been made an executive producer, they all come up in here thinking he's going to give them some role on the show."

My gut told me there was more to it than the explanation Yolanda had just given. But I decided not to press her any further...

It was several days before I stopped by Dutton's office again. I was greeted by one of the stage managers as I crossed the lot. "Hey,

Debbi! If you're looking for Roc, he's in a meeting over in the producers' building."

"Okay, Jimmy. Thanks a lot."

"Sure, no problem."

I decided to stop and say a quick hello to Yolanda before I turned around and left. She was buried in some files as I peeked my head in the door.

"Hey, Debbi. Charles isn't here, but come on in."

"Yea, I ran into Jimmy. He said Dutton was in a producers' meeting. Hope he's not over there going into a fit again."

"You know your husband. He's still on a rampage about this new script. Sometimes when the producers see him stomping across the studio lot in a huff, flinging that script in his hand, they act like they want to lock the doors and hide."

"Do you think they might get fed up with Dutton's behavior and cancel the show?"

Yolanda smiled demurely. And then took a moment before she responded in her diplomatic fashion. "As long as *Roc* continues being a success, they won't have any problem trying to keep Mr. Dutton happy."

I guessed Yolanda had a point. But I couldn't help but feel a bit uncomfortable at the bullish reputation my husband was garnering.

"Yolanda, is James still here?"

"No, I put him on a plane this morning." Yolanda looked sad.

"I'm sorry we didn't all get to do something together. You two make a beautiful couple."

The sadness that reappeared in Yolanda's eyes didn't necessarily seem to be about James's departure that morning.

"Yolanda, everything's okay with you two, I hope."

"Oh, yeah. We're fine, now."

Yolanda didn't seem like she wanted to expound, and it was not like we were the best of friends, so I certainly wasn't going to press her. But then Yolanda let out a gentle sigh, and continued on, as if she needed to.

"I was thinking about this same time, two years ago." I didn't say anything. I waited to see if Yolanda felt comfortable enough opening up to me. "I found out James was having an affair."

"Oh, Yolanda, I'm sorry." Seeing the memory of the pain that was still in her face, couldn't help but remind me of the pain I'd caused Ellis's wife... no matter that I'd loved him dearly.

"Yeah, it was pretty shocking. The kids and I moved into my mom's place, but it was way too small to accommodate all of us so we went back home. But I made my husband sleep on our living room sofa for an entire year."

"Wow, that must have been really tough on the kids as well."

Yolanda stared off into space as if recapturing that very moment she discovered her husband was cheating.

Sadly, I could relate to her pain. I had my own fears. Dutton and I had begun sliding into old habits. His phone consultations with our therapist had all but come to a grinding halt, and the intimacy that'd I'd thought we'd finally recaptured had yet again begun to wane. Coupled with that, there were times I felt a true dislike about the person my husband seemed to be turning into.

Sometimes he could be downright mean, and a big bully to anyone he felt like intimidating. That was directed at quite a few of the people he worked with, and eventually would spill over into his attitude toward me. To others, he remained a charmer, someone people still flocked to, still impressed by his fun-loving nature, his sense of humor, and the times he'd readily offered to help those in need.

But this began to trouble me, because soon I'd begin to see that alongside the Dutton I'd fallen in love with, was another Dutton, one with a very ugly, very scary side.

Chapter 50

"Dutton, I don't understand! What is it?! Are you gay or something?"

His lips receded above his teeth, and his eyes became narrow slits. I suddenly wished I could take back what I'd said. My frustration with Dutton not making love to me had gotten the better of me.

"I'd have killed a muthafucka for saying less than that. Do you understand me?"

"Ye-yes," I said, my voice quivering. "I didn't mean what I said. I'm sorry, Dutton. But I'm so frustrated. Aren't you? We haven't made love in almost four months."

"I'm not sitting around counting the time since we last fucked, okay? I'm busting my ass trying to keep this stupid-ass show on the air and maintain some damn dignity and respect with it! Because if I don't do that, you won't be able to keep moving us all the time, and spending all my damn money on new furniture. So I don't know what the hell you're complaining about!"

We'd sold our home in Sherman Oaks, and moved to a luxurious rental home in Nichols Canyon until we found something else we wanted to buy. It was the only thing in my life at the moment bringing me any joy. And though it was easy for Dutton to throw this in my face, if he'd been opposed in any way, I didn't hear him complaining about our lifestyle.

I'd gotten to the point where I felt like I was walking on eggshells with my husband. The climate in our household was beginning to feel too much like my childhood home. I never knew which Dutton would walk through the door on any given day, quite like my father. Quite like my mother had experienced with her father, too. I would come to see that there was one inherent difference: while Dutton could be quite frightening, he was never physically violent with me. Still even when Dutton was in one of his charming moods, I couldn't relax because I was constantly waiting for the tide to turn.

Six months earlier, my dentist had discovered a rare tumor (an ameloblastoma) during a routine X-ray. Because there were no symptoms involved, my doctor informed me that had I not had the X-ray, I might have lost part of my jaw. I shuddered to think of that possibility.

My stay in the hospital was all of four days. Conni Marie had driven me to Cedars-Sinai, and held my hand as the nurse took me in to get me prepped for surgery. "Don't worry, Deb, everything is going to go fine."

Dutton informed me he couldn't get out of rehearsal. This struck me as an odd excuse because producers certainly had the power to rearrange rehearsals, certainly one who was also the star. I'd gotten to the point that I didn't know when to believe the words coming out of my husband's mouth.

After the surgery to remove three of my lower right teeth, and some of the bone in my jaw, I underwent a second surgery to remove bone from my hip that was implanted into my jaw.

Dutton only visited me in the hospital once. No flowers. No cards.

Following the surgery, I hired a woman named Nirankar who came highly recommended by a previous caterer. Nirankar reminded me of a jolly, light-skinned Aunt Jemima. She was chubby and round, and was always covered in white from head to toe, as was the custom in her religious belief as a Sikh. We took such a liking to each other that even after I was completely well, I begged Dutton to let me keep Nirankar on as our cook/and my personal house assistant.

Now that we'd moved to the huge property in Nichols Canyon, it was really great having Nirankar around. Our house was in a very woodsy area up in the hills, and Dutton was rarely home. Often I'd talk Nirankar into staying over in the guest house.

One afternoon, Nirankar was baking some of the homemade biscuits I loved. The telephone rang, and Nirankar wiped her hands on her apron to answer it.

"That's okay, Nirankar, I'll get it. Hello? Hello?"

"May I speak with Roc?" a bitter female voice said.

"He's not home. Who's calling?"

"Is he at his office?" she demanded to know.

"Who is this?" I countered.

"Mary. Why do you ask?"

"What do you mean, *why do I ask?* You're calling *my* home, and this is his *wife.*"

"And that's supposed to mean what?"

"Excuse me?!"

"Yes, excuse you."

I couldn't believe the woman had the gall to be calling *my* home and speaking to me like that. "I don't know where you get off calling *my* house looking for *my* husband, and giving me attitude on top of it. So I'll tell you this, don't you ever call this house again."

"And I'll tell you, I'll call there any time I like. Roc gave me this number to call him, and if you have a problem with that, then you need to take it up with him."

The woman hung up. I felt the blood rushing to my head.

"Debbi, what is it?" Nirankar asked.

"That was some woman calling here looking for Dutton. And she had the nerve to be nasty."

Worry crossed Nirankar's face. "Must be the same girl who called here the other day."

"What? You never told me."

"Well, that's because Charles was here. When I asked the woman what the call was in reference to, she got hostile. So I told her to hold on. When I went into Charles's office and told him who was calling, he immediately picked up the extension. I didn't think any more about it."

But from the look on Nirankar's face, I could tell she'd probably thought a lot about it.

"Nirankar, I'll be back. I'm going to take a drive over to the studio."

I was enraged. It was one thing for Dutton to withhold sex from me because his plate was so full with business. But if he was seeing other women, giving them what he wouldn't give me, that was another story.

Sometimes, I wondered if Dutton had the Madonna syndrome like Elvis Presley. Priscilla Presley had often talked about the fact that once Elvis married her, he no longer treated her as a sexual being. She was his wife, this pure object that wasn't intended for sexual gratification.

When I arrived at the stage, the show had just finished its taping. A young, attractive woman ran up and threw her arms around Dutton. I wondered if this was Mary, the rude woman on the telephone.

Dutton was grinning and whispering something in the woman's ear. When he looked up and saw me, his mood changed to irritability.

"Okay, Janice. Don't worry. I'll give you a call about that. And have a safe trip back to San Francisco."

"Thanks so much, Roc!"

This obviously wasn't the woman who'd been calling the house. She ran off without Dutton even introducing us.

He was staring at me now with venom in his eyes, as if I'd been the one caught doing something God-awful. "Why are you showing up here all the time? You act like you're checking up on me and shit."

I was so taken aback by his reprimand, I almost forgot why I *had* come. Dutton had never questioned my dropping by the studio. What was different now?

An actor by the name of Clifton Powell walked up and Dutton was all smiles. "Hey, Roc. Thanks for everything, Man. It was great working with you."

"You bet, Clifton; you bet. And we're going to do it again. I'm definitely having the writers write more of a story arc to bring you back."

"That's solid, Roc. Solid."

"Hey, Cliff, you know my beautiful wife?"

"Yeah, I've met Debbi before. I have a lot of respect for her work. How ya doin', Debbi?"

I lied, "Oh, I'm great, Clifton."

"I'm gonna let you guys go, Roc. But I'll be looking forward to doing this with you again."

As soon as Clifton was gone, the hard look returned to Dutton's face. "So why do you keep showing up here?"

"What are you talking about? Are you saying you have a problem all of a sudden with my coming to the studio?"

Some older ladies were walking toward us, obvious fans. Dutton put his arm around me. "No, Babe. I'm not saying that at all. But let's not get into it here. We'll talk about it in my office."

"Oh, Mr. Roc. You are too crazy! We love you!!"

"We sure do. Can you sign this autograph for my sister? She was too shy to come over. See her standing over there in the pink dress. Now you know that pink dress don't go with her orange hair. And I told her anybody who had the nerve to walk around with orange hair and a pink dress on, ain't got no need to be shy."

The two ladies cracked up laughing, and then the first one glanced over at me. "Lord, have mercy! You're Angie! Honey, I watch you every day on *All My Children!* You and Jesse!" I didn't have the heart to tell the woman that she couldn't possibly be watching us every day because Darnell and I had been off the show for years.

"That's right. Ain't this your wife, Mr. Roc?"

"Yes, she is."

"She sure is a pretty thang."

Dutton hugged me. "She sure is."

His arms around me felt like they belonged to a stranger. When the women left, Dutton immediately dropped his arms and started off. "I'm going to my office; are you coming...? So did you decide to stop by for a specific reason?"

"I didn't know I needed one."

"You don't."

"Why did you attack me like that when you saw me over on the stage? Was it because that girl was hanging all over you?"

"Who, Janice?"

I waited for his answer.

"Janice was one of our writers. She was leaving to go back to San Francisco to help her mother take care of her father. He's dying."

All I could think about was that Janice seemed pretty chipper to me. "And who is Mary?"

"Mary?"

"Yes, *Mary*. She called the house today looking for you, and couldn't have been ruder. She said you told her to call, and that if I had a problem, I needed to take it up with you."

Dutton looked like he was getting impatient. "I don't believe that woman. Carl Gordon and I are working on an idea for a script, and we were thinking about hiring this woman to write it. She sent in some sample scripts, and they were pretty good. But then she started acting kind of kooky. First she started coming on to me, and then she started coming on to Carl. I'd already given her the home number before I realized she might be sort of a nut case. I'm sorry, Babe. I should've never given her the home number. That's all my fault."

Now he was back to the normal Dutton. But how long would that last?

Chapter 51

"Hey, Pretty Girl, guess what? I've gotten the writers to write a great part for you on the show."

"Really, Dutton?"

"Yeah, it's the part of a pregnant, homeless woman. Tommy Davidson from *In Living Color* is going to be playing your husband."

"Oh, Dutton, that's great!"

As usual, Dutton's mood shifted from moment to moment. I'd never really pressed for him to give me a part on the show because unless it was his idea, it'd probably never happen. When I read the script, I was very excited. People considered me only a dramatic actress, but given the right material, I could pull off comedy as well.

However, my initial excitement began to deflate rather quickly. When Dutton and I would arrive home from rehearsals, he'd start chewing me out about what I was doing wrong. I started feeling like being on the show with him might not be a good idea after all.

And I wasn't the only one struggling with Dutton's personality. Tommy noticed Dutton's irritability as well. After enduring Dutton's cruelties, Tommy finally came up to me one day and asked, "Debbi, do you know what's wrong with Roc? Is he upset with me or something?"

By this time, Dutton would walk right past Tommy without so much as a hello. It made me feel terrible for Tommy.

"Tommy, you keep trying to bring as much to the role as you can.

That's all you need to be concentrating on. Dutton has so many things he's dealing with, sometimes he can come off like he's irritated or pissed off. But it really has more to do with him than you."

One particular Friday afternoon, I was with the costumer trying on a few outfits for my character. I'd already finished my rehearsal for the day, but Dutton was still on stage rehearsing some scenes with Rocky Carroll. Before I left the studio, I walked over to the stage to say goodbye.

When I got there, Dutton was sitting in his chair with his back to me, as Rocky crossed over to us. I put my arms around Dutton and winked at Rocky in a gesture of a friendly hello. Dutton looked up at me at that moment, and then threw my arms away from him.

"Hey, Debbi."

I regained my composure. "Hi...hi, Rocky."

"You finished for the day?" Rocky asked me.

"Uh...yeah...yeah." I managed to mutter despite still being startled by Dutton's reaction. "I just finished trying on wardrobe."

Rocky looked at Dutton. "Roc, let's start that scene again. I'm going to go out and come back in."

Rocky slowly crossed back through the *Roc* living room set.

"Get the fuck outta here!" Dutton said to me between clenched teeth.

"What on earth is the matter with you?" I gasped.

"I said get the fuck off this stage, and get the fuck off of this lot. And don't bring your ass back here, either."

I backed away, completely baffled by what had transpired. Driving home, my hands were shaking so badly, I had to pull over. I looked up at the hillside's dried brush that'd turned brown from lack of sufficient rainwater; it hadn't been nurtured, thus it was dying... just like me. I was being abused in an insidious and calculated manner. I was dying inside, a slow, emotional death.

That night I never heard when Dutton climbed into bed. A mountain of tears had forced me into a deep sleep. But when I awoke at nine o'clock the following Saturday morning, there was a note beside my pillow.

You're going to be real sorry for that wink. I don't know who you think you are, trying to pull that kind of shit over on me. And you can forget about being on the show. I'll be talking to Stan Lathan about us recasting the part, immediately. Let me make myself perfectly clear; you are not to show up at the studio. And I mean just that!

I stared at the note, trying to make sense of it. But the way my life had become living with Dutton, it was difficult to make sense out of anything anymore. What wink was he talking about?!

Suddenly, I remembered. It was when Rocky Carroll had walked over to us on the set. I'd winked at him. *My God!* Was Dutton really threatening to oust me from guesting on his show over something so ridiculous? How could he be serious? But I realized he was deadly serious.

When he came home and I tried to broach the subject, he immediately shot me down. "Get the fuck out of my face. I don't want to hear a lying word you have to say. You think I'm so stupid I didn't see you flirting with Rocky when you thought I wasn't looking!"

"Dutton, you've gotta be kidding me!" I cried.

"Do I look like I'm fucking kidding? Now get out of my face!"

I went upstairs to our bedroom and wept. The frustration and fear over the predicament I found myself in was too much. How had things gone this wrong? Yes, we'd had our share of sexual problems for some time, and there'd even been infidelity, which had existed on both sides, but what was happening now was way beyond any of that.

Dutton didn't speak to me at all over the entire weekend. Yet I woke Monday morning to a cheerful Dutton. He stepped out of the shower, toweling himself off. "Hey, Babe. We have to be at the studio by twelve noon today."

I was too afraid to ask if this meant I was back on the show. Though Dutton's mood had changed from the monster mood it'd been over the past few days, I didn't trust it not to come right back, depending on what I said.

The next day, as I prepared to tape the show, Dutton gave me a huge hug. "Have a great show, Pretty Girl." It was as though nothing bad had ever happened between us.

Everyone was on pins and needles because the show was airing live—Dutton's idea. All of the stars on the show had come from theater. They were perfectly fine without the reshoot safety net. Having starred in theater, I, too, was comfortable with the live show. The guest stars, however, had their nerves tested like never before.

Thankfully, we made it through the show without a hitch.

"Hey, Pretty Girl!" Dutton lifted me up in the air. "You were fantastic, Babe! I'm going to be talking to the producers about bringing you back. You were great! Listen, I'm going to invite folks back over to our place for a little get-together, okay?"

"Yeah, that sounds great."

Since I'd come through on the show with high points, I had the pleasure of spending the evening with the loving, sweet version of my husband again. But I was all the more anxious and sad; I was convinced it wouldn't last.

I called our new cook, Seta, who'd been hired by Nirankar, with a heads-up to throw some snacks together.

A short while later, everyone was gathered in and around our huge pool house. The singing divas, En Vogue, who were singing the new title show track to *Roc*, had been invited over as well.

I was having a pleasant enough time when I heard a familiar voice. "Debbi."

I turned and saw Rocky Carroll sitting off in a corner beckoning me over to him. I was scared to death to go over to him. Dutton had given me hell about Rocky, and now he'd invited him to our home, and why shouldn't he? The two were close friends. But what was I supposed to do; ignore the man in my own house?

Rocky looked at me puzzled, probably wondering why I was standing there not moving. I turned back and looked across the room at Dutton. He was in a deep conversation with Dawn Robinson from En Vogue.

I turned back and slowly crossed over to Rocky. "Hi, Rocky."

"Hey, Debbi. Are you okay?"

"Yeah, I was looking around to see if anyone needed anything."

"Oh, here, sit for a minute."

I looked back at Dutton, who was still chatting with Dawn. So I sat down next to Rocky.

"Debbi, you were terrific on the show. Roc said he's definitely bringing you back on. You were cracking me up!"

"Thanks, Rocky. And that scene I did with you and Carl in the kitchen when I first started going into labor was so funny. It was all I could do to keep a straight face."

Rocky and I started laughing and then I glanced across the room. Dutton was staring at me with dark, steely eyes.

"So, Debbi, you know what I wanted to ask you to..."

I jumped up from where I was sitting next to Rocky without so much as an *"excuse me."* I could only imagine what Rocky must've thought about my rudeness. For the rest of the evening, I stayed far away from Rocky. At one point, I caught him looking at me with complete bewilderment in his eyes. I felt awful.

Many years would pass before I could tell Rocky the reason I'd been so rude and had rarely spoken to him that night.

After everyone left, I quickly went upstairs to get ready for bed. Dutton followed behind me.

"So what were you sitting in a corner and giggling with Rocky about?"

"Dutton, why are you doing this? We were laughing about the show tonight, and you invited him here. What was I supposed to do? Ignore him when he tried to talk to me?"

"Oh, shut up. I don't want to hear your bullshit."

"Dutton, may I please ask you a question?"

The way he was looking at me almost made me lose my nerve.

"What is it?"

"When I winked at Rocky, it was totally innocent. It was just the way I was saying hello to him. You couldn't possibly think I'd be flirting with Rocky, and with you sitting right there?"

"Since when do you wink at people to say hello? I've never seen you do that before."

Dutton was right. It wasn't something I normally did. But that still didn't mean I was being flirtatious with Rocky. And I would've bet my life on the fact that Rocky never took it that way.

He continued, "And besides, you didn't know I was going to turn around and catch you either. That's why you did it behind my back. But I think it's best for you to drop it before I get pissed all over again."

"Okay, Dutton, I'll drop it. But I want you to know that however it might've looked to you, that is not what it was, not at all. I would never disrespect you that way. I don't, and never have had feelings like that toward Rocky in the first place."

"Well, I know what I saw. But I told you I don't want to fucking discuss it anymore."

"Okay, Dutton. I'm sorry."

Why was I sorry? I'd done nothing wrong. But, of course, I'd never really had much confidence or security. I'd become withdrawn and unsure of myself, very symptomatic of a battered wife. Just like my mother. Just like my grandmother. And following that same pattern, I would stay and suffer, becoming as fearful of leaving as I was of staying.

Chapter 52

"Nirankar, I have an appointment for surgery at eight o'clock Thursday morning. I'm going to need you to drive me and pick me up. I don't want to ask Dutton."

"Surgery? What kind of surgery?"

"Cosmetic...liposuction."

"Liposuction? You've got to be kidding me! And where are they supposed to be taking the fat from?"

I was too embarrassed to tell her my husband had actually called me "fat" and had even suggested that was probably why I hadn't been getting work lately.

"Nirankar, you see how flabby and fat my thighs have gotten." I pulled up my skirt trying to convince Nirankar I knew what I was talking about.

She chuckled. "Like I said, where is the doctor taking the fat from?"

"From here...here...and a little around my hips...right here. I've been working out really hard with Constance and I still can't get rid of this." I poked around at what must have seemed like microscopic deposits of fat and cellulite to Nirankar.

"Are you doing this for your husband?"

I looked at Nirankar with shock. "Where did you get that from?!"

"Because I know you, and I'm aware of how insecure you've been. I hope you don't mind my saying it, Debbi, but it breaks my heart to see the way Charles treats you. You're such a beautiful, sweet lady, and he doesn't seem to give you the time of day. I've never said anything, but I have eyes, and I can see how much pain you're in most of the time. I hope you're not doing something foolish like this for his sake. There's nothing wrong with your body."

Nirankar couldn't have been any more frank. I couldn't even look her in the face as the tears rolled down my face. And she was right. Who was I doing this for anyway? Dutton wasn't interested in me. It didn't make sense that I should care one way or the other what he thought of my appearance; but the truth was, I did.

I could hear the panicked voices of the doctor and the nurses working above me. Their stricken faces looked distorted. But I couldn't feel anything. I had a sense that things weren't going according to plan. I wasn't afraid. In fact, I rather enjoyed the calmness that enveloped me. But I did feel sorry for the terrified doctor and nurses as they fought to get things back under control.

Eventually, the pitter-patter slowed, the voices quieted, and there was a lull in the sound of their movements. My eyes fluttered opened to a sterile room. I heard the sound of a door opening, and then there was the friendly, familiar face staring at me.

"Hi, Debbi. Do you think you might be up to getting dressed now?"

"Yeah, Nirankar. I think so," I managed to mutter.

"Okay. Just hold onto me."

As soon as my feet touched the floor, the room swayed. But I held on tightly to Nirankar as she helped navigate me into a big, fluffy robe.

We managed to get out to the front lobby, though it seemed to take hours. My lower limbs were unbelievably stiff. Nirankar stood me near the door while a desk nurse gave her my prescriptions.

Suddenly, I felt like someone was tugging my legs out from under me. I began to slide down the wall.

"Oh, my God! Someone help me! She's falling!" Nirankar rushed to me, but it was a male attendant who'd run up and kept me from sinking to the floor.

Now the desk nurse and one other nurse were by my side.

Nirankar was quite alarmed. "What's the matter with her? Should she be passing out like this? Are you sure she's okay to go home?"

The desk nurse put one arm around me, and the male attendant took my other side as they helped me out to the car. "Yes, Ma'am. She's fine. Just probably feeling a little weak. Get her home and into bed. Make sure you get her prescriptions filled right away. If there are any problems, you have the doctor's number. You can call him."

Jesus! Mercy! Getting me into the car and sitting me down was like trying to sit an elephant in the seat! The drugs hadn't worn off yet, so I wasn't in any real pain. But my upper thighs and hips were wrapped with so much bandaging, not to mention that tight-ass girdle. My stiff movements couldn't be more uncomfortable and awkward.

Nirankar was speaking to me on the drive home, but her voice seemed like it was coming from outer space. I only caught snippets of what she was saying. I heard her make a comment that I didn't *seem right* to her. I tried to tell her that I'd be back to myself in a few days, but I didn't have the strength.

Sometime later, I woke to a stinging, parched throat and an incredible urge to urinate. "Nirankar, Nirankar," I whispered.

"I'm right here, Debbi. What do you need?'

I hadn't even seen her sitting off in the corner of the room. She'd been there all this time, waiting until I woke.

"I have to go to the bathroom. And I am so thirsty."

"Okay, let's get you to the toilet first, and then back to bed. Then

I'll get you some liquid. Plus, it's time for your medication anyway."

I felt a jolt of lightning go through my body. The pain was excruciating.

"Nirankar, I need my pain pills. It hurts so bad."

She called to our housekeeper, "Chata! Bring Debbi up some water."

Now I was in horrible pain. And I felt like I couldn't hold my bladder another second.

"I have to pee, bad."

"Okay, okay."

But just as we got there, I seemed to slip right out of Nirankar's clutches.

"Oh, God! Chata! Chata!"

I saw Chata run into the bathroom as I stared up at them from the cold, cement floor.

"She slipped right out of my arms, Chata. Here, help me unsnap the bottom of her undergarment before she goes to the bathroom on herself."

Chata shrieked, "Nirankar? What is all this blood?! Should she still be bleeding like this?!"

"My Lord! Chata, run downstairs and get some rubber gloves."

Things became hazy after that. Slow motion, fragmented. I remember being set on the toilet, and then sliding off the toilet while pee ran down my legs. A frantic voice saying, "Call nine-one-one!"

As I regained consciousness, I realized I was lying flat out on the bathroom floor with a pillow underneath my head. Chata was kneeling over me, patting my forehead with a damp, cold washcloth.

"Don't worry, Miss Debbi. We're going to get you to the hospital. Don't worry."

Then Nirankar returned. "I finally got a hold of her doctor, but he told me not to call nine-one-one because it'd probably be all in the press by tomorrow. He said we have to get her into the car and bring her to this private facility. He's going to meet us there.

"I keep calling Charles's office but Yolanda said he left a long time ago. I didn't want to say anything to her over the phone. I asked her to have him call home as soon as possible."

I screamed "Noooooo!" in my head, but Nirankar didn't hear me. Now I was back in total reality. I'd forgotten all about Dutton. There was no way he could see me like this. But God disagreed with me.

The three of us heard the front door slam, and then Dutton's gruff voice. "Debbi! Why the hell is Nirankar's car parked out in the middle of the damn driveway? I couldn't even get around it! Debbi!"

Apparently, Nirankar had forgotten to move her car after she and Chata had struggled getting me into the house earlier.

Terror moved across all our faces as we heard his frightful steps approaching. It sounded an awful lot like my daddy's footsteps as I lay trembling underneath my covers. Now I was trembling on the cold bathroom floor, and fraught with pain.

"What the fuck?"

Nirankar said, "Charles, we have to get Debbi to her doctor's. He's given me the address where we should meet him. But I didn't know how Chata and I were going to manage getting her up and out to the car by ourselves."

"Will you stop it with all your babbling! What the fuck is she doing on the floor?! What happened to her?!"

Nirankar took a deep breath. "Well, she had a little surgical procedure."

"Surgical procedure? What kind of fucking surgical procedure?!"

"Liposuction," Nirankar answered reluctantly.

"You took my wife to have fucking liposuction?! Are you crazy?!"

Nirankar remained quiet for a few seconds. Chata kept her gaze on me, never once looking up at Dutton.

"I'm sorry. But I think something is really wrong, and she's in a lot of pain."

Dutton waved his hand for Nirankar to shut up, and stared down at me with fury in his eyes. "She wouldn't be in no damn pain if she hadn't gone and done some stupid shit like this!"

"Charles, can we just get her into the car?'

"Shut up talking to me! I heard you!" Dutton fired back at Nirankar.

And with that, my charming husband snatched me up and threw me over his shoulder like a sack of dirty laundry.

"Ohhhhhhhhh!!!!" I tried to protest.

"Shut up! That's what your stupid ass gets...some fucking liposuction!"

The pain was beyond unbearable, and it took everything in me not to make another sound, because it seemed the more I cried out, the more brutal he was. I felt every bump in the road as we raced down the Canyon, and finally we pulled into a parking lot where a nurse and an attendant were waiting. They gently lifted me out of the car, and onto a gurney.

I recognized my doctor, who took a quick peek down at me. "We'll take good care of you, and you and I will talk tomorrow."

Just as I was whisked off, I heard Dutton say, "Hey, Doc! I wanna word with you!"

I remembered nothing else until I woke the next morning in a beautiful, sunlit room.

"How do you feel?"

I immediately turned my head at the sound of the familiar voice. Nirankar was stretched out on a pretty paisley chaise in a far corner of the room.

"Good morning, Nirankar. I'm not in any pain this morning, thank God. Did you stay here all night?"

"Yes, there was no way I was leaving you."

I loved this woman so much, and she knew me very well, knew from the look in my eyes.

"He's not here. He left after he finished scaring the bejesus out of your doctor."

Nirankar recounted the night's events and every lethal word my husband had uttered.

'There was a time I would've slit your throat before you got to say one fucking word! You better pray don't shit happen to my wife tonight, 'cause if it does, you don't have to worry about your license being revoked, 'cause nobody won't be able to find you.'

I'd been in this quaint convalescent home, which was a beautiful hideaway for the rich and famous after their secret plastic surgeries, for almost a week. Not one call had come from Dutton.

On the last day, I finally heard his voice outside my bedroom door. I watched the doorknob turn as he slowly entered the room.

"I thought I heard your voice."

"Yeah, I was talking to one of the nurses about how much this damn place is costing me."

Thankful that he hadn't belittled me, I ventured, "You haven't been to see me since I've been here, and I haven't been able to reach you at the house or anywhere."

"I haven't been here because you pissed me the fuck off! What would possess you to do some dumb shit like this?"

"You said I was getting fat. You said I was putting on weight," I tried to refresh his memory.

"You shittin' me, right? So what? You put on, maybe five pounds, and yo' stupid ass gonna have damn liposuction? I should've fucked that doctor up. He know doggone well yo' ass wasn't big enough to have no damn liposuction...now, *my* ass is a different story. You think he'll give *me* some liposuction?"

We both stared at each other, and then broke out into huge laughter. He'd switched in the twinkling of an eye, and was back to the charming, funny man I'd fallen in love with.

"And the reason you haven't been able to reach me at home is because me and our chauffeur, Charles, have been parked in front of Yolanda's building, trying to catch her damn stalker."

"Stalker?!"

"Don't go mentioning this to any of your friends, but Yolanda has been getting some threatening letters."

"You're kidding! Where have they been leaving the letters?"

"Outside her door at Park La Brea."

"But I thought you had to go through a security gate to get into that place."

"That's why I'm thinking it might be somebody who works on the property. I've been having Charles hang around after he drops her off in the evenings to see if he sees anybody. But I had a meeting yesterday with the chief of police, Willy Williams, and now he's got detectives on it."

"My God! I'll give Yolanda a call."

"Definitely not! I...I mean, they don't want to risk anything leaking out. After we catch the bastard, then you can give her a call."

Then Dutton leaned down and softly kissed my lips. "I love you, Pretty Girl, and I'm sorry if what I said made you go and do some stupid shit like this."

One minute he was calling me *Pretty Girl*, the next he was cussing me out. I was in such a deep, dark hole, I didn't know which way was up. I hadn't worked in ages and all the money coming in was Dutton's. I needed to start making my own money again, so I could gain back some semblance of independence.

I called my agent and asked him to give ABC a call to inquire about a return to the show. He called back two days later, and said that ABC wanted to know if I'd be interested in going on the *All My Children* spinoff, *Loving*. I really wasn't because it was a fledgling soap, but what choice did I have? I jumped at the offer.

When I told Dutton I was going to New York to work on the soap, he acted as if he were a bit sad. But he couldn't possibly be. He sat down with me the night before I was to leave.

"Babe, you sure you want to do this? You've never really wanted to go back on the soaps again. And what are we going to do about this place? You know our lease will soon be up. We need to think about buying another house. Anyway, I'm going to miss you being here at home every night, Pretty Girl. That's for sure."

And now I was sure...that I was married to two different men.

Chapter 53

Alpine, New Jersey

"Debbi, Roc's on the phone for you."

"Thanks, Cindy. I'll be right there."

I was staying temporarily in Alpine, New Jersey, with some close friends of Dutton's and mine. I'd originally met Cindy and Bob Kaplan many years before through Dutton. When the two of us were living in Englewood, we spent a great deal of time with Cindy and Bob, but had been out of touch after we'd moved to California. When I called Cindy to let her know I'd be coming to New York to work, she opened her home to me. The rambling, four-bedroom contemporary was sort of empty after their two children had gone off to college.

I'd had my BMW shipped back East. It was an enjoyable drive back and forth from New York to the quaint town of Alpine on the days I had to work. Dutton and I managed to speak a few times a week. So far, our conversations had been normal, under the circumstances, that is. My husband told me that he missed me. I found that hard to believe. But maybe now that I was gone, he was mourning his abusive treatment of me, and feeling sorry.

I didn't realize that I was still experiencing the battered wife syndrome. As soon as my spouse expressed a bit of kindness to me, I started making excuses and falling into that trap once again.

I was lying on the sofa in the sun-drenched living room with its walls of glass when Cindy called me to the phone. I was engrossed in a juicy thriller—my favorite kind of book. I walked through their huge dining area into the kitchen to pick up the phone.

I'd installed my own personal line up in the bedroom I was sleeping in, which used to belong to Cindy and Bob's daughter, Karen. Dutton had probably called on my phone first, and not getting an answer, called on the house phone.

"Hi, Dutton."

"Hey, Babe. I tried calling you on your line, but I didn't get an answer."

"Yeah, I'm downstairs. I couldn't hear my phone. Dutton, what's wrong?" He didn't sound right.

There was a moment of silence before he answered. "Mom called... Vernon just died."

My heart broke for him. "Oh, Dutton. I'm so sorry."

Vernon had contracted the AIDS virus from his years of intravenous drug use. He'd been placed in hospice and had passed away in his sleep.

"I'm on my way to Baltimore to help Mom get the funeral arrangements set up. Are you going to be able to make it?"

"Of course! I'll let them know at the studio that there's been a death in my family. I'll meet you in Baltimore."

"Okay, let me know your flight arrangements so I can have someone pick you up. I'm going to get us a hotel suite. There will be so many folks coming in and out of Mom's house."

"Yeah, you're right. Dutton, I'm really sorry. I know how much you loved Vernon, and he knew it, too."

"If only I could've gotten him off that shit, Babe. If only I'd been able to do that."

"Dutton, you know in your heart that you have no blame in this.

You tried so many times to help Vernon. But ultimately, it was up to him."

"Yeah, I guess. Anyway, I'll see you when you get to Baltimore."

"Yes, you will, Honey. Goodbye."

I hadn't called Dutton *Honey* in ages. But it felt so right at this moment.

When I arrived in Baltimore two days later, a limo was at the airport to pick me up. Dutton was finalizing everything for the funeral services that would take place the following day. Mom Gloria was exhausted and had taken to her bed.

Aunt Gwen met me at the hotel where Dutton and I were staying. I wanted to change for the viewing that was taking place that evening. It seemed like all of Baltimore turned out for Vernon's funeral the following day. But I had a sneaky suspicion that a lot of folks were there to gawk at Dutton and me. There were fans standing curbside when we exited the church, waiting for autographs. It amazed me that even at times like that, the thought of getting next to a celebrity was all that mattered.

My mom, Cindy, my friend, Camille, and two of my cousins had also come in for the funeral. We'd all held hands with tears streaming down our faces as Dutton stood at the pulpit, speaking of all the difficulties in Vernon's life. Dutton connected Vernon's life to all those in the inner city who'd lost their way, and talked about what we, as a society, and as African Americans had to do to bring about a change.

I looked at this man standing at the pulpit orating in the style of the great Martin Luther King, Jr., feeling the depth of his words, and the way he held everyone in that church in the palm of his hand.

Where had this man been for the last four years? How could someone be so completely different, depending on the setting and the audience? I would learn later, in therapy, that this was the kind of man I'd grown up with—my father. The kind of man my mother grew up with—my grandfather. In both cases, the first men in our lives had mastered the art of emotional manipulation. And we, the women, had done our best to live and love in between the good and the bad times.

My family and friends all took a flight back to New York after the burial. I'd be leaving the following afternoon. Sitting in Mom Gloria's home until the late hours, I watched as Dutton and some of his buddies consumed lots of alcohol. Dutton was apparently trying to drown out his sorrows. Around one o'clock in the morning, Dutton and I went back to the hotel.

I took a shower and being pretty exhausted, crawled into bed for a good night's sleep. But Dutton, strangely, seemed to have other things on his mind.

He stepped out of his clothes, and climbed into bed beside me.

"Babe, I want to thank you for being here with me."

Dutton was staring at me with glazed-over eyes.

I wasn't sure where this was going. "You don't have to thank me. It's where I was supposed to be."

He pulled the covers away and pulled me to him, pressing his naked body into mine. "You looked so pretty today. I was so proud being with you," he whispered deeply, close to my face.

I wasn't sure if this was the alcohol talking or Dutton.

"Pretty Girl, forgive me. I think I've had too much to drink to get anything working here. But I still want to make you feel good."

Dutton slid down the bed, pulled up my short teddy and parted my legs. I was in total shock. Then he buried his head, deeply, between my toned, liposuction thighs.

I couldn't remember the last time my husband had performed such incredible cunnilingus on me. At first there was so much confusion in my head, it took a minute to get with the program. But as Dutton worked his wet tongue with an expert's skill, ultimately bringing me to an explosive climax, all things in my head and body felt in perfect order.

Afterward, he clung to me in a spoon position, and that's the way we slept the entire night. When my eyes opened the next morning, I realized the fantasy was over.

I had been so caught up in my own drama that I had lost touch with my sister, Terry. But word got back to me through my Aunt Shirley (who was so much like a big sister to me that I simply called her *Shirley*) that Terry wasn't doing well. As soon as I hung up the phone with Shirley, I called my sister.

"Debbi, what is it?" Dutton was looking at me with deep concern etched across his face, but I was frantically trying to dial my sister's number. Twice, I'd punched in a wrong digit.

I finally got the number right, and my sister answered the phone. *"Hello."*

"Terry, it's Debbi."

"Hi, Debbi! How did things go with Vernon's funeral?"

"It was sad. But everyone got through it."

"Debbi, are you okay? You sound upset."

"Terry, what's going on with you?!"

"What do you mean? I'm fine."

"I just got off the phone with Shirley."

My sister fell silent.

"Terry, I need you to tell me what's going on with you."

Finally, she spoke. *"I have lupus."*

"Lupus?" I repeated.

My sister began to cry as Dutton sat across from me looking alarmed, and mouthing the word, lupus?

"Terry, please don't cry." But I didn't know how I could tell her that

when I'd begun bawling myself. Dutton had to take the phone from me.

"Terry, it's Dutton. Listen, is Charles there? Let me speak to him... Hey, Man. Howya doing? So what's going on with Terry? I see...I see... Well, look, hang in there, Man. Let me talk to Debbi for a minute, and we'll get back with you guys."

After a brief round of conversations, my sister and her husband, along with Dutton, decided that we'd fly Terry out to L.A. to be seen by Dr. Cynthia Watson, my physician, whom Terry had seen due to complaints of exhaustion the last time she visited me.

I managed to get the soap to write me out of the show for a few weeks because of a family emergency. When I saw my sister, it broke my heart. She didn't look like she even weighed ninety pounds. The joints on her fingers were black and swollen, and she could barely grip anything with her hands. The pain in her leg and knee joints was so strong, she could hardly walk.

Dr. Watson performed a battery of tests and concluded that Terry didn't have lupus, but seemed to be suffering from rheumatoid arthritis, another autoimmune disease. Dr. Watson informed us that sometimes autoimmune diseases mimic one another because they are all under the same umbrella. She immediately referred my sister to a rheumatologist.

After she was definitively diagnosed with rheumatoid arthritis, the specialist wanted to begin treating Terry with a series of medications. He was alarmed at the way her fingers were already beginning to curl up. The doctor wanted to start her on heavy dosages of prednisone immediately.

Yet the holistic practitioners we consulted were all against Terry going on heavy prescription medications. We got her to take their advice. Terry began taking different kinds of herbs and vitamin drips. Then we found an alternative doctor in Pacific Palisades, Dr. Jean McClain, who began treating my sister with injections inside her mouth and around the front of her skull.

On days when she wasn't feeling up to par, Nirankar would stay with Terry while Dutton and I searched for a house. Our real estate agent found us a sixty-five-hundred-square-foot Country French colonial in Studio City. Yes, this was the dream house I'd been waiting for!

It had a gated, cobblestoned driveway surrounded by fruit trees. There were four bedrooms, a wonderfully large kitchen with stone floors, and French doors leading out to a patio. There was a maid's wing, four fireplaces, a huge pool and pool house with an adjoining room, and a luxurious spa. At least Terry would be able to use the spa every day to help loosen up her stiff joints.

Dutton had been the kindest he'd been in ages. He and my sister had always gotten along and he went out of his way to seek out treatment for her, and to make sure she was comfortable. It was a side of him that I'd longed for. I really began to feel like things might be turning around for us. It was nice not having a burdensome marriage on my shoulders with everything going on with Terry.

Listening to bits and pieces of Dutton's phone conversations, I could tell things weren't going well with Yolanda either. Things seemed to have heated up even more intensely with her stalker. And Dutton had begun coming in again at almost daybreak. I felt sorry for Yolanda and this ongoing saga.

The day before I left to go back to work, Terry felt well enough to get out of the house. She rode with us to the new place in Studio City to meet a floor crew. They'd be inspecting all the wood floors in the house.

"Oh my gosh, Debbi! This place is unbelievable!" We walked through the twenty-foot vestibule into the living area, where there was a commanding circular staircase going up to the second floor. "And look at this staircase. Wow!"

The sellers were holed up in the pool house, so I was able to give Terry a grand tour of the main house. When we were done, my sister and I sat on the staircase looking out the huge, floor-to-ceiling window. Dutton was in another part of the house with the floor guys.

Suddenly, my sister spoke with a bit of sadness in her voice. "Debbi, do you know what that big tree right outside the window is?"

"No, I'm not sure."

"They call it a Weeping Willow. And they say that it can evoke much sadness for those who live near it. They say it brings many tears. Didn't you tell me that every time you come here, it looks like the wife has been crying?"

"Yeah, I did. But I've never heard that about a Weeping Willow before."

"Debbi, are you happy?"

"Sure, I am, Terry."

Both of us were guilty of keeping secrets we were afraid would cause the other concern.

"And you and Dutton are doing okay?"

"Well, we've had some ups and downs. But things have started going much better lately."

"I'm glad then, Sis. And forget what I said about that Weeping Willow. This house is gorgeous, and you and Dutton will be very happy here."

Two months later, we were all moved in. My friend, Tony, had begun turning our new home into a Shangri-La. The walls were done in an expensive gold faux; there were beautiful and sumptuous down sofas; a baby grand piano; large, oak tables; and Dutton had acquired some beautiful paintings by Romare Bearden. Tony had hung them with picture lighting, which gave off a soft and elegant glow in the evenings.

The master bath was so large and the ceilings so high, Tony had the gardeners place a fifteen-foot ficus tree underneath the huge skylight. There'd been an enormous, unfinished attic that I'd had the contractors finish off. Tony turned it into my closet and dressing suite. It was bigger than our master bedroom. At first I thought Dutton would surely balk because his dressing suite was on the small side. But he actually joked about it.

"See what I mean, Tony. She has a damn gymnasium for her dressing suite, but she had you put me in the broom closet!"

Tony was happy to convey how much he felt Dutton loved me. "Debbi, you don't have anything to worry about. That man loves you so much. He told me the other day that I could do whatever you wanted me to do with the house. He was giving you carte blanche."

When I got back to the East Coast, Conni Marie was on her way out to the West Coast to try and book some auditions. I told her I'd asked Dutton if she could stay at the house. There was certainly plenty of room. Not only that, Terry would have company—someone to help look after her when Nirankar couldn't be there.

Dutton had no problem with Conni living at the house at first. But shortly after she got there, he went home to see his mother. That's when California had the January '94 earthquake.

In the wee hours of that January day, the entire house rattled violently. Terry woke up screaming frantically for Conni Marie. Her legs were too stiff to jump out of bed. Glass could be heard crashing throughout the house, and my sister said she'd never experienced a worse nightmare.

Conni managed to get them both out of the house to safety. Other than some glass and a few other broken objects, the only serious destruction was a major crack in the chimney. But hearing of the 6.4 earthquake was terrifying for me, especially when neither Dutton nor I were able to get through to anyone at the house for two days. All circuits were down, and we had no clue if anyone had been hurt. When Nirankar finally phoned that everybody was fine, I broke down with tears of joy.

By the time I got another break from the show, I came home and was in shock to see how much worse my sister was. Obviously, the herbs and the vitamin drips had done nothing. Terry could barely walk to the bathroom. I had to leave the room so she wouldn't see me bursting into tears.

We had scheduled a meeting at the house with Terry's doctors. The topic of discussion was Terry's admission into an alternative clinic down in Mexico. We sat around for well over an hour waiting for Dutton to come home. I was a bit ticked off that he'd not even called to say he'd be late. When I heard him pull up in the driveway, I excused myself and went out to meet him.

"Dutton, where have you been?! The doctors are here. We've been waiting for you for over an hour. Where've you been?"

"Will you calm the fuck down?! I'm here now. I was over at Yolanda's going over some business conferences I have coming up."

"At Yolanda's? I thought she was back in New York."

"She was. She just got back and settled into her new place a couple of days ago. Now if you're done with the damn third degree, we can go into the house and talk to the doctors."

Terry would be going down to Mexico, but she'd need someone to be with her. Patients stayed in a nearby hotel and were carried by a van back and forth to the clinic each day. Shirley had flown in to help look after Terry's two small boys, Donovan and Denmark. So of course, she'd have to remain in L.A. I was working in New York. And it wasn't anything I'd ever ask of Conni Marie. It was too much of a responsibility. In the end, it would be Mom who'd take a leave from her job and go to Mexico with Terry.

The fear I had about the change in Dutton's attitude toward me was not unfounded. Of course I had no idea what brought it on; I never did. But his timing really stank. I kept trying to keep my spirits up where my sister was concerned and think positively. And now

Dutton was starting his manipulation again. He'd come home and barely speak to me, and when he did, his words were mean and hostile. I started feeling so uncomfortable in his presence, that it was difficult to even share a bed with him. I ended up sleeping on a futon in my dressing suite.

Then one day, Dutton became livid because of something our driver, Charles, had told him. According to Charles, Conni Marie had given him some kind of an order like, *you can't wait in the house. You need to wait out in the car.* This sounded absolutely absurd to me, and I didn't believe Conni Marie had said any such thing. Conni had seen Charles sitting in the house many times. But Dutton ordered me to ask Conni to leave.

"She's been here long enough anyway. And I don't know where the hell she gets off giving orders to anyone around this house."

It was up to me to tell Conni Marie she had to leave. I felt horrible. The last thing I wanted was to put any kind of a wedge in our relationship. We were as close as sisters, and I hated Dutton for what he was making me do. But Conni had been very observant of the change in Dutton's attitude. She'd been thinking it might be best for her to leave anyway. Conni Marie ended up moving in with her close friend, Roxanne.

One night, before I had to fly back to work, I found Terry propped up in the family room with Shirley...the boys were in bed, and my sister and aunt were glued to the television set watching the events of the day of the O.J. car chase.

"I have an early flight. I'm going upstairs to bed," I said. "Mom should be getting in tomorrow night."

Terry turned her attention away from the television. "I think her flight gets in somewhere around eight o'clock. Debbi. Are you going back to sleep up in your closet?"

"It's not really just a closet, Terry. It's a dressing suite, and it's huge."

"That's not my point. Shirley and I were talking about it. It probably wasn't a good thing for you to move out of your bedroom. You guys might be having some problems, but, Debbi, you're probably making them worse by moving out of the bedroom."

My sister and my aunt had no idea of how ugly Dutton had been treating me because he always managed to make sure other people didn't see him at his worst. As far as Terry and Shirley were concerned, we'd had some spat, and I was retaliating by not sleeping in our bed.

"You guys really don't understand. But I don't want to talk about it right now." In retrospect, my husband's public persona was so very well tailored, it was hard for people to imagine how cruel and downright scary he could be. I'm reminded of how so many people thought Robin Givens was overexaggerating when she tried to tell people that her husband, Mike Tyson, was abusive. It wasn't until Mike Tyson bit off Evander Holyfield's ear, in front of the world, that the public finally saw what she saw.

The next night, when I was back in New Jersey, I got a call from Mom. "Honey! This house is gorgeous! I'm sorry I won't get to spend a little more time enjoying it. Dutton is driving Terry and me down to Mexico first thing in the morning."

"I'm sorry, too, Mom. But there'll be other times. Listen, I'm glad you're the one who's going to be with Terry. I'm praying to God that the doctor down there is going to be able to cure her."

"Debbi, your sister has lost a lot of weight and she's having a lot of tenderness in her joints, but I'm not putting any focus on that. We're all going to think positive. Terry is going to leave that clinic healthy as a horse." I could tell by Mom's voice that she was fighting hard to believe her own words.

"When will you be coming down to see us?"

"I won't have any more time off for about another month. But I put in for a two-week vacation around the end of July."

"That's great, Honey. And I'm sure by the time we see you, your sister will be greatly improved."

"Yeah, I'm sure, too, Mom."

Of course, my mother, sister, and aunt thought Dutton was the next best thing after Jesus since he was paying for my sister's medical treatment. That's the thing about people like Dutton: when they're good, they're really good; but the flip side can be Dr. Jekyll and Mr. Hyde!

I arrived back home for my vacation. I'd just walked in when the telephone rang. I ran and picked it up in the kitchen.

"Hello!"

"Hello, may I speak to Roc?"

It was a man's voice. "He's not here at the moment."

"Gee, I've been trying to reach him, but he hasn't returned my calls." The man sounded flustered. "Do you think I might be able to reach him on his other number?"

Other number? "Yeah, you might want to try him on that number. Are you sure you have the right one?"

He rattled off a number I'd never heard before. I quickly jotted down the digits and pretended to confirm, "Yes, that's it. You're most welcome. Goodbye."

I immediately pushed down the disconnect button and dialed the number I'd just gotten from the guy looking for Dutton. A cheery, automated voicemail message played. *'Hi, it's Roc. Leave a message, your number, and I'll get back to you as quickly as I can.'*

I'd discovered my husband's private phone service. Of course, he'd never fess up to having an extra phone line to aid in his philandering. He'd say I was crazy. Get defensive. Treat me like crap on the bottom of his shoe, but smile in my family's face. The mental manipulation made me question my own stability at times.

One night I'd struck up the nerve to ask Dutton. "Why do you feel the need to be so cruel? Why are you doing this to me?"

He'd responded in kind.

"Doing what? I'm not doing anything to you. Anything being done to you, you're doing to yourself."

In retrospect, Dutton was right. *When was I ever going to take responsibility for what I'd allowed to be done to me, not just in this relationship, but also in my life?* This question only began to scratch the surface... but it would be a question that would ultimately take me very far.

Chapter 54

Studio City, California

"I guess Dutton's going out of town."

Shirley's eyes looked toward the vestibule where Dutton's leather suitcase was sitting.

"Yeah, I guess so. Not that he's said anything to me, of course."

"Debbi, have you guys sat down and tried to talk about whatever problems you're having?"

What could I say to my aunt? The whole situation was almost inexplicable. I wouldn't even know where to start. I shrugged my shoulders and walked up the stairs.

Dutton was heading down the staircase. "I'm flying to Chicago for a meeting."

He didn't even look at me.

The following morning, I came downstairs and found Nirankar in a bit of huff. She'd gotten into a confrontation with our cook over something I'd asked him to make for lunch. It was quite silly actually because Nirankar felt he needed to be discussing the menu with her. After letting her know in a very nice way that I thought she was out of line, Nirankar apologized.

"You know what, Debbi, you're absolutely right. I've always been accustomed to the employees dealing directly with me."

"Of course, Nirankar. Let's drop it. I'm not upset with you."

"Well, you can be assured it won't happen again. I'm giving you my thirty-day notice."

"What?! What are you saying, Nirankar?"

"I've been thinking about leaving for some time now. Things have gotten so out of hand I can't stand being here anymore, as well as having to face you every day."

"What does that mean?"

"Your husband, Debbi. I'm sorry, but the man is slime. The way he parades these different women in and out of the house is a disgrace. And it's been going on for almost as long as I've been working for you."

The look on my face must have beckoned for Nirankar to continue.

"When you first started going to New York, he'd be bringing women up to the house in Nichols Canyon, and Terry was asleep right in the downstairs bedroom. I caught him coming out of the door with someone twice. He made up some half-cocked excuse. And I can't tell you how many times the housekeeper found condoms in the trash basket. I never had the heart to tell you, but when I fired the other girl, Jape, she told me that when we sent her on the film location to be Dutton's personal chef, he had literally chased her around the hotel room trying to get her to go to bed with him. She swore that even though she didn't want to lose her job, nothing ever happened. But then I ended up firing her anyway. Even before that, I'd walked over to the pool house one day to check the bathroom toiletries, and found him up there with some woman."

Now I understood why, over the years, Dutton had taken such a dislike to Nirankar. I guess he thought if he'd come out and tried to have me fire her, she might expose everything.

"And when you all went to Mexico to see your sister last week, he had someone in here before you'd even gotten out of the door good. That's when I decided it was definitely time for me to go. I can't continue working for you, knowing what I know, and having to look you in the face every day. I'd be lying if I said that I didn't hope you'd find the strength to walk away. This man does not deserve any good to ever pass his way. Maybe you'll end up staying in New York, and I can come for a visit."

I hugged Nirankar tightly. Then we stood back looking at each other for the last time. She reached up and brushed a tear from my eye, and I brushed one away from hers. I watched through the window as she got into her ancient, white Volvo and drove through the gates.

"Shirley, something seems to be wrong with my car. I'm going to take Dutton's Mercedes."

I drove out toward Manhattan Beach to clear my head. How many more tears could I shed? What good had they ever done anyway?

Dutton's car phone rang, snapping me back to reality. I'd almost decided not to answer, but the caller tried again.

"Yes?"

"Debbi?" It was Kathy, Yolanda's assistant. "Yolanda said you need to get back home with Dutton's car. He has a meeting in half an hour. Charles is on his way over to the house to pick up the Mercedes so he can get Dutton from the airport. Apparently, Dutton's flight was late."

There was no way I'd make it back home in all this traffic that quickly. It made more sense for me to pick my husband up. I was only ten minutes from the airport. I'd never let on to Dutton what Nirankar had told me. Not yet anyway.

"Tell Yolanda to call Charles back and tell him not to come to the house. I'll pick Dutton up. I'm only ten minutes from the airport. I'll never make it all the way back to Studio City in all this traffic."

Two minutes later the phone rang again. This time it was Yolanda. "You need to get Charles's car home, immediately!" *Click!*

The witch had hung up on me! How dare she speak to me that way...what the hell was going on?!

And then it hit me. Dutton must have been coming into the airport with one of his mistresses, a mistress whom Yolanda, Charles, and everyone other than me knew about. They were all trying to protect him. *Well, I'll be damned!* But it was Yolanda of all people whom I couldn't believe. *Debbi, Charles knows I would never tolerate him being disrespectful in front of me.* What bullshit! Yolanda had probably sat and lied right to my face about catching Dutton with other women in his studio office late at night as well.

This time I could not care less what his reaction was. I'd be right at the airport as my husband exited with his flavor of the week.

The phone rang again.

"Hello!"

"It's Shirley. Debbi, I don't know what the heck is going on with Dutton, but I'm getting nervous. He just got off the plane and called home. He went off because Charles was not standing there waiting for him. I told him that you were on your way to pick him up. He said he didn't want you picking him up, and what the hell were you doing driving around in his damn car anyway. Charles said Yolanda called Jackson Limousine Service to pick him up."

And just as I pulled up to baggage at American Airlines, Dutton was exiting through the glass doors. He looked me dead in the eye and jumped into his black stretch limo, alone.

I lay in bed listening to the sound of the quiet room. It was after eleven p.m., almost six hours since I'd seen Dutton at the airport. The telephone rang. I couldn't stop the strange tremble in my hand as I picked it up. Somehow, I knew it was him. I didn't speak.

"I had a very interesting trip back home today. I'm sitting there reading the paper, waiting to hop on my last flight back to L.A. when I notice this white woman staring at me. I could tell she recognized me from television. She comes over to me and says, 'Your wife had an affair with my husband and practically destroyed our life, and my little boy's life.'

"Do you know someone by the name of Ellis Horne, a Las Vegas singer?"

I lay like a piece of stone and could not speak.

"Answer me!"

"Yes, yes, I know him. I'm sorry. I didn't mean for it to happen...I just, I don't know. I don't know what to say to you."

"I'm on my way home, and when I get there, you'd better have all your shit packed, and all the rest of your family's shit packed because first thing in the morning, I want every last one of you out of my house!"

I'm not sure how long I'd been lying there in a half coma when I glanced up at the television and saw the flashes of Nicole Simpson and Ron Goldman under those bloody sheets. Then I heard the door downstairs slam shut, and his feet barreling up the stairs. I watched him enter the room, and slowly move toward the foot of the bed. He didn't say anything. He looked at me with eyes that seemed like they could reach inside my head and rip my brain out! *Run, Mommy, run!* Run, you stupid woman! *Run, Debbi, run!*

I tried with every ounce of strength I had to move, but I couldn't even part my lips! And then I thought of my beautiful mother squirming over in a corner about as terrified for her life as I was right now...because he was moving around to my side of the bed... reaching down over me and grabbing...!

"Noooo! Please! Please! Somebody help me! He's going to kill me! He's going to kill meee!!! Help meee!!!"

He grabbed the covers away. "Kill you? Ain't nobody gonna touch you, but I should rip your fucking heart out! *And don't think I'm giving you one red...*"

I could see his lips were still moving, but I couldn't hear shit! Because his words were suddenly drowned out by the thoughts in my head of where I was in my final moment of being fearful. I don't know where I got the strength or the fortitude. Maybe I was so damned drained, so tired of being bullied, and being afraid since almost the day I entered this world. But I was ready to let go of all the pent-up emotion that I'd never, ever been able to unleash until now.

"That affair happened over four fucking years ago! We were separated, and I'd filed for divorce! And don't think I didn't know yo' cheatin' ass wasn't fucking all over the place! You even had the unmitigated gall to bring women into this house and into our bed no less! You've had no respect for me, or our marriage, ever since your big-ass head got even bigger thinkin' you all that! *But I got a reality check for you*. If you think for one minute that all those women been fucking you for you, yo' ass ain't looked in a got-damn mirror! *And did you forget what you looked like before I took you to have them vampire-lookin' fang-ass teeth of yours fixed?! Oh, yea, I'll pack all my shit, cuz I can't get out of here fast enough, you fat fuck!*"

Now in all honesty, that last portion I actually said to myself, I mean come on.

And now he was gonna try to switch back to that little boy charm, but I could see right through his ass...

"All right, yeah, I admit it, Pretty Girl, I've cheated. But I'm a man."

Did he just utter that prehistoric bullshit outta his mouth?

"You're my wife, and I placed you on a pedestal when I married you. It might not make sense to you, but that's how it is. You can't do what I do. It's unacceptable. And where I come from, shit don't go down like that, pure and simple."

But then he said the most honest and profound thing he'd probably ever said to me. "I could've never really made you happy, Pretty Girl. I'm not worthy to be anybody's husband, not in this lifetime; won't ever make that mistake again."

I got up at the crack of dawn, looked out the window and saw that his car was gone. I quickly made reservations for my aunt to fly back East, Terry and the boys to Nashville, and Mom back to L.A.

After I was done packing, a letter on the kitchen table caught my eye. I opened it, and began reading. That bastard was suing me for divorce, which meant this shit was planned long before yesterday!

When Charles came to pick up Mom and me for the airport, Dutton, who'd arrived home a short while earlier, remained in his office. We never communicated again. He also forbade his mother and his aunt to ever speak one word to me either.

Charles took the bags out to the car, and Mom took one more glance around the house.

"I can't believe you have to give up your beautiful home."

"Don't let the man of the manor hear you say that. He already thinks that's the only reason I'd want to hold on to him. But I'm part owner of this house. He will be paying me; make no mistake. And you know what, Mom, it might have been a beautiful house, but it was never a beautiful home. Terry was right. There was nothing but tears and sadness here, and even if I could, I'd never want to live here again. Let's go."

I walked out of our beautiful house for the very last time, with my head held high. For all the real love, loyalty, and honesty I never got from this creature, I realized what he had given me was so much more. He'd give me the ability to awaken my own power.

Chapter 55

West Hollywood, California
Late 1990s

"Hi, Debbi! When did you move back to California?"

"About six months ago, Edward."

I was sitting in Borrelli's Hair Salon on Santa Monica Boulevard in Los Angeles having a very relaxing pedicure. Edward, a hairstylist I'd known years earlier, was standing at the very next station. I remembered that for a long time, Edward had been Yolanda's personal stylist.

"Debbi, I have to tell you, I went to see you in *Eve's Bayou*. Girl, you stomped on it! I was so amazed by your incredible performance. I went to see it three times!"

"Thanks so much, Edward. Well, you know I received a sweet note from Yolanda. But she didn't leave a return address, so I couldn't write back. She told me she'd seen the movie, and was deeply touched by my performance, and wanted to wish me well. It's been almost five years since I've seen her. Do you know if she's still living out here in L.A.?"

"No, she moved back East. But I can't believe she'd have the audacity to write to you."

"Why would you say something like that?'

"You know what, Debbi, forget it. It's too funky to even get into, not to mention a waste of energy."

"Now, Edward, how are you going to make a statement like that, and then leave me hanging?"

"I know. I shouldn't have even brought it up. So anyway, are you working on anything at the moment?"

I could tell Edward was determined to drop the subject. But whatever he was trying to keep from me, I needed to hear. I was a good enough actress, so I was going to use my skills.

"Of course I know, Edward. I just didn't know how many other people might know."

"I guess that's why she left before a lot of other people found out."

"How did you find out?'

"When she sent me this card announcing the birth of Charles S. Dutton the second."

I almost fell out of my chair! To say I was shocked beyond comprehension would've been a mouthful. If Edward had this right, it would all make sense! It would explain why Dutton had been his most vile in those last weeks. And why he'd played FBI, coming up with something on me, although he'd had to go back four years to do it! If Yolanda was carrying his child, he had to find a reason to get me out of the house, out of California, and out of the marriage before I somehow discovered what was happening.

And when I thought about all the stories he'd told me: how his dog had tried to warn him when he'd gotten busted with the guns in his car; the incident when he'd gotten in the car with a bunch of thugs after getting out of prison; the incident that'd happened the night he'd stabbed a boy to death; the events leading up to Dutton being stabbed in prison; and the aftermath that'd occurred with the man who'd stabbed him. Now I had my doubts if all had happened in the way Dutton had told me. There were so many stories he'd told that'd probably never even happened at all.

I thought of all the times he'd subjected me to his dual personalities, turning on me like a grizzly bear without any provocation. It was like something out of the thriller novels I was so fond of. But this wasn't fiction. It was real... It all happened...to me. Also, for him to kick us all out of the house, stop paying for my sister's clinic, and file for divorce over an affair I'd had four years earlier when we were separated! It wasn't rational.

Even given Dizzy's and Charles's drug addictions, at least I always knew who they really were. Neither man had ever pretended to be someone they weren't; nor had they been frightening or calculating.

Looking at Edward and trying to keep up the innocent act was one of the most challenging performances I'd ever pulled off.

"I know, Edward, you can only imagine how I felt when I found out."

"The last time she was ever in here, it was obvious she was pregnant. But it couldn't be her husband's because she'd told me a year earlier they'd separated. The woman already had a herd of damn children! I said, 'Girl, what's up?! When did this happen?' She was real secretive about it, but I kept trying to prod her. Finally, she said it was some man she'd been seeing back in New Jersey. But I was thinking that unless it was a one-night stand, I didn't know when she'd had time to cultivate that kind of relationship, because she was always here. She rarely went back East anymore, even to see her children. She was in the salon once a week getting her hair done."

"What about her family?"

"When her family found out she was having the baby, they all turned against her. I heard that her oldest son doesn't even speak to her to this day. And when I found out, I stopped speaking to her trifling ass myself. When I think of all the times she'd been up in your house, and up in your face. I'm telling you, I was outraged when I found out about that mess. As far as your ex-husband goes, that's another story. I never cared for him anyway."

I thought back to Yolanda's supposed stalker. Who knew what was true? *My God! Could Dutton have such an incredibly twisted imagination?* And if there had been any truth at all to the stalker story (I'd never really know for sure), Dutton had certainly used the situation to his advantage. It was a great excuse for having to supposedly spend most of the night guarding Yolanda's front door, while now I believed with a great deal of certainty they'd been in bed fucking each other's brains out.

I also thought back to that day in Yolanda's office. She'd sat with me relating the sad story of her and her children catching her husband in the mall with another woman. It looked like Yolanda and Dutton deserved each other.

A short while after my marriage to Dutton had ended, I sought out therapy again. Sitting in my therapist's office one afternoon, I was crying my eyes out over how horrible my life had been.

"Debbi, as far as your ex-husband goes, you can't spend that kind of time in prison, especially at that age in his life, get out and become an almost instant celebrity, without ever doing any emotional work on himself. It's too difficult to know how to function in the outside world. Where do you get your moral ethics? You don't. Your husband was most likely devoid of not only morals, but also guilt. And to keep from ever having any, he constantly had to look for ways to take the focus off of him and put it on you. But don't for one second think it ever had anything to do with you. He'd be like that with any woman. When he first met you, he might have very well gone into the relationship with the best intentions. He was incapable, ill-equipped, and didn't have the necessary tools to ever pull it off."

I remembered the last night I'd slept in the house. Dutton had said: "I could've never really made you happy, Pretty Girl. I'm not worthy to be anybody's husband, not in this lifetime; won't ever make that mistake again." It'd been a moment, just a moment, of real honesty.

"I'd be surprised if he ever even married again," the therapist commented.

Her words confirmed what he'd said to me.

"Now getting to you, which is the real issue here. I suspect you've had some deep traumas, fears, and insecurities that have prompted you to make a lot of decisions in life, accordingly. So we're going to take this one step at a time. I think if we can go back and begin to explore some things from the beginning, back to when you were a small child, maybe even discuss your family's relationship patterns. We can start to find some answers..."

Epilogue

And I found the answers. I had started life at a disadvantage. There had been incredible emotional shortcomings, seemingly implanted with each sperm cell connecting to its egg, from generation to generation. Some call this a generational curse.

Yes, my childhood had been fraught with fear, insecurity, lack of self-confidence, neediness for love, constant protection, and given a psychologist's evaluation, the list could probably go on and on.

We all know we're here for a reason. But if we were all destined, doomed to repeat history and become the sum total of our pasts, then what would be the sense of it?

Though I'd undergone therapy following my divorce from Dutton, I still had a few more glitches in my relationship system.

I married *Husband #3*, a talented photographer, whom I never, ever should've walked down a 7-Eleven aisle with, let alone a *church* aisle. But he wasn't an actor, he wasn't into drugs; he should've remained...a photographer who took beautiful pictures of me. With him I would lose my home and have to file chapter seven bankruptcy. On top of all that he'd had an affair with an impressionable nineteen-year-old.

Now I know what you're thinking: *'My God, woman! I thought you'd evolved! What about all those damn therapy sessions!'* But I had! I was faster this time! As soon as everything came to light with the tricky Bahamian photographer I'd married...his ass was out the door!

The second leg of my healing journey came through penning this book. It has been a fifteen-year journey of incredible pain, laughter, joy, and courage. This therapy of words in dialogue and drama, the very essence of my professional career, finally brought me to a profound awareness. Alex Haley had been right after all. In order to understand my present, I had to understand my past, understand the line of women and men before me...a seed is the root, the germ, the beginnings. Both my mother and I had been seeds of domestic violence, children who'd grown up as spectators to both physical and emotional abuse...watching, hearing, listening, but not fully comprehending, therefore rendering us incapable of stopping the cycle.

Along my literary journey, I discovered that it no longer mattered that my home life as a child had been laden with abuse. It no longer mattered that I'd been partnered with drug addicts, and had most often lived in fear of the men in my life. It no longer mattered that I'd always been so desperate to be loved that I'd overlooked whatever stared me square in the face. And it no longer mattered that my neediness for love and attention allowed my own breaking heart to break another's.

The only thing that mattered was the revelation gained from this experience: *I am responsible for my life.*

We've all had our burdens in life to bear, and many, far more unspeakable than mine. But I could no longer put blame on my father, my mother, the men in my life, myself, or even life itself. There was no blame. I finally realize how counterproductive blame is. It keeps us stuck.

Instead of blaming my predecessors, I took what I could from their stories, paralleled them with my own and realized that I am here to learn an important lesson from all the tumbles in life.

I had allowed the fear of fear to rule me, to determine who and what I allowed into my life because...well...that was all I knew. My mother taught me and her mother taught her to be afraid...afraid of outbursts, afraid to upset people, afraid to demand respect because that might lead to loneliness, lovelessness, not being liked. So as long as I believed that lie, it was my truth.

Creating a new truth by choice opened my heart and my eyes to my past, present, and future.

My dad has been dead for so many years. But when I think of him now, it's no longer with sadness about the past. It's with a longing, wishing I'd gotten the chance to know him as an adult. I'm sure he'd be a very different man today than he was back then. There's no need to further define each of the husbands in my life. We attract all people and all things in our lives for a purpose. And they each had a purpose in mine, a purpose for helping me get to the place where I am now.

For all I've come through, I especially have a deeper understanding, respect, and undying love for my mother, and what she went through. I honor her, and my Grandma Rosie. They're my true heroes.

I've laid to rest the disturbing memories, the menacing fears. And I've traveled a great distance to get here, stepping into the light of loving wisdom, flowing all the way through me and spilling over into a relationship with someone who knows what real love is all about.

Enter Mr. Jeffrey Christopher Winston. *He is...say it with me...Husband #4*. The man and the partner I knew deep in my heart I'd finally attract. He gives me the space to continue to grow and spread my wings. Yet he keeps me confined by the security of his love and embrace. This is the happiest, most peaceful, most content, most respectful and loyal relationship I've ever, ever had with a partner.

Now don't get me wrong, we argue. Sometimes we piss each other off, like any other "normal" couple. I'm so glad to finally be able to use that term, "normal" couple. But the difference is not only in the loving marriage I finally have. I can't say it enough: the difference is really in *me.*

I once read that the price you pay to be who you are is exactly what it cost. I have paid the price, trailed that long arduous journey to be wholeheartedly in love...with me.

And guess what? *I FINALLY GOT THAT MONKEY OFF MY BACK!*

About the Author

Debbi Morgan was born in the small Southern town of Dunn, North Carolina and raised in both Harlem and the South Bronx of New York City. She is an accomplished and award-winning actress whose career has spanned more than three decades. Debbi has played opposite both Denzel Washington in the biopic, *The Hurricane,* and Samuel L. Jackson in the acclaimed indie film, *Eve's Bayou,* for which she won the Independent Spirit Award and the Chicago Film Critic's Award for best supporting actress.

Her other film and television credits include *Love and Basketball, Asunder, Charmed,* and her iconic role as Dr. Angela Hubbard on the long-running daytime drama, *All My Children,* which won the hearts of millions all around the country, solidifying her huge fan base and along the way garnering Debbi an Emmy Award for best supporting actress, three more Emmy Nominations, and the prestigious 2009 Gracie Award honoring noteworthy women in media. Debbi most recently became a recurring character on the hit Starz series *Power* playing the role of "Estelle."

Now Debbi has stepped into the publishing world writing her first book, *The Monkey on My Back,* along with performing her one-woman show of the same title to sold-out audiences. Both book and play detail the autobiographical account of her difficult past and how she finally found her joy.

Acknowledgments

To Jeffrey Winston, my loving husband. I love you madly! You're a real man's man with a strong spirit, engaging personality, and enduring love for me that I've felt and experienced every moment of my life with you. Your compassion, your fairness, your sense of humanity, your sexiness and your quick wit always keep me in love and loving you. And in helping me complete this process, you've offered your continuous support, patience, and belief in me. I thank God for attracting me to you at what was the right time, the most loving, the most respectful, the best of the best...I thank God for Husband #4!

Thank you to my sister, Terry Morgan Grant. Sis, you've had your own burdens to bear, but such is life, right? However, you've always been such a fighter, possessing the fearlessness that I had for so long envied. Many nights you laughed, cried, or remained steely silent as I read aloud to you chapters of this book, a reminder of many of the horrific details of our growing up. But you've supported me to the utmost through this endeavor. These past years have brought us closer than we've ever been. I cherish you as a sister, and respect you as one of the most intelligent, wise, and incredible women I know.

Shirley Boleware...Aunt Shirley, mom's baby sister, but always more like our *big* sister than an aunt. You'd been there through all the ups and downs, supporting me and being my rock. But upon completion of this memoir, we'd endured so much, Shirley. You'd lost yet a second sister and we'd lost our mom. But beyond all the heartache, pain, despair and family strife, there was still a deep familial love that could not be broken...because time heals and love endures. Simply put, I love you. Aunt Shirley, today, tomorrow, forever!

Thank you, Sara Camilli, my wonderful literary agent. I don't think I could've ever asked for a more interested, receptive, and incredibly kind and generous person to represent me in this new field, that of author, which I've now added to my resume. Sara, you've been on my bandwagon with this book from day one. During all those times I was saddened and disappointed when yet another publisher had turned down the book, you never let me give up the faith. You never had one ounce of doubt you'd get me a deal because you so believed in me, my writing talent, and the importance of this story being told. Thank you, Sara!

To Karol Stackhouse, my personal assistant and one of the most beloved friends I've ever been blessed to have in my life. Karol, there aren't enough pages to write all that I would like to say about you. I sincerely don't know what I'd ever do without your dedication, hard work, and stick-to-it-iveness in getting things done. You know how to take care of business, Woman! I want you to know how deeply I appreciate and respect all you do on my behalf, and in representing me with the utmost professionalism, protection, and kindness. Our business relationship goes without saying. However, on a personal level, you are my champion and I love you like a sister! I thank you each and every day.